The Purpose is
Love

Felicity Rose Mackinnon

Copyright © 2024 Felicity Rose Mackinnon

All rights reserved, including the right to reproduce this book, or portions thereof in any form. No part of this text may be reproduced, transmitted, downloaded, decompiled, reverse engineered, or stored, in any form or introduced into any information storage and retrieval system, in any form or by any means, whether electronic or mechanical without the express written permission of the author.

The views expressed in this work are solely those of the author and do not necessarily reflect the views of the publisher, and the publisher hereby disclaims any responsibility for them.

ISBN: 978-1-917129-47-3

About the Author

Rei-ki Master and attuned Rahanni healer she is also the author of two non-fiction books *'Essential Connections. The How and why of your Personal Energy'* and *'Body Mind Connections. The Essential How and Why Book'*. She lives in Hampshire and continues with her writing.

Dedicated to those I love and especially my beloved Mama and my beautiful daughter Caroline.

Introduction

Each individual has their own personal path to follow for the spiritual learning or awareness needed at this time in Human history. The need and awakening are increasing across the world with each passing year since the cosmic energies began changing for the Age of Aquarius.

Thus, each individual path is tailored and determined by factors related to, suited to, each Soul purpose and the chosen personality so that all aspects are recognised and worked with for the best outcome. In that personal recognition, comes the willingness to follow it.

This then is my own that I am wishful of sharing with you, the extraordinary experiences and the beautiful insights that I have been privileged to receive from the loving Dimensions who care for us.

The more we know and are aware of these, the more hope we can hold on to. We need hope in the complex and troublous times we live in.

There are many like myself who have felt the need to keep such experiences and happenings private for fear of judgement, scepticism, even ridicule. I was lucky in that I had a few people I knew who could accept it all. It is so hard because one wants to feel free to reveal the wonders of it, especially to those who matter to us. Even to be free to be that person in one's own very ordinary circumstances.

So, this account is also for all those who too have felt that they must conceal their experiences and their own connections to the Dimensions. We are ordinary people who are privileged in this way. We are not saintly beings leading extraordinary lives. But that is the significance of this privilege. The ordinariness is what really creates the validity. It is always the small parts of the machine that move the rest. And move forward Humanity will, regardless and certainly in spite of all the things we are given to know about Man's inhumanity to Man on a daily basis.

So dear reader, these are the wonders and joys I have been part of, loved being part of, since my own spiritual learning showed me the path I should take and how I followed it, most willingly. Sharing them with you is very much part of the joy.

Felicity Rose Mackinnon 2019

Chapter 1

It all started at the millennium.

Who would have thought, – least of all me – that it heralded an astonishing personal turning point.

So, just as our millennium was about to end and another begin, a positive *jolt* with a right-angled turn was on its way to me. What followed was not only to change my life, but my view of life and awaken something in me in extraordinary ways I was totally unaware of even being possible.

Any right-angled turns wouldn't really surprise me, as this has been happening to me at intervals for most of my life. I ought to have been on the look-out but each time I've been caught unawares. Those changes might be new and untried paths before me but there were always similarities and familiarities that made adapting fairly seamless; recognisable territory as it were. But not this time.

So, dear reader, it is because of the wonderful and amazing things that I experienced after that astonishing abrupt turn, that I am writing it all down here. Rather I am distilling it because there is so much that occurred, so much I learned and became aware of. What happened needs to be in context, so here I'd like to lead you along the path that unravelled before me and share some of those marvellous happenings and especially what was revealed to me. They are a true gift.

Some of you will have similar experiences, resonate with, and/or be encouraged by what I write about. For some it could enlighten or come as a complete surprise, even just intrigue. But sharing it with you is almost to re-experience it which can only be a pleasure and a joy.

But oh! that jolt that led to it all!

Just as the world was on the brink of the millennium, there was I, obliviously and happily jogging along and all unsuspecting as usual. I was busy with an enjoyable full-time job and about to take the final exam of my much-loved studies with the Open University. Then, to my horror and with, to me, absolute suddenness, I fell apart. Whatever the cause, it had caught up with me and laid me low. A low I would not wish anyone to experience, but sadly so many do.

It was many weeks later, on Boxing Day in fact, that thanks to my prescribed medication, my brain suddenly cleared. I'd found *me* again. So, I was able to greet this brand-new millennium after all, albeit gently! Life held promise once more, it *could* get back on an even keel again. The relief was amazing. I'd had a big glitch but now I felt certain that I was going to be able to settle back gratefully into my normal life.

Well, I'd had the bombshell; now Life had another surprise tucked up its sleeve. Barely three months into the new year and, yes you have it! – that abrupt sharp right-angled turn. How could I know that a chance remark would have me not only facing in a totally undreamed-of direction, but into a different way of being? A way that was to be preparation for things wonderful, fascinating and at that time, unbelievable. But yet still amaze me.

Thus, it transpired, that a close friend, Julie, asked me had I heard of Rei-ki? No, I had not. She told me it was a form of healing energy, that she had had a healing session with someone a friend had recommended and it had been wonderful. Would I like a session? She would arrange it at her house if I'd like to. Somewhat intrigued, I agreed.

How could I guess that I was on the starting block to a whole new beginning? A simple first step to the amazing things that followed.

And a Rei-ki healing session I had. At Julie's house, as promised – and it *was* wonderful. I had never experienced anything like it. It was over an hour of, I can only say, bliss! Sheer bliss!

After coming slowly – and reluctantly – to from this delicious zone this Rei-ki healer had put me in, I remarked, 'What an amazing gift!'

'Oh no!' she replied, 'You learn how to do it.'

'Really?'

'Yes, like you, when I first had a healing session, I said the same thing. Then I found out that you could learn it and get training for it and here I am.'

I was very surprised at this. I had no idea one could learn such a thing. I asked her how one went about this. She advised me to get a book on the subject first and read up about it to see if it really was what I wanted to do. I couldn't wait!

That was easier said than done. There was nothing at my local library – we are very lucky as it is a good one, – so I tried our local book shop. They had nothing in stock and had not heard of it. In the end, they found two Rei-ki books on their lists and one was quite expensive.

I ordered the cheaper one, a practical guide to Rei-ki. That sounded fine to me. While I waited for the book to arrive at the shop, I arranged to have another Rei-ki session.

Then at that second healing session another element was added to my life that was to have a profound effect on me and what lay before me.

This lovely healer told me that I was carrying a great deal of sorrow in my heart. Her perception surprised me; she was quite right. She then told me that as well as her healing from the Rei-ki discipline that she was offering me, there was she added, something I could do to help myself.

I was intrigued – this was a new idea entirely.

'Whoever or whatever is bothering you at the moment', she continued, 'close your eyes and visualise them or 'it' in front of you. Then look to see if there is anything between you or you are attached to them or it. Then either remove or cut right through whatever you see. Try that and see how you go.'

Astonishingly, the very first attempt brought up *the* most vivid mental picture with extraordinary multiple attachments. And did it take some cutting through those attachments *and* several attempts at it before they went away! Boy! Was I impressed with this! How could I have had such an image in my psyche from a situation I was sure I had put behind me? Not only that but I had felt an amazing relief after it. Indeed, as if freed from this person that I had found these bizarre 'attachments' to.

Suffice it to say, I took to this 'helping myself' method like a duck to water. I was I admit, not a little fascinated to discover what would come up next in my mind's eye when I brought to mind someone or something that was either a source of anxiety, anger or distress to me. I discovered the most extraordinary 'attachments'.

That my brain had manifested these from my concerns, negative perceptions and experiences was most intriguing. Thinking about it now, I did not find myself questioning them. I simply marvelled and then was intent on their removal as quickly and as thoroughly as possible. I gave myself no time to think about whatever it was, I just determined to removed it. That I was carrying these 'manifestations' around in my psyche appalled me. Out they were to go!

All unaware, for I hadn't the least idea, this was actually preparation for the incredible changes awaiting me.

I was happy to take up this method because it was a way to restore my equilibrium. But also *helping myself* made me feel better. In a burnout breakdown, one feels life is out of one's control which is very unnerving. Doing this was positive and gave me active control of myself for myself which was very therapeutic.

So, I found time and worked at it, but the bounty came after my efforts to get rid of these images. I had a great sense of being unburdened and lighter of heart afterwards. Consequently, I cleared everything that came to mind whenever I had the chance to sit quietly and see what I could find.

I rolled up, scrubbed out, eliminated and detached everything that I visualised. Some took a deal of shifting. I soon gathered that the problems, experiences and traumas etc throughout my life, had made a very deep impression on me and then had been nicely buried in a distant archive in my memory banks. I became really quite adept at this clearing. And keen! Also, having several sessions now and then, funds permitting, with my Rei-ki healer, I felt happy indeed to be taking some responsibility for my own healing, that I was actively playing *my* part in it.

I'd heard the phrase 'emotional baggage'. It was one of those phrases tossed around that didn't seem to have any real meaning. Well, I was learning fast. There *was* such a thing.

The 'baggage' came in different forms and I could 'see' it quite plainly in my visualisations. Now I had been shown a really effective way to deal with this baggage that was patently obviously part of my 'crash'. It would be folly not to use this method to my advantage. Especially since the images that arose were interesting and surprising.

It soon occurred to me that my fears, anxieties and troubling memories had had, and would still have, a powerful effect on my health and wellness. Healing, it dawned on me, was about something quite different now. *Realisation and responsibility* were key to it too.

This really was a revelation to me. Healing was in the hands of others, wasn't it? Doctors, hospitals, the pharmaceutical industry, therapists, they either took responsibility for it or dealt with that surely? Playing a conscious part oneself to aid that healing, now that was new. What other aspects of health could this work for, I wondered?

An entirely new perspective however, had opened up for me; the undoubted emotional impact on the body head to toe.

And now, awareness and releasing the complete body from the weight and pain of negative experiences meant that my body was better able to take care of itself. Moreover, through my own efforts and choice to do so. I was to learn a great deal more.

It was my fascination and the surprising things I saw that kept me very focussed from the beginning. Thus, it didn't take me long to realise that its effectiveness lay in the 'looking' to see what appeared in my mind's eye, not the *thinking* about the problem after the initial thought.

All my concentration had to be on removing whatever it was that I could 'see.' I became quite imaginative in my methods too! And something always did appear, much to my astonishment. Whatever the emotional problem was, the brain manifested an image to express it.

How clever! Seeing something in 'form' for a negative emotion, which is an abstract, was amazing. The psyche part of the brain, the Mind, gave one something tangible to remove in order to eliminate the abstract problem. This was quite a discovery for me.

I had been obedient to something new from the idea of helping myself, but I had made a discovery that opened my mind and, little did I know it, another door. I was unaware of it but I was being led surely and gradually, step by step, towards something entirely new, extraordinary and exciting.

The upshot of the work I did on myself and the Rei-ki sessions to boost my system and entire body, was that I was back to work. And two months later I was off the medication I'd had for my burnout without weaning myself off it and with no ill-effects. I had been on them for about 7-8 months by this time.

Although it was essential help at the time when my body could not manage without artificial aid, I deemed it much better not to have to stay reliant on a chemical source if it could be otherwise. I was so pleased to be free of that need and any possible dependency and felt as if I had truly become myself again. I was well, and able to consider myself ready for anything. I applied to the Open University to re-do my last year in a fresh subject in the coming September and was accepted. Life was good.

Meanwhile with my introduction to Rei-ki through the book I had ordered I was enjoying learning about it. It was a neat and concise practical handbook on Rei-ki so it was extremely easy to read, mark and learn from.

The actual Rei-ki principles are wonderful, quite aside from the whole ethos of the methods used to ensure that the Rei-ki energy benefited the client fully. I was also intrigued to think of being 'attuned' to the Rei-ki healing vibration. To be a healing 'instrument'! What a wonderful thought.

I was very eager to take this up. Suddenly my life had a completely new, and totally unplanned, prospect that jumped me over the moon! I had no idea how different my whole life was going to be. Or, indeed, that it would in fact, lead me further yet, to something extraordinary.

Chapter 2

Some ten years previously I had toyed seriously with the idea of training in Reflexology which in the 80's had come into notice as a complementary therapy, but claims of children, home and work put that desire on the back-burner.

At the time, I saw Reflexology as a physical application to physical nerve endings. I hadn't taken in any concept about energy per se. But this new healing method, Rei-ki, which was deemed 'energy' healing, interested me very much.

It was so new to my thinking. It was really due to having experienced its wonderful energy and how my body and my whole being had responded that was the influence. It made an impact I could not ignore. I now longed to do this for others.

Thus, at one of my healing sessions, I mooted this to my healer who said she would put me in touch with a Rei-ki master whenever I felt ready. I was making use of the book to learn the positioning of the hands and making some sense of their significance: I was full of questions. Now, I just felt as if life was opening up for me with delightful and hopeful experiences.

I was completely unaware that I had in fact reached a fulcrum point in my life, a point that everything turned upon. I didn't know it, but something was just ahead that I could never have imagined; nothing was ever going to be the same again.

So, it was very soon after this that my hands started to get extremely warm and then hot. My feet soon followed suit! I had to put them on a cold hot-water bottle if you please. I didn't know what to do with myself or why this should be happening. I hadn't been attuned or even met a Rei-ki master. What was all this about?

I was really needing to get this sorted, so since I knew that my Rei-ki healer worked in a nearby crystal shop and that it would be possible to have a word with her there, off I went, hands and feet sizzling away and the rest of me feeling as if I was about to go off like Vesuvius.

As I entered her work place – a particularly fine minerals and crystal shop, – I saw there was a man with her standing behind the counter and obviously her work colleague. It was near the end of the day and luckily the shop was empty of customers. He startled me by remarking with a chuckle on the huge orange energy blazing out and around me.

It transpired that the man was a Rei-ki master! With a surge of relief mixed with astonishment, I knew I needn't even have to explain the problem; help was at hand.

Between his and my healer's instructions I was told how to ground this extraordinary energy surging through me.

Apparently, it was going around in a loop and recharging itself. I believed them! It was a very strange sensation.

After several tries under their tutelage, I began to cool off. What a relief! I then told them that I hadn't as yet been attuned so I was rather surprised that this had happened right out of the blue. I wondered if my healer friend had triggered it. She then told me that when we met initially and I shook her hand, a jolt of energy had shot up her arm. She was a little puzzled at the time but it certainly portended something remarkable

This interesting colleague of hers then produced a book on Rei-ki he had with him which he said was the best there was. He offered to lend it to me as he was about to go on holiday and it would help me understand what was going on and please to return it in two weeks.

I was very grateful and thanked him. I was delighted. It was by an American, Diane Stein and was the other and expensive book I hadn't ordered. I was so absorbed and fascinated by what had transpired that it was only on the way home that it dawned on me how amazingly apt the whole encounter was.

I returned home, considerably cooler and intrigued by the whole event. I was also rather excited about reading what Diane Stein had to say. This was a book with more depth and insight and made fascinating reading.

She is an amazing woman whose passion for Rei-ki was apparent in every word. More reading, marking, learning and inwardly digesting. Then I came to the section on the symbols one was required to learn and use.

These were in Japanese and looked far too complicated to me. I felt convinced that it would take me a month of Sundays to learn their names and strokes by heart.

I knew already through my reading that these symbols, which were Japanese words, represented certain aspects of ill-health and should be learned and where appropriate, used during the healing session. These are used by the therapist to focus the healing energy to enhance it.

It seemed that attuning the energy enabled one to connect into the positive vitality of the Universal Life-force we exist within, which flows through and vitalises every living thing on the planet. This made perfect sense to me. Even those with a secular view of the world have to acknowledge that there is such a thing as a life force.

I was surprised to discover later that some people believed these symbolic Japanese words were part of the dark arts, to be feared and avoided; even fearing the word Rei-ki, which in fact, translates as 'Life Force.' That people were still superstitious and fearful in this day and age, that some were either dismissive or simply just wary of the practice, had to be accepted without comment or concern. I felt no such alarm, only belief that this focussed Life Force, could only be loving and healing. How could it be otherwise?

I was very keen to learn and channel this wonderful energy. In my view, it is purely love and as such, comes from God who is the source of *all* Universal energy. As I heard later, '*Healing is a loving act, an act of loving*'.

If I was to take this up and learn it, I felt sure that the way forward was an approach through 'the channelling of a gentle energy' without any spiritual reference. Many people find any aspect of God or any Spirituality off-putting and many are suspicious of it.

Up to that time, esoteric books and reading material had not really been my interest. Although years ago, I did read and love The Prophet, by Kalil Gibran. A wonderful work I felt everyone should read. It was a present from my sister Grace otherwise I would not have known of it.

I certainly and unequivocally believed in the Soul, the inner Being; the indomitable part of Man, that Human spirit that rises above all things, gives us love, tenderness, compassion and altruism. I also readily believed in re-incarnation and the reality of other invisible Dimensions. This seemed to me to be only common sense. There was much that was unexplainable otherwise. For me the mechanistic and purely mathematical concept and approach to life and Man didn't satisfy or answer at all.

But these aspects were a somewhat unexplored part of my learning, just there to be touched on at times. My belief in God and the teachings of Jesus, were always part of my thinking, my view of and approach to life and humanity. It was more than belief, it was a 'knowing' that I cannot explain better than that. That 'knowing' had sustained me through all the twists, turns, experiences and vicissitudes of the preceding years. Indeed, had held me together during that burnout I spoke of. I had just got on with life and living, caught up in the ordinary everyday practicalities of life as most people are. There was simply a spiritual philosophy more or less at my shoulder that was a part of my thinking and approach to life in a general sort of way.

I speak of these things in brief basically to give an idea of where I was coming from, to coin the modern phrase, up to that time.

Reading then in Diane Stein's book about Guides helping with healing and channelling loving energy was very easy for me to accept. That was not entirely new to me. But my idea of them was quite nebulous and associated with very sensitive, spiritually connected people. In this healing approach it seemed to be very much a part of Rei-ki and the whole field of 'energy' healing.

Energy healing. That aspect *was* new to me. I was fascinated and felt a rightness about this even though I felt myself sadly ignorant of the chakras and the wider world of esoterics and metaphysics. All I knew was that I recognised something here that resonated with me despite my ignorance. I now felt in my bones as it were, that I wanted to channel, be a part of, understand and offer this loving energy to other people very much indeed.

I sat with the book on my lap and relished what I'd been reading. But those symbols daunted me somewhat! Oh well, I thought, I'll leave those for the moment. Plenty of time for that. I need to take the book back anyway so it's a good place to stop.

Fate took a hand of course. I got to the shop and lo and behold, the poor chap had caught the flu on the journey home and was to be off for a further 2 weeks. I had not met the lass who served me before so I felt it was only courtesy to return later and give the book back to him personally rather than just leave it there.

Hmm! I thought, when I got home. So why have I still got this book?

I decided to open it at random and see what came up. Surprise, surprise! The title page of the section marked, 'The Rei-ki Symbols'. Not even the page with the symbols on, but the elaborate page where the words alone stood out boldly! Sigh! No escaping them! So, I've got to tackle them, have I? Come on booby I said to myself. Get to it!

I learned them in ten minutes – all three of them *and* their pronunciation, (others came later). I could not believe it. Diane Stein had put little lines and arrows showing the direction each stroke took and it all just settled into my brain as easy as winking. What was I afraid of for goodness sake? I was thrilled to bits. I knew I was going to love this.

Then the most extraordinary thing happened.

For the first time in my life, I had the strongest 'perception' – I can't call it image, more a transparent 'picture' before me of three pairs of small hands.

I am not psychic, I've never seen a ghost or apparition nor had premonitions or anything remotely psychic – though I must admit I have frequently thought, 'how interesting if I could!'. I certainly believe and know, some people do have psychic ability.

Now I sat on my settee and really felt with this odd, vivid perception that before me were three pairs of small hands. I felt curiosity; not alarm or anything like that. I was intrigued, fascinated. Were these my Guides I asked myself? Again, I had a feeling that they were. Had I become a channel then?

Naturally doubts assailed me. Nothing like this had happened to me before. I'd never, to my recollection had a 'perception'. Had this 'perception' therefore been merely imagination prompted by reading about Guides? Was it all wishful thinking and hoping that somehow something special had happened to me? Was this all my ego prompting me to think I might become a healer?

What was certain was that I did not want to *be* prompted by ego. I did not wish to make the claim of 'I am a healer.' I really wanted to be a channel for this wonderful loving energy and work for it and with it. *Was* it because I wanted it so much?

My mind went around and round, trying to sort out my thoughts and get a proper perspective on things. One aspect however kept coming to me. Why were all the hands small? Weren't Guides adults? Surely not children? Surely too, if I had conjured them up from imagination, the hands would have been adult-sized?

I had no-one to talk this over with. I lived alone. Another concern was that if I did speak of it, people would think I was delusional or losing my marbles. Had I not had a serious nervous collapse, several months previously? I couldn't bear the thought of their judgement. And so, I wrestled on with my thoughts for a while in some confusion.

Getting nowhere I decided to give it up, have a cup of tea and think of something else.

When eventually I went to bed, I wasn't particularly tired so decided to read a novel – a favourite pastime of mine, before I went to sleep. I read a whole page. Nothing went in. With a resigned sigh I leaned back and closed my eyes.

Unbidden, I saw, rather in the distance, the image of a man in silk robes. He was wearing a green tunic over a longer gold-coloured garment and had his hands folded into his sleeves. He seemed to be in semi-profile and had something tall upon his head and I 'knew' he was Japanese. Also, from ancient Japan.

Hardly daring to breathe, I held my focus looking ahead in my mind's eye; I didn't want the image to fade. Then to the left of me on the periphery of my vision I was aware of another image, a tiny old lady in a chair in long dark garments.

Again I 'knew' that she was from Tibet and a long time ago. The certainty of this knowledge was very strong. It was almost as if they had told me what I was discerning about them.

I found myself sitting very still and trying hard not to let my mind work on this or lose my focus. This was amazing! Two people who undoubtedly had small hands! I could scarcely believe this. The effort to stay looking and not thinking was quite hard. What was going on? No don't think, look!

But it was tiring. I had to open my eyes and rest my brain for a minute. This was extraordinary I told myself. A little bubble of something rose in me. Could I trust this? Some odd feeling of certainty told me that this was real. Something had been triggered. What or how or why I didn't have a clue. Just this weird sort of knowing! If I closed my eyes, would 'They' come again?

How on earth had this happened to me, I wondered? Perhaps this hot energy in my hands that had started up out of nowhere had triggered this. Healers had Guides. Was this then how they discovered them? I couldn't resist trying again. Yes, they were there but fainter.

I was still rather doubtful and afraid that I had let my imagination run away with me so I settled down to sleep.

The following evening however, I thought – will I see them again? Are they still there? I closed my eyes and looked inward. Yes, they were! Then just as I looked, something else appeared on the periphery of my vision but this time to the right. I saw a pair of small feet encased in calf-high moccasins and just above, the hem and part of a pale skirt. – but no further.

Oh, come on, I thought, this *is* imagination! An 'Indian Guide'? That always seems obligatory!

I opened my eyes scoffing at my gullibility. Then to my utter astonishment I heard someone say – inside my head. 'I am Eyes-of-a-Doe'. I nearly fell off the bed! What on earth was happening? At the same time, a certainty filled me that this was a shy and very young woman. The third pair of small hands!

My head was in a spin. I thought, this is real! I can't believe it, but it's real! No one will believe me but it is real! I sat there marvelling and not a little pleased. How, by all that was wonderful, had this happened? Did it happen to everyone who worked with this healing energy? Had it *really* happened to me? Suddenly, I had no doubts. My life had just shot round the bend onto a new branch-line.

Chapter 3

Although this amazing mental perception, for want of a better description, was nearly 20 years ago, it was so astonishing and such a profound experience that I assure you I recall it perfectly. It is as vivid to me today as then. That is why I can be so precise as to what I perceived and what occurred. How could I possibly forget something so profoundly different, an experience that I could hardly have believed would happen, least of all to me? What it heralded I had no way of knowing of course. But it changed my life irrevocably.

The following day though, was back to work and life as usual. I so wanted to talk to someone about it. Of a certainty, especially in the light of my recent nervous collapse, I couldn't talk of such an experience to anyone, friends or family!

In the days between, I couldn't resist going inside my head to see if these lovely people materialised. To my relief and joy, they did and I believed again that they seemed to speak to me.

I cannot remember these details but I found it reassuring. I do remember it took a lot of concentration which was quite difficult after a day at work so I didn't 'listen' for long. although I found this fascinating. I was a trifle concerned that my imagination was doing overtime and that this was wishful thinking. Was this real?

I had booked a further session with my Rei-ki healer and was looking forward to it. As usual, my Rei-ki session was a wonderful experience.

After it I talked with her about some of the things that were happening to me. She accepted what I told her and was beautifully matter-of-fact with me which was deeply reassuring! She also gave me the name and address of someone who could help me understand more. This was a very experienced lady who dealt with all aspects of healing and metaphysics.

The upshot was that I went straight round that evening to this lady's house to put a note in her door asking to see her. Is there ever any such thing as coincidence?

Luckily, she had just arrived home so seeing the note come through the letter box, opened the door and invited me in. On meeting, I naturally put my hand out to shake hands. As we did so she said,

'Oh! Rei-ki healer?'

Too astonished to think clearly, I said,

'Ah – um – yes!' and left it at that. When later I asked her how she knew, she said she could always recognise it as it had a particular vibration and that she herself wasn't keen on it. She thought it too strong. For her own use she preferred the etheric healing energy that she channelled.

I didn't tell her I had not been attuned, or go into that, as I was more interested in my questions about the Guides and that possibly I was hearing them speak. The relief at meeting someone who might answer my question on Guides was too important to discuss anything else for the moment.

She accepted without a blink my saying that I thought I had encountered some 'people' in my head and asked if they could be my Guides? Yes, they were, she said, 'they' had just told her they were.

It transpired that she had Guides she knew, loved and worked with in her own healing work. She heard them speak quite clearly in her head. She said it was 'clairaudience.'

What a relief that was! It does happen to people! I told her about the young Indian girl and how I'd heard her name but that was the only one I knew, but I believed they had spoken to me. I then said there seemed to be others but I didn't say who I thought they were, I just asked if she could tell me anything about any others.

She then said one was Japanese, a man, also there was a little old lady. The bubbles of joy were rising in me now! Could she ask them their names please? She came up with a very odd – obviously Tibetan name first. I couldn't grasp or pronounce it so I asked, could she ask if I could call her Tibetan Grandmother, please? Apparently, the little lady chuckled and said yes that would be acceptable.

Then I asked for the name of the Japanese gentleman. That came over very indistinctly but she caught part of it that sounded rather like Ja, so I asked if I could call him Ja-San! Yes, he was quite happy with that.

If I had been less in a kind of wonder-zone I could have got a better notion of their names. My own contact was too fragile and immature for me to establish them myself. Later when I became properly attuned to this listening/hearing ability these names had become their identity to me and as such, very personal which I'm sure pleased them. They were always happy to use them. I never did find out their full names. It never seemed necessary.

The healer I was visiting then said with a laugh.

'You can ask them yourself you know! Speak inside your head, they hear you quite clearly.'

Well of course! Silly me! But this was all so new and frankly incredible that I couldn't take it fully into my own keeping. I was so involved with my contact with her that I couldn't bring my concentration to hear anything myself.

We had a very interesting conversation in which she told me of her own three Doctor Guides and the work they did together. It was riveting listening and she was obviously a very experienced healer. She was also an astrologer and offered to have a quick look at my natal details.

Two things stayed with me. First, she said she had not seen a kite in anyone's chart of my natal year. This seemed to interest her, though she didn't explain. Then she got out a fascinating map of the constellations and galaxies and after looking at it a while said 'Hmm. That one's a new one on me.'

It didn't register much with me as she then went on to tell me a few interesting aspects in my chart and the moment passed. There was so much to take in and so much was interesting that my brain was whirling.

On my way home, somewhat in a daze I have to admit, I recalled her feeling Rei-ki energy through my hands. Could I really already be a channel for attuned Rei-ki energy? She had been so clear about it, had recognised it as specifically Rei-ki energy, hadn't she? All of this was so much to take in.

On the one hand, I didn't know what to make of it all and on the other marvelled at what had transpired and what I'd learned. How could I ever dream that I could have just had the conversations I'd just had? They were far beyond anything I'd known of before. This was going to take some time to really assimilate.

When I did get home however, I couldn't wait to sit quietly and get mentally in touch with these lovely people *if* I could do so again.

I had never heard the words clairaudience or clairaudient before nor that people were able 'hear' in this way. Naturally I knew of clairvoyance, the seeing of spiritual aspects of life, people and other Dimensions which was all I knew of it, but this was *entirely* new! Without my mixture of a strange certainty which came from heaven knew where, and awe, I would have found it hard to believe quite frankly! I felt blessed in meeting this woman who vouched for its authenticity. As for myself, would it continue for me, I wondered?

What happened and developed from that day I will come to and talk of again for there is much to tell you. It was intermingled with my working with this energy flowing so well through my hands.

I was trying it out on myself as, according to the books, the start of using it was for Self-healing, a pre-requisite of the Rei-ki method of learning to practice this.

How wonderful and truly sensible that Self-healing comes *first*, to learn not just theory, but from the *experience itself,* before you offer it to others, Then, that you offer not only your technique but your personal experience as well with the healing practice. To create an empathy in this way seems an excellent approach to healing. On top of that you are approaching the person you are working on in a better state of health. How good is that?

Moreover, to experience for oneself this wonderful loving healing and also to know what one's future clients will feel too, makes this unique. And, most importantly, to discover the effect that focussing the symbols had on oneself before one offers them to others.

For some inexplicable reason however, I had already been attuned to Rei-ki energy, and I presumed, level 1.

I remember feeling a kind of bemused acceptance of this as my Guides assured me that this was so.

At the beginning, since the energy was flowing very freely already for me and through me, I was in fact enjoying practicing this lovely self-healing every day. Plus of course the Rei-ki symbols quite happily on myself. And for my own benefit – and joy.

I found this all so different and exciting that I found myself utterly absorbed in it. That things even more so lay ahead in the field of Rei-ki I hadn't the least idea of.

I couldn't wait to channel this warm flow of energy coming from my hands for other people, so it wasn't long before I was offering this warm loving energy to friends and family at every opportunity! I was undoubtedly over-eager but mostly they were very patient with me!

But things were also developing with regard to my clairaudience and that was just so beautiful and profound that I loved this part of my developing life very much.

As they talked to me, I started to take it down in writing: there was so much they wanted to convey to me that I couldn't wait to get a large pad and a pen ready each night.

As soon as I could when I was finished for the day, I settled down to focus my listening to inside my head and my inner eye to look to see what might reveal itself.

Surprisingly, this did not take much effort. Possibly it was because I now had no resistance, no fear that it was unreal. Clairaudience was a fact. Seemingly I had been blessed with this amazing ability. My eagerness was much appreciated by my Guides and I soon had pages and pages of their wonderful wisdom.

I was also beginning to get detailed guidance from these lovely Guides in learning about the way to channel and enable this Rei-ki energy. I knew with certainty now that for some reason I had been attuned in some way other than through an 'earthly' Rei-ki Master.

Now they were to teach me comprehension of the energy through fully-focussed channelling. Their advice and guidance were how to make good use of my feelings, instincts and awareness. There was so much being conveyed to me even to using the techniques of self-healing and what I could learn from the energy in my hands and my body's response.

Their words below are so wonderfully apt; their teaching very precise and particular. Tibetan Grandmother's voice seemed the strongest guiding voice. I would love to quote much more of them to you, but this would become practically a treatise on Rei-ki which is not my aim.

'...you will learn to feel the difference. This will come as you focus your inner self on the energy in your hands. You may question us as you feel the difference and we will help you to understand and come to 'know'. Take your time with this. Question it every time in the stillness of giving Rei-ki. You must use this to focus, feel, learn, question and learn again. It will be a slow process. Let it come slowly. You will come to the 'knowing' better, more strongly. The 'knowing' will take much practice which is why it is important that you are able to do it. We will help with this. - yes, in self-healing much can be learned. Yes, it is valuable to practice the focussing and the difference in your finger and palm chakras and doing the questioning and asking and feeling. Yes, when your hands are on your own body, use the opportunity to do all that we teach you. Yes, do not concern yourself at this stage with any medical knowledge. Do not think of the organ under your hands only what the energy and the chakras tell you. You can then learn to feel for the deeper levels. Think of it as tissue, not an organ with a function. Think of the position of the chakra. We will show you how to balance that to bring the energy centre into correct status for beginning the process of healing. Do not make your mind overshadow your feelings. Use the mind lightly - in this way the light will come on and you will be able to 'see' with your inner self. It is your 'inner' self that will learn and direct your Rei-ki healing energy. That stage will be the next one......'.

It became apparent from the emphasis of the teaching that vibrational energy was the focus. Rei-ki was certainly the surest method for me to learn about in all forms. Partly because it contained so many aspects of this field of knowledge, but particularly because energy could be *personally* and *physically* experienced through my own body and the response from others who received it.

There was much encouragement, and indeed emphasis, to work with real conscious awareness. Their guidance was so comprehensive. I felt there had to be a deeper purpose.

I began to realise that this was not to make me a professional Rei-ki Therapist, full stop. This was a very deep grounding. It was, in effect, essential for the many things I needed to learn and which unfolded for me as time went on.

With the addition of clairaudience now, I was learning to focus on and understand the inner, the place within. And such a lovely new way and very important way, of doing it.

'....now there is much that is different to learn and you have been given this gift to help with the clarity you have always looked for so hard – yes, we know – it has been seen that you learn well this way...'

I had a great deal to learn and my mind had to, in fact needed, to be attuned, to get to grips with all that was to follow. Little did I know then that this was to enable me to really encompass metaphysics and energy and acquire a fresh viewpoint on everything.

'this is a different learning dear one as it is not of the intellect - that has been developed. Now is the time for the heart and the inner spirit. These require different methods – gentle absorption like oxygen from the water flowing through the gills of the carp. No striving – no effort......your intellect once connected to the heart chakra and the 3rd eye will flourish afresh.'

'...be patient with yourself for although you have a lot to learn you must go gently and that means with yourself also. You are full of enthusiasm but you must not run at knowledge, you must let it come to you through us and the workings of your own mind and what we teach you.....we know you are going gently with the practicing and thinking over what we have given you to the fullness of your knowledge...we are always with you helping to watch over you because we care for you and you love us too. Let your mind follow its own ribbon for a while dear Happiness – yes, Ja-San – it will be good to see what is revealed.'

What sweet encouragement this was. How fascinating life was promising to be!

Chapter 4

Meanwhile I was agog with curiosity of course about these 'people' who had entered my life. By this time Ja-San came to me facing me, though his features were indistinct. He had sometimes made references to his time as a Samurai to illustrate a point in regard to balance, focus and the use of principle to guide actions that he was patiently teaching me. One evening I asked him about himself and he told me,

'I was a Samurai and spiritual teacher to the pupils of my master and Prince in whose service I was for the defence of his realm – yes in Ancient Japan which we called O'yashima. There I taught the spiritual principles of the use of the sword through oneness of mind and body and inner being. With this oneness the sword was forged and so in oneness it should be wielded for Right and Good. A principle of movement to defend the weak and make wrong right swiftly, so the mind was with the sword not the enemy for that would make it a personal act of vengeance which corrupts.'

Ja-San told me how, in order for him personally to accept the training and necessity of taking life, he had conceived this philosophy of his own. Coming from a tradition of Samurai, that way of life was chosen for him in part and eagerly accepted by him as a very young man.

He had a strong inner spirituality however, and to him love was the ultimate spiritual truth. Therefore, love had to be part of what he did. Thus, love as a consciousness, of every aspect of the Samurai way of life, made it possible for him to follow it until he was permitted to be a teacher of his philosophy as part of the training in his principality.

When he spoke of this I was very aware of the sincerity and commitment through the timbre of his voice. At the same time, I was given a perception of his world and the ambiance he was in. This perception was beautiful and quite fascinating.

It is so hard to find words adequate enough to describe a measure of this experience. I felt very privileged for this glimpse into the world of his last incarnation. Also, into another and very different culture of which I knew very little. Theirs was an ancient world and the way of the Warrior was very important but Ja San's teaching of respect and love of the skills and the purpose gave enlightenment to a necessary way of life. His principles used in that lifetime were relevant to everything I was learning.

As Ja-San put it so succinctly,

'The concepts of harmony, balance, focus, oneness, are integral to all things Japanese but the fulcrum of these is balance. Once that is right, then all is *good*. Use this principle to enable you to see situations and events clearly. With clarity comes all understanding from understanding comes focus and from there the correct action for the purpose.'

To illustrate this Ja-san spoke to me of the sword that was used in his profession.

'The secret of the Samurai sword is in the balance in all the elements worked into its shining beauty. Only great masters were able to achieve this because the tuning of this balance was only possible from a lifetime of skilled craftsmanship. The hand, the eye and the third eye in unity and harmony judged the balance of the blade as it was worked on. The focus was deep and intense and was not allowed to waver – the end result was as near perfection as it was possible to make it. In this way the unity in the sword responded to the unity in the warrior and they then became one in the purpose which both Samurai and sword were fashioned – preparation - each one was in the hands of a master guided and prepared by the same principles.'

Ja-San told me that all disciplines required principles. Part of his guidance was to be about the principles of healing and the understanding of vibrational healing. His voice was cultured and serene and his phrases were like that of a gentle teacher. He called me Happiness. I loved that. His whole essence was so loving and gentle. He said that he spoke Japanese to me but it was transposed so that I heard it in English and that it was suited to my particular understanding. It was thus-wise with all the Guides from different countries and eras that came to speak with me. Communication was thus assured. Speech patterns and vocabulary were always suited to the recipient clairaudient, they said. It had to be appropriate to each person. What suited one person, would not suit another. Thus, each person was accommodated perfectly. Guidance naturally needed exactly the right communication. I was riveted by all of this I can assure you.

And dear beloved Guide that he was, Ja-san sometimes wrote little poems for me. They are in the style of haiku and I copied them out into a special little blue book. This pleased him. He said they were only moderate as he was not a haiku scholar but I love them. Perhaps one day I will create a little book from them and do my best to illustrate it as they are such an endearing gift to me.

I treasured everything they said to me so I was glad that I had decided early on that I must write down what they said to me as I heard it. I didn't want to lose *anything* they said – also their words needed to be recorded because what they said was too precious to be lost! I would always have them to re-read at any time and 'listen' to their wise words whenever I needed them. Now out came the book and pen every night.

I took down dictation with great anticipation at every opportunity. I wish I'd thought of this from the very first few nights but I was too caught up with listening and so some beautiful conversations were lost alas. I had, and still have pads and pens with me always, in handbags, side tables, beside the pillow, in the car, everywhere. I'd listen and write on the train, in cafes, sitting in my parked car. There was so much I had to learn and so happy was I to hear their dear voices and gain their guidance.

'...yes – it is good for us in our hearts that you draw so much from us. We find it easy to talk and give you this talk –

yes, Tibetan Grandmother this time. You good listener you want so much to hear us and learn. It is good for our hearts and minds to come to you this way. It makes us feel good in the heart chakra for it beams with love for you and the work we do. We feel raised up inside as you do and this is a good feeling and makes our brains work. That is good too. We know we will all accomplish much together so sleep good, sleep and be happy in your heart too for all is well and you are much loved by us – yes, we feel your love and how it has grown as has ours for we are now a part of each other in love and wisdom, sleep now.'

I wish you could have heard her dear sweet voice. What beautiful reciprocity and how happy I am to be able to re-read these lovely words and copy them out for you too.

'...trust and believe in the strength and love within you. Hold it in your mind and you will find answers will come swiftly but make the stillness principle a part of your thinking too for clarity and knowledge and the 'knowing'....'

This came from their collective voice. Clarity, Trust, Knowledge. These became my watchwords through their loving help. I was blessed indeed.

When I asked Tibetan Grandmother about herself, she told me that she was from a long time ago and was to share ancient knowledge with me. She was always seated. I asked her why. She told me she had lost both legs from mid-thigh. They had been severed during a terrible time when her people were brutally attacked and they had lost their homes; whole villages and many lives including her own. She was always very sweet and serene with a laconic way of speaking that was always to the point. She called me Granddaughter and I loved her and had immense respect for her sweet wisdom. Here are a few examples of her special idiosyncratic wisdom that I'd like to share with you

When talking together on the difficult way of life of someone I knew, she replied:-

'The traveller seeking the top chooses his own path up the mountain, otherwise all would be in line and single file and reach the top only in turn.'

'Feeling love for what you are doing will bring much light – use it to dissolve any doubt – no good to us, only dark side! Be good to yourself and make best use of wise words.'

'..wisest not to feed dark side at all. better they starve than you lose light. To lose light is to let dark side win. No good for anyone dear Granddaughter!'

'Instincts were given to you before your abilities to communicate, therefore trust them. You have learned how the mind can provide distortion. Yes – instinct comes first! Hold on to it lest it escape like the cricket from the cage and be gone and unseen. Question the instinct for truth. Not for doubting!'

When speaking of focus and clarity of mind she invariably used nature as a metaphor to make her point. And very concise it was too! The 'pictures' she gave made the point very clear and without fuss and were always most apt.

'…Our eyes are like that of the eagle. We see far and comprehend much. His flight is keen and true. He is not an aimless wanderer. He knows all that is necessary and right. – you will see the way forward – it will resolve itself. No effort. Save energy!'

'Wise beast is mountain lion! You think like her; think her stillness; think her patience in all things this is good and wise advice.'

'Very good Granddaughter. Pursue the work as the hawk pursues that which pursues its young.'

Her especial wisdom was to help me understand how to use the stillness within to guide my decisions and actions. To benefit from patience as the animal kingdom does. That preparation and clarity of thought were the most helpful tools and to be made regular use of, especially if they saved energy which animals fully understand! These were her guiding principles and very necessary for me to take heed of being the impulsive, eager for action charge that I am. I have found a perfect example of her delightful ways to illustrate what she was teaching me.

'You have worked well to deal with the negativity dear dear one – but used too much precious energy dear Granddaughter trying to unravel the tangled thread. The mountain lion goes for easy prey. He has wisdom to refrain from pursuing that which will elude him – learn from wily hunter dear Granddaughter. Wait in still and quiet place till better quarry comes – so. He does not rise and pace up and down while waiting for that which is needful – once in a good place he waits in patience even though his belly rumbles with hunger – for he will go away empty if he loses patience dear Granddaughter and the hunger will gnaw at his belly and teach him better next time – and this is an animal with no knowledge of God within him. Yet he is wise in this. Yes, wise lion will find a place of comfort for waiting. His 'now' is good.
....Even the lion growls and snarls sometimes to show his feelings. Voicing them is to relieve them and then they are gone on the wind where they belong – for they will find no place to stay for the wind is restless and blows all things into dust. You worked wisely to take out the pain dear Granddaughter but refrain from pulling it back for inspection. Let the kindly wind blow it all to dust in high places of clean air and the face of the sun to burn away the dross and render all renewed – yes, better to drop thought and count blessings instead. Happy use for energy – better for you, better for ether, better for all!'

Worlds of wisdom in dear sweet Tibetan Grandmother. She was always such a delight! What wonderful ways of expressing her guidance, always to the nub of things.

It is hard to convey how the information from my Guides was imparted to me. It was very clear and I heard the timbre of their voices clearly too; their voices and speech were distinctive. I could hear their words of wisdom and take down every word with such immediacy that I marvelled at it. It was so clear, so fast. There was also an instantaneousness in my thinking and theirs and I experienced such clarity of thought, such a grasp of concept that segued with theirs as we explored so many things together; it was incredibly stimulating. A truly in-depth method of conversing that is impossible to convey satisfactorily. Thus, it wasn't like ordinary listening at all.

Their multiple-voiced guidance was fascinating too. Together they called me 'dear dear one'. Their voices segued into what they were conveying to me and then their individual voices with their particular contributions came to the fore. It was wonderfully caring and personal. I was so blessed.

'Look always within for thinking, feeling, knowing. All is within to make right that which is without. Thus the material physical world benefits the Being not masters it. Far better dear dear one not to be mastered by the material or the physical. To overcome mastery takes much energy dear Granddaughter. Better be still and let benefits come to you! Wise old woman!'

'.....Walk slowly, savour the journey and see much! Otherwise dust will obscure what is vital to progress.'

'.....As you bring things into 'realisation' so they are brought into existence and the momentum starts from the moment of creation. – until that moment there is only stasis and the energy is trapped with nowhere to go.'

'.....Knowledge without comprehension does not 'realise' itself. Truth lies in the heart for it is felt within therefore becomes 'known.'

'.....Going within for answers is wiser than searching the mind which will look in areas of association for knowledge and bring confusion and doubt to make the road long towards finding the truth......bring the intellect into the heart – thinking with the heart is to use heart chakra energy, not to think with the emotions. Guilt against the self seeks to prevent that which is greatly valued in the physical plane.' (ie: all forms of mobility, physical independence.) Being positive with the mind is not enough – only when it comes from within does it unravel before one and find the right response. Gentleness is more lasting for it dissolves negativity so it is less likely to return.'

'....truth always lives in the heart dear one and that is where one looks for it if one is wise......truth and love cannot be destroyed or cast out only covered and obscured – both are stronger than all things.'

These are just a very few excerpts of their wonderful guidance and wisdom which they gave me to reassure me as well as to prompt my understanding of the subtleties of things. Everything they said warmed my heart as well as stimulated my thinking.

What was so brilliant was that their sentences flowed so beautifully, lucidly and concisely. Everything they said was pertinent, nothing extraneous or irrelevant. Reading through what they said to me was so perfectly syntaxical and hardly needed punctuation. I knew incontrovertibly that quite apart from what they spoke of, how they spoke of it, could not and did not come out of *my* brain! Oh, that it could! If I had to teach or make a speech, I could not come out with the information needed so seamlessly without endless note-making well beforehand, or indeed, explain something significant so lucidly. Even trying to paraphrase what they say is hopeless.

It was a constant joy to me to take down their wonderful words and to be in conversation with them. It was very exciting as well as stimulating when they picked up my thoughts instantly and fitted them into what they spoke of to me; my occasional questions and simultaneous connections with them I couldn't write down, I was taking dictation after all. The majority of the time I wrote seamlessly without a break. It was and still is, an amazing experience.

Because this is the most intimate way of communication, one's hearing and participation is from truly within oneself. This means that one is very connected to the speaker and the dimension that they are coming from. It is a sharing that has no equal in human terms because there are no barriers. It is synchronous and spontaneous with no pre-conceptions or analysis. I cannot explain how wonderful it is. Yes, it is the communication of words, for they are clear, but also a communication through the senses through one's hearing, through the feelings that arise as you communicate on this interior level with 'people' who are purely loving.

Here they explain it perfectly!

'.... it is very subtle dear dear one. We need your mind to be free for our way of working – yes the way that is so satisfying to us dear dear pupil for our minds act in unison and you receive perceptions and subtle vibrations that enhance your comprehension in a way that is very dear to us. We love this method and your love for it brings joy to our hearts and minds. It is therefore most precious to us.'

Their different personalities, which came through their 'voices,' the timbre and their own phrasing, made them very real to me. This could hardly be otherwise in so intimate a way of communicating. Learning something of and gaining a feeling of their last 'lives' enhanced this for me. It also gave colour to their way of conveying what was needed and this gave everything a special impact and a beautiful quality that resonated so sweetly with my own thinking and being.

Between the 'lights' that seemed to come on in my head when we covered certain topics and the expansive feeling I experienced around the region of my heart at profounder moments, (which gave me abundant proof that there was indeed an energy centre there that was very responsive indeed,) you can appreciate my joy in it all.

Chapter 5

Because it was all so beautiful and profound, I so wanted to share it. At the beginning, this could possibly have had an element also of needing reassurance that the words were really not mine.

There was one friend in particular I felt positive I could trust. Lesley. She is a very good friend who had been wonderful to me when I was in, and trying to recover from, my burnout (as I discovered it is often called). We had known each other very well and closely for some years. She is lovely; she had no agendas or ego hang-ups. A truly good friend. She is also a very pragmatic lass with a lovely inner calm. She made me feel safe so I knew I could trust her judgement implicitly.

Naturally she was very familiar with my interest in – not to say passion, for Rei-ki. I had been helping her with her hay-fever to good effect. She seemed the perfect person to confide in.

So, I went to her and asked her if she would read something I had written down. When she had read a page, she remarked how loving it was, how different from anything else she'd ever read. So, could she tell me whether she felt I had written them, that they were my words?

Without hesitation, she said they didn't 'sound' like me. She said the flowing way it came across was exceptional. I told her all about hearing these words and taking them down. She believed me totally. It was an incredible relief. Now I could share this wonderful happening with someone who felt the joy I had in it.

It wasn't long after this, for I was by now hearing very readily, that I asked in my head if my friend had a Guide and would they talk to me? To my utter delight my friend's Guide came to me and said she would be delighted to. Her name was Amanda.

When she introduced herself to me, I saw her so clearly. I am always given an instant perception of the Guide who comes to me and it is difficult to explain how I perceive the person and simultaneously receive certain knowledge.

She was standing, leaning back on the rail of a large ship, her face to the sun in part profile to me, thick blonde hair lifted by the wind, the long deck before her. I felt her exhilaration, her vitality and joy in life, the bright sun, the freshness of the sea air. She was in a white uniform and I knew her for a Navy nurse and that this was wartime in the Pacific in the 1940's.

Just as I was 'seeing' her, the front of the ship suddenly exploded into an inferno and I knew that she did not survive it. It was quite a shock but she spoke to me and said 'but I was unaware and full of life and joy so please do not be concerned. Now I am a Guide to my precious charge, Lesley.'

It transpired she was Canadian and had been very eager to join the war using her nursing skills. She was so suited to my friend, also blonde, full of vitality and a very sporty-outdoorsy lass, English but brought up in the Australian sun. My dear friend was delighted to have Amanda made known to her. Although she can't hear her, she frequently talks to her and feels comforted. She seemed a perfect counterpart.

This was something I found over and over again in my encounter with the Guides who were so happy to talk with me, especially those I had worked with during my healings. They always suited their 'precious charge' as if they were an aspect either of them or their chosen path. There were always clear connections. I could not have made them up; their stories were about things I had no knowledge of. Also, I certainly do not have the talent to instantly and lucidly 'create' a counterpart in character to the person whose Guide I am eager to connect with. The connections are really only apparent to me when I re-read what the Guide has said to me because the dictation I'm taking down is very rapid.

This was answered beautifully on an occasion when I marvelled to my dear Guides how our thinking and concepts were so lucidly and swiftly connected when we were considering some aspect or another. They spoke of them being attuned to my aptitudes.

'....Reciprocity dear one, even without conscious awareness has to be part of the equation of Guide and Soul-part's personality – the guidance is attuned to the attributes so that there is a naturally attractive connection – vibrations always find their receptor – it is their nature. They can be pulled out of alignment, they can be lowered in pitch, they can be blocked by negative energy barriers but they always find their receptors. That is why once a barrier is removed, in other words negativity released – the vibration will reach the receptor very rapidly. This enables the Guide to be in close contact with his or her precious charge on the un-conscious level that most operate on.'

Thus, it is obvious, that affinity was essential and was also relevant to the path their Soul, their inner being, had chosen to learn from. We all know that in our physical world those closest and dearest to us in life have an affinity with us.

I will also mention here that during my healings I do not 'hear' anything as I do when listening and talking with Guides. Instead, I am 'given' information that is needed in a subtle sense of 'knowing' that is very clear and precise.

It is this preciseness that gives me the certainty that it comes from those who know; ergo their Guide. When it is important I 'perceive' events that need healing. I do not conjure them. I am not psychic. I am given the information that is necessary in that moment of need for me to work with the person. I never know what will transpire or whether or not I will *receive* or *perceive* (or both) at any given time or healing session. The Guides know all. I don't, so I do not guess. As one of my dear Guides, a Dr Ying Po said. 'To speculate is to invite incorrect conclusion.' What a beautifully-put truism. I think of it often.

Another Guide I spoke with, called Melanie, (the Guide of a very bright young woman I met), reveals her sweet personality and the way that clairaudience 'works' – for want of a better word.

'You are developing your clairaudience so quickly that you are absorbing our thinking into your hearing and your own thinking dear Felicity. Please do not worry that you are using your own imagination. Your thinking processes are very fast that is all. Trust and believe in yourself. You are eager and willing – you are being guided to be wise with it. They love being busy for you and I love talking to you and thinking with you too. It is great fun for me.........(We 'thought about' Soul choices)...Oh yes dear Felicity without the Soul's direction the personality *would* be without essence. Thus the essence of the Soul imbues the personality with whatever qualities that Soul needs to enable the personality to help its development. Yes, it is hard to define it exactly! We all try but it's sort of elusive isn't it?'

I absolutely loved meeting all these remarkable and sweet 'people'. They were all so happy to talk with me and I was always interested in who they were of course. The vastness of this closely interconnected network grew ever more apparent. That I had a channel into it constantly amazed and delighted me. And still does.

~ . ~

I knew something of Ja-San's last lifetime and a little of Tibetan Mother's although she was reticent about hers, deeming it unnecessary to dwell on. She had things to say to me so why waste energy on unimportant things, she said. She was really good at giving me lovely metaphors for not wasting energy!

I loved the way she illustrated this very important aspect to me. I could see her sweet tiny face crinkle up with a smile and her little dark eyes full of amusement when she admonished me for using my energy wastefully. How easy it is to do! She was adorable. I imagined kissing her dear sweet face which she liked very much.

During the times I sought to listen to my Guides, Eyes-of-a Doe became more revealed to me too. She was very young and slender and always appeared standing half facing a tepee. She appeared quite shy and reserved too. It transpired that her father was the Medicine man and healer of the tribe and that he had trained her in the healing arts from childhood. Later I learned that she was married and the mother of a little boy, Running Fox

He was only a little child when he fell sick and nothing she could do could save him. She naturally blamed herself; she obviously wasn't good enough. When she spoke of it to me, I had a most profound experience regarding this as I was writing down her words and I would like to share it with you for it was beautiful and cathartic too. Only her own words can convey the actuality.

'Years ago I learnt that I was not invincible in the arts of healing. This brought much sorrow to my heart and I turned away from men to the animals whom I could love without pain. They gave me their loyalty and I loved them with my whole heart and wished to heal them of every little illness or pain because they had no voice as my baby had no voice. Let the tears flow because you wash away my guilt and pain too, so I thank you for your tears for they come to me out of your loving heart and for this I love you very much and will help you all I can in all that you do. (suddenly this brought acutely and vividly to mind, the death of my dearly loved dog (in 1970) who was badly injured and taken to the vet. I couldn't go with him and when the vet phoned later and recommended he be put to sleep I was devastated but more so because I wasn't there with him and felt I'd betrayed him.) – she continued – 'I know, this was unplanned – it came from your memories of your little dog and I felt your guilt and remorse and helplessness to prevent death and shared your sorrow. Because I am now a part of your experience, we were and still are joined at the heart and so our twin sorrows fled across the ether one to the other so that each of us could wash it all away. Yes it is deep but trust us, we are all a part of something special so we will not let you be unhappy. Pain is sometimes a bottomless well but love saves us from drowning and your love for me and my little baby – yes, dear little baby – a son – Running Fox – has taken the pain and cast it into the ether forever. So has the guilt and pain you felt for your innocent little animal. Now I must learn to trust my abilities to heal men, human beings, for they are our task.'

This lovely Guide, Eyes-of-a-Doe, spoke with such sweetness. She had a pure healer serenity as did my other Guides. After that experience, I always perceived her as facing me from the entrance to her Tepee.

In that lifetime, due to her grief and the belief that she had failed her beloved baby son she had retreated emotionally from her people. Consequently, she had not moved on with them after her earthly life ended; she had chosen to be a Guide and thus worked with healing on the plane appropriate to this work. Through resolving that karmic and deeply sad incident from that incarnation it meant that she was able to move to the Dimensions that her darling son and her father and brother were awaiting her.

Later, my Guides reassured me, 'Eyes-of-a-Doe is happy now and with her father now while her baby sleeps. She is eager at last to learn and extend her knowledge of human medicine. Her brother is with her too now. Running Fox is happy too.'

Eyes-of-a-Doe then came to speak to me. 'I have been learning with such joy. ...I can return and work again amongst men for which God and my father have prepared me through the great gift of healing. We became part of a great love you and I when you took my pain away and made me believe I was worthy of my son and my healing arts....I will be with you for a while....I will be going to a place of waiting and preparation soon. We are all working together in love and each has his task we are all working for. All is well here and soon I will speak with you of these things in more detail. I am safe now and in love with a good purpose thanks to your loving tears and therefore being able to receive my baby back into my empty arms and heart.'

My Guides then added, '...Eyes-of-a-Doe is with her baby now because you made her believe she was worthy – she could not accept this from another who was not in her heart experience even though she tried – but that was from you...she will be back from time to time when you need her,......by being with her baby and being now in a happy mind and heart healing and knowledge will expand into the human realm and grow so that she can truly work with her father and learn skills for human beings properly at last......'

It seemed she had moved into another plane or dimension because of being re-united with her family

Through the network she still joined her voice with Ja-san and Tibetan Mother, visiting the mental plane I was connected to in order to add her wisdom for my guidance for a while longer. And always that sweet essence she had was imparted in her words. Lovely Eyes-of-a-Doe.

This seemed to be part of her Soul path. I was also told she would be able to move on to the Halls of Preparation where she would eventually reincarnate with her son, no doubt as members of the healing profession and working together.

This made her even happier. I seem to have played a specific part for her, a healing her personality needed so much and I was honoured to do it for her, although I did not know why I was able to. It was also a perfect example of the reciprocity which is inseparable from spiritual work, in that I received healing regarding my little dog too as well. That is quite apart from the joy in being a part of such a crucial healing and an intensely beautiful experience in an *amazing* exchange of love.

Chapter 6

I was continuing with the visualising techniques as often as possible and finding different ways of getting rid of the elements that came up in my mind's eye.

As I cleared the major stuff as it came to mind, I began to notice all sorts of everyday negativity. This new sharpening of my awareness made me see how much there was of it, that also, I took it for granted. It is surprising how easily we overlook it, how much we do take for granted and worse still, accept as the norm. I certainly did. I began working on this on a daily basis from then on to keep it at bay.

In due course I discovered another method of dealing with this but meanwhile I was working on expanding my understanding of the body physical - more of this later. In the course of a query, a new voice came to my inner hearing to answer the question as I puzzled over where to find the answer.

He introduced himself to me as Dr Ying Po. He said I could call upon him to help with anything in this field. Very soon he joined my three lovely Guides on a regular basis and eventually called me dear pupil as I furthered my understanding of the physical body.

Once upon this singular and metaphysical road, many more realisations were coming to me. Angels and Archangels were coming more into my consciousness too. This was a beautiful development.

I was aware by now of my Guardian Angel whose name is Michelle which she has kept from her last time on Earth, for Guardian Angels come down to experience the earth plane at some stage so that they have the empathy necessary for their close link to us. Many return to their Angelic name of course and many were identified to me by their Human name for those people I helped with Rei-ki.

Michelle however, was made known to me through automatic writing. This I had to cease because it is easily interfered with. I was sorry this had to be as it was so lovely having her guide my pen.

It is quite an extraordinary experience. This came about through a lovely psychic lass I knew and was able to share my clairaudience with. She was clairvoyant and very etherically connected. She was hugely reassuring for me and I missed her a lot when our paths diverged. Her Guide, unsurprisingly, was a lovely and very interesting young woman.

Connecting mentally with your Guardian Angel even if you do not know their name is always helpful to them. So many thoughts and wishes crowd one's mind which take a bit of untangling from the rest of the stuff birling around in one's head.

'Angels and Celestial Beings find great joy in having specific requests made to them – it is a strengthener to the vibrations they receive if there is some particular help they can work on and all direct communication is received with joy, also for being in the consciousness of humans is *good*.'

It is much easier for your Angel to help if you make a clear, definite request to them in your mind. You will find that the conscious connection gives instant comfort. Thus, immediately you know that someone cares unconditionally for you. This is especially when we humans feel we are alone. We are not.

Uriel was a very special helpmeet in guarding the channel of my clairaudience, particularly in the first years when there was quite a concerted effort by the interferers which was rather irritating. He is a lovely gentle Archangel and always happy to help me. I'd send him armfuls of daffodils when they came out. He loved that. After that I went to him often and still do in my meditations and temple visits: (more of that later). I still frequently send him flowers.

I meet dear Sandalphon at the Temple too and both help in healing sessions as well. Of course, during healing sessions Angelic help is always there. The lovely gentle Haniel is always ready with her beautiful healing which she is so happy to do. Her soft hands are amazing in visualisation sessions. It is so beautiful working with them. Angelic help came to me for my channelled healing too. I heard his name, Zadriel, and thanked him for coming to enable the healing.

'The Angel Zadriel sends love and blessings dear one. He is a very experienced healing Angel from the family of Archangel Gabriel - He says he is very glad to come and help you....'

This was so lovely to know that he was there to work with my channelled energy as it developed and strengthened - and still does. This made it even easier for the Guides to respond.

And of course, I called on dear Archangel Michael for help when things were particularly tough at one stage. He is always available for help when called upon of course. There is no saying how many others of these dear Beings participate, not only in the healing sessions but in ways unimaginable too.

But at this time these were the significant Angelic beings I was encountering in lovely and loving ways. Even just writing about them makes me feel, as Tibetan Grandmother would say, 'glowy'!

~.~

One weekend I was staying with friends and as usual before I settled to sleep, out came the pad and pen. Much to my surprise, someone new greeted me.

He introduced himself to me as Khatumi. He was he said, a Master and the network I was connected to was in his especial care. He had a great interest in and oversaw all that was happening to guide me along my new path of spiritual understanding.

He assured me, after I seriously questioned who he was, that he applauded my doubt but he was indeed the Master Khatumi. I was a little overawed for the timbre of his voice had an indefinable air of mastery as well as deep wisdom. With clairaudience I was finding, one could detect very subtle differences.

I marvel now at my level of acceptance of the extraordinary. Here after all was a Master who had come to help me. I was just delighted to encounter a fresh mind and another source of wisdom. He came often and what we shared was always stimulating and exciting. Many times Khatumi and I explored many wonderful synchronous concepts and subjects. Before long he was a beloved friend.

'Yes dear friend, I am here to guide you to enlightenment as always.' was a greeting that meant something interesting was about to unravel before us. Whenever we were exploring concepts and I made a particular connection it would turn a Light Key in the network which pleased him very much. The first time he told me that it occurred I was so happy to have played such a part. No wonder my brain fizzed along and my heart expanded with this 'thinking'. We loved this kind of work.

He came often and added to what my dear Guides were discussing with me when I needed an aspect that my thoughts had prompted. Like my Guides, Khatumi always had something interesting to add to my thinking and comprehension.

'To become a Guide is a dimensional step which is still part of the Soul's path, and incarnation on the same plane can be returned to, to continue to follow the original plan at a fresh point to fulfil all that is needed. These are choices determined by the choices of those they guide. As you have gathered dear friend, the Soul, its template, path and choices are so much a part of the whole that separating of aspects into clear-cut pictures is an infinity of comprehension. This is the fascinating thing about the Earth Plane and Human Beings – the Will and personality effects are extremely complex and aspects are met as things move along and evolve so shifts and adapting are a constant part of the whole.'

So, as you can imagine, my metaphysical life was full and wondrous to experience. The number of A4 pads filling up with fascinating dictation was increasing and I also had medium and small handy notebooks in use all over the place. I have a whole pile of them beside me for reference as I write.

Trying to find the proper sequence of events and wisdom takes some unravelling as sometimes the nearest notebook to hand might not have been the current one. Luckily, I dated every 'dictation' as I wrote it.

I was just so eager to take every opportunity to talk with them. It wasn't only the loving words of beautiful wisdom but the sweetness of the feeling while engaging with them.

I was unsurprised that the plane these dear ones and I were connected to was, they told me, the Mental plane – one is inside one's mind, making discoveries through it and therefore bringing them into it through this beautiful communication with the Dimensions. I was receiving wisdom and insights from an intangible world, yet the subtle perceptions in clairaudience gives these dear Beings tangibility.

That the several minds are working almost as one yet simultaneously with mine is amazing. It is a very elusive reality that mere words can't quite capture. But a reality nonetheless.

It was interesting to realise that '..here the vibrations are 'light' and as you know, this translates into sound when needed.' How well this clarified how the vibrational Dimensions communicate through 'speech' on the Mental plane. The full impact of this came to me much later in an extraordinary way.

~ . ~

Unsurprisingly, the significance of negativity formed a considerable topic in the conversations my Guides shared with me. Through these synchronous conversations with my wonderful helpmeets, I had been learning much about this; it was readily made apparent to me how very important a part it is of all aspects of health and healing.

'The illusion of negativity is that it is correct. Badness has been made into a concept of reality, therefore badness is believed in first and so it generates negative responses. In this way it grows. Positivity just 'is' goodness just 'is,' 'in being,' 'in existence – the light and the love – obscured by negativity but never extinguished. This is the hope and the truth that has been unceasing and held in the hearts and minds of the human race. This is innate knowledge. Negativity is an external force. It has made use of Man's Will and Ego and delicate spirit to obscure truth and hide love. It is all illusion.'

At another time my Guides commented,

'How faulty the memory can be made by negativity. If memory is tied into it, it sticks like goose-grass to the legs of the pony and is carried along unnoticed. Once removed, the pony's legs are free. Yes dear, dear Felicity, learning to disassociate the negative from the memory is part of the healing.'

During one particular conversation with them, once again we referred to this prevalent energy and the importance and benefits of dealing with it properly.

'...your awareness of the invidious nature of negativity is good! Prompted by love all is good. This is wise thinking dear one – negate any negative thoughts that prevents you from doing something from love – it will always bear good fruit – yes dear girl. Yes dear one – we pierce our own hearts with negative thinking – yes, always a sword turned against one's self -indeed - one blade with two cutting edges – yes – external source – this tells one that it is from those whose energy source is using yours – yes positive thinking energy starts in the heart chakra – internal source - yes the Divine within and is sent outward in a beam of gentle energy - not like that of negative energy which from an external source wounds or shadows the heart and then turns to emanate outward to wound or shadow others – indeed, piercingly too. Thus it gathers strength and finds energy by seeking it from others which in rebounding gathers strength and momentum.'

Naturally we had synchronous conversations about the effect of fear which Man has to contend with on this plane.

'...yes - .....that is what the dark side tries to work upon when human emotions become greater than the reasoning control of the Will which makes human beings vulnerable. It is then that fear is stimulated by the negative energy tipping the balance away from positive energy – In the imbalance fear flourishes because it is increased by the heavier negative energy. The inertia that results inhibits the Will and the reasoning so a greater imbalance occurs – indeed dear one.'

'.....goodness is there for anyone and comes to all who are open to receive all that awaits them from the Universe – many feel unworthy to receive and deny themselves all that is waiting. - This is unwise but many believe it. This is indeed a strange thing but it is through this that the truth is learned for it allows the light of truth to be seen in the darkness of fear – yes a dark background can bring something to the attention. Such is the nature of fear, but it is considered a safe place to be, in the dark, just as the womb is dark.'

'...it is good to collect memories, unwise to collect fears.' A good maxim!

And as always, a gentle reminder to myself of recurrences of negative thinking in the course of a day.

'...yes all is understood dear dear one, refrain from negative thoughts as much as possible so that that the dark ones are unable to make use of it. – go within the Divine energy dear one and think of loving things for there is only loveliness within – God's loving arms are there to rest within. Our loving guidance is with you always and your Angels guard and protect you with love and their loving energy.'

'....leave what is no longer beneficial and look forward rather than send the mind backwards through the thinking – this is to waste good energy.........Every moment of the past is behind you – your brain and your Soul have already learned from them to guide you forward dear dear one.'

Such a simple statement. Such succinct wisdom. Oh that we would live by it!

In another conversation with dear Dr Ying Po which, though I actually had at a rather later date, is so apt that I feel it should be included here. It just seems so appropriate as well as revealing the wisdom and enlightenment I received from my Guides.

The sweetness and wisdom of their words were always like balm and yet were invariably thought-provoking too so I feel I must share this with you as well, this being important to our understanding of the human condition.

'...the knowledge that negativity invites negativity is essential for helpful choices dear pupil but someone else's learning will always come from any choice that *seems* detrimental to the personality and indeed enlarge *their* learning also – even though that way is hard and seems dark! For even in the deepest dark man's Soul will seek the light for the light is present in that darkness and can always be found for the light 'is' always and all darkness but passing – yes dear Pupil, the voice of Khatumi was added to ours for these are profound concepts – the nothingness you speak of to describe Man's perception of the intensest negative energy is a helpful concept to comprehend the evil that you ask about that seems to consume some of men's beings – some Souls are consumed by 'nothingness' and tied to the physical plane (through re-incarnation) until the nothingness is greater than the physical but within is the light that has been drawn within as perceived by your scientist and because the nature of light is to be light and the power of light is the greater, since its proportion is greater than the darkness of 'nothingness' its energy bursts forth and light is in creation once more. So it is with the darkest of Man's Souls and all light is God so love is always created from this 'nothingness'.'

As you may have guessed they were picking up my thoughts and perplexity about the intense depths of cruelty Man is capable of. In other words, the extremes of negativity.

As we 'thought' together I was put in mind so much of the black holes in space where dark matter is so concentrated that it seems as if there is nothing there. But of course, there is no such thing as nothing, it is only the way we have of describing this unseen state.

I realised that in the case of those Souls we deem uncomprehendingly cruel that there will be a point, is a point, when the pressure from the extreme density of the negative energy is so great that it bursts and reveals the Light Being that is the Soul and releases it into its original loving form though it takes aeons to occur.

'.....the essential nature of all creations remains an absolute – this is the law of creation – yes. Thus the purity of the Soul will be eternal regardless of the accretions of negativity which serve only to steer a course until the essential nature having reached its optimum stretch will return to the centre and be released into itself. This is the hope for all Mankind.'

I personally found this very hopeful for Mankind for it does seem at times as if very great depths of evil and badness prevail despite so much enlightenment in our 21st century. They are such a contradiction to the loving Souls that we all are.

Naturally we talked further of these things.

'.....already there is a vibration for more care of the planet and its peoples and a coming understanding that violence achieves very little but more violence. – for some it is a releasing of fear and suffering that Man seems to wish to express in blood and death – but all death leads to rebirth and all of rebirth is of hope and change out of the destruction created by their anger........the innate spirit of man is for goodness and peace so it always triumphs in the end. The future is all we can reach for and that is what Man does with every idea and every rebirth. It is the hope and flame of, and for, Mankind so refrain from concern....understanding is also Man's hope and foundation for development. Yes indeed dear pupil /Happiness /Granddaughter. Man needs to develop and also needs to understand that he has chosen suffering for *that*, not for suffering itself.'

Chapter 7

With wonderful insights such as these I now began to really grasp some of the intricacies. Clearly negativity produces a very heavy energy. And we do add to it unconsciously. This definitely influences our energy levels and creates barriers in our perceptions which we rather tend to cling to. They give us a nice illusion of safety.

When we allow ourselves to accept the negativity we create and also that from external sources, there is no doubt we will carry it all with us. And there is an inescapable interplay going on with it. Yes, negativity in all its forms abounds and is inevitable, but we don't have to welcome it on board and feast with it. Once it is tucked into every corner, we get so used to it we lose sight of its impact.

My attention had been drawn to this in no uncertain terms and I had every intention of doing my best not to hang on to it if I could get to grips with it. I didn't fancy carrying it around with me at all! That idea had certainly given me pause for thought.

In the course of this exploration of things negative I became ever more aware of what I had been systematically burying over the years. Everyone does this in order to get on with life of course.

I was finding that as I cleared something an incident would pop up that I hadn't thought of for years! Soon I realised that if it needed out, it would be re-awakened from the archives! It was such a good method because I didn't have to go over the past events or emotions at all. A quick thought and I just had to 'look' at what it had 'created' and get rid of it! Job done!

This in fact was extraordinarily helpful because I had no desire to dig around in my past and re-live the upsets, distresses, sorrows, or simple annoyances that are so much a part of life from childhood onwards. In amongst it are many hurts and humiliations too that I had no desire to revisit and certainly not dwell upon! Yes, they had all become part of and helped to create those attachments that kept them in my energy. They formed the biases, the judgements, the motivation even for how and why I did things and the quality of my relationships.

So, I was seeing patterns of thinking and a view of myself and the events of my life from a fresh perspective even as I was clearing the negativity that I carried because of them. Simply by seeing those patterns showed me the how and why. Also, I had no desire for them to go on determining my life which was an added motivation for having them gone.

In talking with a friend one day about getting rid of one's worries, she told me that she heard that one could write something on a piece of paper and burn it to get rid of it.

I thought I would try this, but rather than physically, I would try it in my mind's eye as a visualisation. I thought perhaps this could be used for those everyday negatives that were coming to my attention.

So, I tried it out with something I wasn't happy with at the time. It wrote up very easily! On a brick wall in fact with white chalk! This image just popped into my mind's eye. I got rid of it alright, then something prompted me to try and see if it would write again. Well, most of it did so I scrubbed it out again. I found that it took several goes before it wouldn't write! I realised then how deep a negative thought could go.

From then on, I made sentences of anything that I disliked, annoyed me or bothered me on an everyday basis. I became very adept at it. It wasn't long before I realised that my Guides were helping me formulate very pithy sentences!

Short and to the point is *essential* as some take a lot of removing! Seeing them go was immensely reassuring. I always took care that not a scrap was left behind. I do still work in this way as much as I can to minimise the negativity that we are constantly assailed with. I have no desire to add to the negative energy of the planet if I could help it.

In this I felt lucky that I had my Guides to help formulate those neat sentences. Then I realised that, since Guides are always there, a person just needs to go quietly into their mind and I feel sure that the sentence will undoubtedly form as their Guide will prompt it from within.

While these visualisation methods meant work, focus and concentration they truly offered that magic key, change. Change was the significance of it all. How else to go forward and make good use of this astonishing right-angled turn, if there was no change after it?

One of those changes was that Cause and Effect now had real meaning for me. This gave me insights into 'attitudes' and 'behaviour' which happily began to erode those judgements and criticisms it is so easy to fall into. It was all certainly illuminating and enlightening.

I was beginning to comprehend things, seeing things afresh and thus gaining a much fairer view of occurrences and the ways of 'being' in my family and my part in their lives. And by family, I mean my parents and siblings. And also, and just as important, the family I had created through marriage and children.

It was like suddenly being given the answers to half-formed questions one hadn't bothered to follow up. This created great changes in my viewpoint. I was learning to *observe* in place of judgement and criticism so that I could comprehend. Observation was a key word.

This was set out so clearly by Khatumi.

'.....the power of the observer dear lies in having no judgement only comprehension. Judgement sets up ties that hold the something judged in place. Observe and comprehend dear – step back and see with the inner eye and the heart. Your comprehension creates the correct vibration dear.'

Thus, the power our 'judgements' have against ourselves!

My awareness of what our fears and doubts do to ourselves was widening all the time. One aspect that my Guides and I discussed was boundaries and barriers to change.

'...The question of boundaries is a complex one dear dear one/pupil. Man seems to feel safer with them and creates them at every opportunity. It is only illusion. To create 'form' from abstracts is to use only energy and the result is restriction instead of safety. To go no further than a boundary is to impede freedom and prevents developments from reaching the person who has set the boundaries for this encompasses change and development which many fear.'

'...taking stock of your boundaries is the first step to dissolving them for once in view the conscious knows they obscure crossing places. Freedom of spirit needs also a mind free from restrictions and limitations and these are the creations of fear.'

I found it was quite an exercise to write down all my own negative boundaries and dissolve them. It doesn't do to get complacent however. We can always build some more very easily!

~.~

Throughout this time, I had also started on my last year of study for The Open University. I really loved my studies so applying myself and writing the TMA's, (Tutor Marked Assignments, their name for our essays,) was no hardship. In fact, I enjoyed it all immensely.

I revelled in the study itself; the material the University provided was really excellent. At TMA time, the effort and focus to marshal my thoughts in order to answer the chosen question, was very satisfying. I had learnt such an amazing amount doing my Arts degree.

Every aspect of the five disciplines we worked on for each period we were studying interested and enthralled me. Learning how to convey my understanding of that study and each discipline was in itself a discipline that opened my mind and honed my ability to express through writing what I had grasped of the subject.

I really applied myself. This was to be my final exam and would determine the type of degree I would attain. Having lost a year, I was eager to do the University and myself justice. It was a completion and a fulfilment of something I had longed to do, a goal I had set myself that satisfied my love of study. And it certainly did just that! When I gained my degree, I was more than overjoyed. I was jubilant!

When the great moment did come to go up on the stage and accept my BA (hons) I had a grin from ear to ear! I could not stop smiling! It was my great privilege to receive it from the hand of Betty Boothroyd who was our University Chancellor at the time. It was one of the most wonderful and unforgettable days of my life. I had reached a pinnacle I had dreamed of. It excited and humbled me at the same time. As I write I have a picture on my bookcase beside me of me in my gown flanked by my youngest son and his wife and the grin on my face expresses everything!

I had the added pleasure that my Guides were sharing this event with me too, as was everyone in the network. And every Guide of all those present too.

I remember vividly being aware that the entire room must have been brimming over with Guardian Angels attending this momentous event with their own dear ones. It was a lovely and stunning thought! But I had to keep that to myself – and my and their Guides! The vibration in the room was palpable to all from everyone's sense of achievement and happiness. It was good to know how much joy it brought to the Dimensions too.

How I blessed these years of university experience for they certainly stood me in good stead for what lay before me in the not-too -distant future.

~ . ~

Through my Guides I was gaining Conscious Awareness. I have put it in capitals because, not only is it vital but it was this that opened my mind so that through it, I became receptive and able to grasp this new metaphysical understanding.

In practical terms, how much had Conscious Awareness of negative energy enabled me to tackle it. Witness my work with my releasing efforts. In spiritual terms, I was realising deeper levels of observation and comprehension.

Experiencing this personal communication that was clairaudience gave metaphysics a reality I could not have gained through reading or studying books. The depth, the breadth, the inner space of it was now part of my consciousness. How could my mind not be opened? I was being given the 'experience' of Dimensions beyond and beyond that; of dimensional beings in this 'beyond-ness' who had a reality like mine, were privy to great depths of wisdom gleaned from dimensional interconnectedness over aeons and more beyond-ness than one could encompass. And although I felt the immensity, I knew even then I could only have an inkling of the tiniest part of it.

Sometimes a voice said something to me from a great distance and I thus had an experience of something further still. I realised later that it was an infinitesimally small impression because within the experience was some measure, some fleeting measure that I couldn't hold on to, of its vastness. And more extraordinary and wonderful than that, a glimpse, an infinitely tiny glimpse of the immensity of unconditional love that abounded there. But yet I felt that love and connection enormously while knowing for a certainty, it was only a tiny glimpse!

There were two occasions when I was afforded a measure of it.

I had just finished talking with the two Guides of a very sweet friend of mine. They told me how happy they were for her to know of them and how much they loved her. Suddenly I felt this surge of love that practically knocked me over in my chair! It was incredible!

I tried to express some measure of it to my friend and wished so much that she could have felt it too. What I did feel had a depth and intensity that is not possible to describe. The realisation of it being unconditional was in a fleeting impression of immensity itself. There is no other way I can convey it.

In that instantaneous communication that clairaudience gives one I was 'told' that the human body was physically unable to withstand the full power of this love that they have for us so they let me experience only an infinitesimal measure of their love for her. I was deeply honoured that these dear Guides shared that with me. The full force of Divine love is therefore quite impossible to contemplate!

The other occasion was after a healing session with someone I had been working on who asked for my help. He had been disempowered for over seven years with ME.

After this particular session, which had been singularly effective, again I was *flooded* with this incredibly powerful love that was a physical wave that again nearly knocked me over on the stool I was sitting on. They wanted me to have a glimpse of their joy at the effect of the session on their precious charge. How beautiful is that?

Once again, I knew positively that its true power could never be felt by human form, that we were too frail by *far* for its strength. One cannot even imagine its immensity or its blissful beingness. But how wonderful!

How can one find words to truly express this? I kept wishing that everyone knew; that everyone could experience and comprehend this. I had to keep what I was being gifted to experience to a very small group of those who would accept and believe me.

That indeed was a comfort but I couldn't let them 'into' the experience. I puzzled over why it was happening to me but mostly I just took every opportunity to tune into it. How often my dear Guides advised me to 'refrain from concern. All would be revealed when the time was right.' Patience, patience and yet more patience!

Thus, the joy of knowing of the existence of Dimensions where 'matter' as we perceive it is vibrational, therefore uncluttered by Will and Ego, was sublime to me. Vibrational also in that there could not be any separation from the form and matter we experience on this earth plane but was simply an extension of it at a different frequency.

'That,' said my friend Sheila, 'is what quantum physics is about.'

This made a great deal of sense the more I was in contact and learning from my Guides and the experiences being granted to me. (And continue to be.)

'...all will become clear as you progress. The light of realism will illumine all and you will have your sense of 'knowing'....your clarity is for what lies ahead in the realm of knowledge for healing and teaching and an understanding of yourself for you are on the see-saw and we will help you find the point of balance....for now you are learning the power of love. It's gentle healing energy is what you need to call upon to do the work of learning. In the calmness of love all will dissolve.....you are making us work and we rejoice in it – you are given a little seed and up comes a sturdy plant – but its quickness is both a delight and a leap for us to catch it and resolve it....I am happy in my heart for our pupil (Tibetan Grandmother) for we know your heart is busy for our task as much as your mind.'

For my mind to be learning through this synchronous communication from such a beautiful source was both exciting and very satisfying. There being no barriers or ego or distractions, there is a closeness in substance when immersed in this communication that has an almost tangible reality of matter so that there is no sense of separation only a sublime unity. 'for seeing with the inner eye, feeling with the inner being.' A sense of thinking into each other's minds. It truly is the joining of minds. Ergo, no separation of matter.

I was assuredly experiencing this Oneness myself through our beautiful synchronous communion. Now I became sharply aware of how much separation there is in many areas of modern life.

I could see now, the 'ticking of boxes', creating ever more specialisms, pigeon-holing, modular learning and ever-narrowing separate 'fields' in all walks of life, even high-rise buildings, vast blocks of flats which frequently lead to isolation. And men do have a liking for taking things apart, both physically disassembling things and mentally in Scientific research; quite apart from War where a great deal gets taken apart.

The ultimate was splitting the atom and discovering ever smaller and smaller particles. This widespread reductionism seems the current way of things, the unchallenged norm. It seems a masculine drive separating itself from the creative feminine.

This seems so at odds with our innate needs. We as humans flourish best in relationships, cohesive societies. Social exchange is vital to our personal and social success in all fields. We create and need unity in many forms quite naturally.

Yet we continue to separate, to reduce, to isolate. This serves only for finding the scientific proofs that seem to exercise the scientific world but separation from the whole is to deny its validity. Quantum physics informs us that we, our world, the Universe is energy and therefore all undeniably one, therefore *in*separable. Yet influential thinking *holds to separation*.

It seemed extremely apt indeed, that apart from the beautiful Oneness I was being blessed with through my Guides, I was now, without doubt, becoming deeply involved with the oneness of the mind, body, and inner being, our vital life force and the oneness of us all. I was definitely on a very different path. Where it was leading I had no idea, I was just very happy with whatever unfolded with the happy acceptance I continued feeling about it all!

Chapter 8

At that time, I was still very new to this quite different 'road' that life was taking me along. There was still my ordinary everyday life with its own needs, demands and responsibilities. Life in its ordinariness went on regardless and flowed along its course.

My life however, seemed to have acquired a kind of two-tier effect with these twin elements of the physical and metaphysical. I was finding moreover, the metaphysical side to my life so remarkable that the thought of yet another aspect of it interested me very much.

Quite apart from the joyousness of clairaudience, I received further marvellous experiences. These came from some advice I received early on from the kind Rei-ki healer who had introduced me to the visualisation way of 'tie-cutting'. She told me at the time that if I was needing inner help I should go to 'the Temple.'

This one could visit by visualising a temple and going up the steps into it, then I was to cross the floor and voice any need or needs I had and see what transpired. It sounded intriguing at the very least. It was very simple and the result rested with me and what came to me there.

It took some concentration to 'see' the temple and the steps and 'feel' myself going up those steps then crossing the floor. Once I'd mastered that though and entered, the floor always looked chequered black and white for some reason.

That accomplished I saw a beautiful column of intense white light ahead of me that I 'knew' somehow, I should walk into. When I did, I felt it swirling through me from the feet up until it came out of the top of my head and poured in a swirling motion down over me again. I stayed there until there appeared a moment when I felt I should step out of it. To my surprise 'someone' came over to me. In my mind, I called them 'The Angel of the Light'. I then asked if I was to be told something or directed to do something.

After all these years I cannot now remember exactly what happened on that first occasion. All I do remember was that I was answered clearly, *'Someone will come to you.'* To this day someone always does.

I realised later that it was necessary for me to learn gradually how to go there and 'enter' the Temple so that I was ready for the significant events that occurred there. As dear Ja-San often reminded me, preparation was everything!

Frequently after that I was directed there by my Guides and also by an intuitive sense that I needed to. After I had been going for a little while, I found that instead of the white light a voice told me that it was time that I 'enter the crystal chamber.'

At the next visit, and obediently focusing as always, I found that once I had crossed the floor, I *was* in a crystal chamber. At that time, sometimes it was rose quartz, sometimes amethyst, sometimes crystal quartz. As I left the chamber, I was now in an inner Temple. This, I realised, was a progression for the Angel of the Light was here and I either asked for help or waited to see what happened.

~ . ~

One evening soon after having progressed to the crystal chamber, my Guides advised me to go to the Temple as someone was waiting for me. Once I was through the chamber I went over to the Angel of the Light. She moved towards me and said someone would come for me.

Two Beings came and lifted me gently up. It was a very strange feeling but felt very real.

Soon we came down into a corridor leading to a chamber. It was rather indistinct – more an impression than anything – but I was totally aware of everyone present and of my own body. I was standing before someone important and a fine gossamer garment was passed over my head. It came down to my ankles. It was purest gleaming white but it had a broad hem of deep violet.

I was told that this was mine now that I was channelling Rei-ki and to visualise it in my preparation for any healing, or desire to contact Rei-ki healers in the Dimensions. I thanked them and was returned to the antechamber before returning through the crystal chamber. This was quite a significant stage I was to discover. I felt very honoured and did indeed visualise it when I did any healings. It made me feel very connected.

Whenever I went to the Temple I was always taken somewhere. Sometimes I was flanked by two Beings and taken along a corridor to someone of importance. This was always in silence but what I can only describe as a calm silence because their presence was loving so there was no need for words. Once there I was required to perform some task, or receive information. My trust was implicit. At no time did I ever feel any resistance in myself.

On an occasion, something occurred that particularly distressed me and gave me a lot of worry. My Guides suggested I went straight to the Temple.

Once there I was taken up and escorted towards a doorway that was framed in beautiful glowing emerald crystal that emitted a soft energy. I went up a couple of steps into a room with a soft pale light. There I saw a group of gentle smiling Beings in white gowns before me. I somehow knew that this was a healing room.

I asked if I could have some healing please. One came forward and took me over to a soft white couch. I was advised to lie down and relax. The Healer then drew their hands down my body in long sweeps which seemed to be going through my substance rather than my physical body.

Each sweep seemed to be drawing out many long threads through my feet. These were drawn together and gently pulled free and seemed to disappear into the floor. This continued until there were no threads left.

The Healer then stroked through my substance from head to toe with healing energy, and said I was to rise as all was well. I felt different, lighter as if something heavy had left my whole being: it had obviously been at a deep level.

I felt such a gentle sweetness coming from the Healer which was healing in itself. I felt happy and safe. No words had been needed to explain what my body had held or why. I had only to accept, not revisit, wonder, analyse or question which was very freeing.

I was quietly escorted over to the door and told to come whenever I needed their help. I thanked them in a rather bemused fashion and went outside to my escort Angels. All my distress and worry had left me in that gentle peaceful room.

It was wonderful to have that taken from me, when I felt I couldn't help myself at that time. I knew that these dear Beings were not to be taken for granted. This was special, not just an easy option. Needless to say, I have visited them again, life becoming complicated as it does.

One evening at the Temple two Angelic Beings led me along a corridor to the right of the Angel of Light. I was taken to a wooden door – it looked very ancient and solid. It opened as I approached. I entered a room with a long wooden table in it. Someone stood at the head and several Beings were seated, several down each side on benches. However, I 'saw' that the last place nearest the door was unoccupied. Everyone there nodded and smiled at me as if they knew me.

The leader smiled, 'Come take your place Felicity. It is your place and you are needed here.' I sat as bidden, perceiving at the same time that suspended in mid-air over the table was a huge motionless cube of amethyst crystal. I was told that I was needed to complete the energy of the assembled Beings to re-activate the static crystal cube.

Wordlessly we 'knew' we all had to focus our energy on rotating this cube. It required huge concentration I found. Eventually it started to rotate. As it gathered momentum a beam of light coming from above shot through it and down through the table and floor. The cube spun faster and faster with our concentrated mental focus. The whole crystal became just a huge blur of movement. We held this focus with intense concentration until it reached its peak of momentum and suddenly a great beam of intense purple energy with a white centre streamed at great speed through it. Every one relaxed and the cube spun unaided holding the beam in place.

Everyone seemed happy. We were all thanked by the Master at the head of the table. In that strange perceptive state at these times, I was made aware that this was the source of their energy there and that the group I was seemingly a part of were needed to re-set or re-energise it.

Then everyone nodded and smiled at me and I knew that having completed the task I could leave them. I was then escorted back and found myself ready to open my eyes.

It was extraordinary! I hadn't the least idea why, only that it was a requirement I was to fulfil. I wasn't informed. It was just an accepted thing that I accepted!

Sometimes if I had to be taken up, – through planes or Dimensions, possibly it varied, – one Being would carry me.

The first time this happened I knew, rather than felt, arms around me and though I had not the slightest expectation of it, a soft beating vibration. Could this be wings I wondered? I do not know. All I do know is that it was intensely real and happened each time I was taken aloft. I thought of them as Angels and that belief has remained with me. The sensation of being taken aloft is quite extraordinary. Coming down to land at our destination always feels tricky – possibly because the Angel, being larger, lands first!

Because these were very personal experiences, I didn't write an account of them afterwards. Possibly I felt few people would believe me and I would be judged as completely dotty. So profound however were they that I remember them and the most significant of them most vividly. Some were very personal and very much Soul-purpose experiences so naturally they impressed themselves on my memory quite vividly.

The last visit I had recently was so extra special that my daughter urged me most strongly to get it written down. It was through her urgings and the added strong recommendation of my special dear friend Sheila, that I am actually writing of my clairaudience and wondrous contact with Dimensional Beings now! I had no intention ever to do so because I was deeply anxious as to how these revelations would be received.

However, the climate for such experiences has changed considerably and is much more conducive to receiving such disclosures. My concern has not abated however.

There was a final prompt to my decision to write about these amazing experiences and my singular spiritual awakening.

I met a remarkable lady called Dr Jude Currivan at a conference at Allanton, the Peace Prayer centre in Scotland. My friend Sheila and I encountered her the evening before and were both much taken with her loving sweetness.

The following day she gave a talk which I found riveting, - and one moreover at a gathering on primarily secular subjects. I could have listened to her for hours! She talked of her own cosmic experiences with such ease and freedom. She spoke of having 'walked between worlds' as if it were the most natural thing on earth. Aside from the content of her talk, this ease and unconcern for judgement or criticism, or any lack of need for acceptance from people, impressed me hugely.

I would have loved to have really talked with her. I spoke to her briefly later however, and she was very enthusiastic about my clairaudience and encouraged me, Yes! - to write about my own experiences, to tell people as an encouragement to all those who hide it, are afraid of being misjudged. How could I not at least make the attempt after that? That really was the spur I needed.

Chapter 9

Moving on from these digressions, I was working full time of course and as I lived alone, had a home and life to run for myself. Naturally this took a considerable part of my time.

Family and friends also had my time and attention. They were frequently very patient with me when I enthused over Rei-ki healing but apart from a couple of close friends, my daughter and one of my sisters, I couldn't confide in them about being clairaudient.

I felt positive that it would be very hard for most of the people I knew and other family members to accept. The gift was so precious I had to keep it private and share it only with those who would accept it unequivocally. On the subject however of this wonderful healing approach Rei-ki, I must have been quite a bore. No-one complained though. They really were patient!

In the meantime, I was working on my Rei-ki understanding, so my life was expanding in a private and interior way that was profoundly satisfying. I was becoming more and more interested in a very different perspective on the physical body. This captured my interest exceedingly.

It was being revealed as having metaphysical aspects which I had not encountered in my nursing studies or were even considered as such, although TLC (Tender Loving Care, always the watchword of our excellent Sister Tutor Bennet) was taught us in the 60's and was always a constant and expected part of our nursing on the wards.

Here in these fresh experiences of energy healing however, a depth was apparent regarding the human physical condition. To this end Dr Ying Po proved invaluable. He was a Chinese physician from ancient China. To his profession, Philosophy and Medicine were one subject; they could not be separated: it was a sacred art. When I asked him about this he said:-

'Yes I was Dr of Philosophy. In my time the body and mind were one science, so as a philosopher I learned of the body also. Yes it was all a combined Science not separated as in your times. I taught and practiced all aspects of mind and body and channelled the various fields into one conceptual whole. The mind and body together were the point of learning. Medicine as a sacred art could not function without the knowledge of the etheric and the mental, both conscious and unconscious thought. We knew how much these two concerned the body and its healing needs. Also the medicinal needs were more harmonious to the body if the mental and the etheric were both understood and treated with healing. This ancient art of healing has been cut up into small pieces that are disconnected. There is no harmonious whole in your modern 'sciences'.'

This oneness of the etheric, the mind, the emotions and body I was beginning to see very clearly. Now my mind was expanding like a flower opening in the sun. There was so much I wanted and needed to know. I asked many questions of course but I only ever got answers on a 'need to know' basis. They spoke of my queries,

'..like butterflies they fly up through the boughs of your thoughts.'

Sometimes it was very frustrating, I wanted to know everything possible! I had to abide in patience. Of course, the dear Guides that they were, understood me completely.

'All knowledge that is needful will be revealed to you as you need it and where it is useful to you – in this way the correct ground will be covered otherwise there will be so much learning that you will be distracted from the work you have started. Trust and believe as always dear one. Gently with what you need to learn.'

How could one hold on to impatience with such sweet and gentle reasoning?

'...letting go of the desires for the Self is to let go of the Will against the Self for the Self needs to be 'in being', neither served nor indulged but nourished from within.'

Re-reading and copying this out for you dear reader shows me how appropriate this little truism is to many aspects of daily life. I'm glad I found it. Putting the Will behind the action rather than letting it lead you by the nose as it were is really tough sometimes even when gently reminded by one's Guides.

Talking with them was always beautiful and immensely fulfilling. So much love flowed between us; the feeling within my heart chakra was so lovely, so expansive and profound. It was (and is,) a constant joy. When the connection came from somewhere deep in the Dimensions, the experience, the sensation within was even more profound.

Part of me however, my naturally practical, pragmatic me, knew full well that life had to be faced on this Earth plane not escaped from. A sense of perspective was essential. It would have been so easy to prefer being connected so consciously to their beautiful loving vibration. I could see how it could become a little addictive.

I was put in mind of those anchorites of old who had states of ecstasy. That was definitely not my way though. But I was aware, – probably made to be aware by my Guides, – that I had a lot to learn yet about the human condition *from* the human condition.

An idea was propounded centuries ago that has been turned into a belief, that the flesh being 'weak,' is to be despised: it is corrupt, sinful, denotes the beast part of human nature even, its substance is not worth much nor to be valued. Some quite spiritual people even resent the physical state as being an encumbrance.

No wonder there is so much lack of self-worth and regard for the body itself. This seems bred in the bone so that taking care of ourselves is therefore irrelevant. It certainly seems so. We certainly take our body for granted.

As long as it fulfils our desired activities, we give it little thought. How many people are quite careless of their physical state of health and abuse it readily with poor if not ruinous diet, alcohol and all other ways imaginable? We need to take a real measure of care of our 'vehicle' where we can.

My Guides naturally see its value.

'....knowledge of the physical plane has to be imbibed through experience of the physical. This is so dear Happiness. It has been chosen as the vehicle of learning therefore its learning capacity needs to be known through the physical world…..love is goodness, love denotes value. Indeed dear girl - denial of the glory within the physical is to put all out of balance……'

The corporeal state therefore, is the only way for the Soul to experience all that is important to evolving the individual and humanity. It is the perfect vessel for the task, equipped with all the senses, emotions and intellect needed for learning of the human condition: all the possibilities for the unity of the Soul with the Divine through knowledge.

As for the personality we have, it also plays its vital part.

'The Self has chosen the personality for its aptitudes so that those issues it wishes to address, *do* occur. Therefore to consider these very aspects is to learn of what the Self needs to resolve or address or discover for the Soul's journey. From the knowledge of these aspects conscious awareness brings comprehension of them, therefore the answers are revealed and learning can take place. Thus the personality is the 'book' to read for the knowledge that one does not remember from part lives. This is the voyage of discovery that is available from the lifetime one is conscious of. Comprehension of the journey is to discover the destination and recognise the signposts as they appear.'

'………the physical body manifests these things, the heart knows and comprehends them and is the seat of the Divine to bridge the two. It is within the heart chakra, the Divine and the loving energy from it that does much to clear karma– how else can each Soul help itself dear pupil? By clearing the negativity ….. much can be done ……..it is knowledge of the Divine and the importance of the heart chakra to the whole system that is essential for the Soul's development and resolution in the personality it has chosen………the way to passing this 'knowing' to others is part of the task we all have.'

'…refrain from anxiety that there are those who do not recognise fully what is needful. However once it is the physical realm in physical and material form it will be recognised and acted upon by those who need to in their correct time under their Soul's guidance – God uses Man's Will to keep him 'on task' so even though his 'Will' appears to set a person against help of this kind it is only because of unreadiness.'

Since everything has a purpose, being here on the physical plane therefore has its purpose. We need to value our experiences rather than let negativity destroy their value to us. And those experiences can only come from the physical state of being.

Only the corporeal state has emotions and the senses. It is through these that the Will, the Ego and the Heart are explored and learned from. And all three have the greatest energy, especially the heart.

On this occasion an aspect of this purpose is beautifully put, as always, by my Guides conversing collectively with me.

'We hear your questions and perplexities dear dear one. Understanding the Will is a great task and takes time and much knowledge. It has great power. It drives and controls the Self, it is wayward and undisciplined and disciplined at the same time - the Ego and the Intellect play their part as does the imagination and it veers between all three under internal and external influences and energies. – because the Will therefore does not act as a separate entity it is also creative and it is this creativity that makes the complexities that need understanding. To acquire the knowledge of these complexities is the task of the Human Being, Mankind, as we have discussed before. It is difficult to separate these 'creations' as they are being worked upon by the Ego and the Intellect and imagination of observer and observed and all 3 elements have 2 sides – the positive and the negative also – these elements are put to use by the Dimensions of the Light for the purpose of learning – they are not created by the Dimensions of the Light – only by the Will – through the heavy negative energy created by the Will, and 'generated' by the dark side, come dark creations that the Will drives and attracts to the Self. This is its dual nature – goodness is good and darkness is darkness – 2 sides of the Universe separated but in being like two sides of a coin. That is the dual nature of the Universe held together by the created energies of love and the Will - all that is against the Self is used by the dark side – yes dear dear one – but made use of by the Dimensions of the Light for learning of the Self and Love and the Will. Your understanding of this is *good*. The Will creation is very powerful for it is under 'attraction' – indeed dear dear one – nothing is in isolation so situations of complexity are the working through of many Soul aspects at the same time - indeed and is under choice and Will for the Will is bound into 'the freedom of choice' also - indeed, the choice of 'part to play' is also under the Will but is from willingness rather than Will-driven. This is also the duality of the Will. Ah! There is also illusion and delusion which are the tools of the dark side dear dear one. And the dark side use their entities to create both from fear and any negative aspect – such as the fear or dislike of pain attached to the need or desire or belief in punishing the Self – that is so dear dear one....'

'The human condition is to gain all 'knowing' of the human condition through the Will for the 'knowing' of the Will. – the dark side use the imposition of the Will for the purpose of creating negative energy on which they nourish their existence.'

It is hard to explain this unifying of thought while simultaneously making connections; the even greater depth of communion at profounder moments with one's Being as well as one's mind's activity, their insights and wisdom matching exactly with it. A truly astonishing experience.

I don't recall ever having a 'question and answer' type conversation with them. (The odd question at some rare lull, yes, as an extra thought was triggered.) Whatever I was thinking about in relation to all that I was learning just set things off, frequently of course regards the Human condition!

'Michael and the Angels are very happy to help with your work on Will and Desire dear dear one. – all this will clear the way and help with the 'now' of things so that barriers will dissolve and the Universe will be able to reach you. All that is for all waits in the Universe for there, there are no barriers, walls or doors except those created by Man's Will and Desire. The Universe is the natural home in which we all reside so therefore all is there for all. The planes within are levels which we rise through transition as the Soul's needs are fulfilled – the Portals through which they move are merely channels for the purpose, for form needs to exist even in the Dimensions for we all have form even as does a vibration. Indeed dear one each one for a purpose for form is order and order holds things to the form that is necessary for the purpose. Each dimension is a world but not as we on Earth see it although for the purposes of comprehension it translates to a certain extent, for the 'knowing' from one dimension is for all the Dimensions, so form needs continuity also for we are all one although different aspects of the one for the purpose. Indeed dear one good connection dear girl/pupil.'

Everything that we explored together in the interweaving of concepts, ideas and connections that set off trains of thought unravelled so beautifully each time they came to speak with me.

'....the cloth is only created from the materials to hand dear girl – it is from finding divers materials that together with the imagination can find the pattern for the purpose. The creative mind is that touched by the spiritual in whatever form is needed for the purpose – for all purpose is God's - only Man distorts it with his Will but he will always be for the purpose as his Will is put to use as are the threads in a tapestry or colours in a painting – for do these not illuminate dear girl? Are not colours and shapes not all 'broken light'? Thus variety is both to see and learn from but also the physical manifestation of what to look at and learn from – so it is with the variety of Man's experiences of the Will, for these fragment the light and create the pictures of our knowledge for the enlightenment of all.'

'…..All beginnings are with God, so it will be with all knowledge and all endings – the dark side's efforts are an attempt at delays so that they can retain their sense of power for as long as they can – but it is all for the purpose of 'knowing' for God and with the 'knowing' comes all 'Beingness'. The dark side work with energy not knowledge for all 'knowing' is God's - their dark energy is from dark energy and uses dark energy for energy – they see energy as power for that is their beingness. But energy is fuel for action and activity and this is for the 'knowing' which is God's, so *all* is used for the 'knowing', for God and Love are in Beingness without end, which is God and the word is the 'knowing.'

I found this particular passage intensely moving. It encompasses so much, yet is so concise, so perfectly expressed. It is a privilege and a pleasure to share this with you dear reader.

Bringing these extracts to you from my precious notebooks brings back some of the deep pleasure I had at the time of writing it all down. Sharing them with you adds to that pleasure by bringing their wonderful enlightenment to you.

Chapter 10

Aside from my own dear ones I was blessed to be in touch with the Guides of others, particularly those of my children and sisters. It was delightful to know their names and of their loving care of those I love. Also, something of their last incarnation and personalities, though naturally nothing of their guidance. That was their purpose for them, just as mine were for mine.

I was also fascinated to discover something of the lives of those Guides of people for whom I channelled Rei-ki. Their help was invaluable so I so wished to 'meet' them.

Naturally I was curious to know how a Soul became a Guide. I learned that those Souls who choose to become a Guide are those of ordinary people who have had all the experiences common to us all. When the time comes however for becoming a Guide, they have to remove *all* negativity from their Being before they can graduate.

Revealing something of themselves and their lives gave them substance to me. These dear souls who had chosen to guide and comfort us here are real 'people' closely connected through their own knowledge of the joys and vicissitudes of life on Earth, not just a 'something' or 'presence' from the Upper Dimensions. It was through their last personality there came the choice to become a Guide at that point. Though they are in vibrational form, the reality of their 'person' enables that beautiful contact within for their precious charge.

Because there is no negativity in their realms, though they speak of troubled times, the glimpse they gave me and their words, barring a subtle perception were naturally devoid of the harsh realities.

A lovely Guide who was a nurse in the First World war and sadly died from Typhus while working in a field hospital on the Front, talked to me about this.

'...Guides help with 'how', remember, not what - this is jolly isn't it? Oh yes – we worked our way up to the mental plane since it was our choice for this time (in their Soul's journey). We had our time in the etheric too and learnt all sorts of things there. It's an excellent transition place actually – our contact with the physical plane has to be re-aligned so that we leave grief and remorse behind and have a truer understanding of the difference between the physical and other Dimensions. This helps us to understand the level of the physical from a quite different viewpoint. Otherwise our learning to be Guides would be too far up into the mental/spiritual and we'd forget the essential physical to make the 'whole'. We retain the knowledge of what it is to be human so that we have full comprehension for our charges. The 'whole' – all the elements are needed for balance to create the harmony we all need to develop – the spiritual, mental, heart/love – and physical – body/earth. Does that help? It's getting a little busy here so we'll talk again soon. Blessings and love dear Felicity.'

I now understood why their personalities from their last incarnation was still vividly with them. They were thus subtly linked to the physical understanding needed to guide their earthbound charges.

Because they have experienced fully the human condition it must be hard work to remove all last traces! There is no Will or Ego in the Dimensions, therefore no judgement or criticism, only pure loving energy, truth and goodness. As they said,

'...Will and Ego need linear time to work out their purpose.'

If anything else comes through then it is not through the voice of your Guide. There are many negative entities I have discovered who will slide things in to feed the Ego and bring in doubt or to confuse what is being said to you or tell you what you shouldn't or can't do in those terms. Guides speak positively. If they do say not or no it is in a positive context. *Guidance* is their purpose and task.

Clairaudience needs great concentration to listen carefully and discern the untruthful as well as the truthful. At certain times, when we needed to share important insights or specific information, then a Guide I knew with a distinctive voice or accent came to speak to me to dispel all doubt.

For example, a lovely Guide, Jalal who has a soft accent from northern India, comes to help. If an interferer tries to slip in, they sound like Peter Sellars with an Indian accent so it is pointless to try to fool me!

Another, Guide, dear, lovely Sophie, is from Paris with a very distinctive Parisian accent that again can't be imitated by the interferers, as I call them. You also learn to recognise the timbre of the voices of the true Guides and you quickly hear when a new voice has something to say. I always ask for verification. Clairaudience isn't frivolous; it is a beautiful privilege and always for the purpose. It has been and still is the most wonderful asset and gift in my life.

One evening after we had been talking in this wonderful synchronous way on something quite profound and beautiful, my Guides said,

'.....Someone who was with us wanted to speak this to you because you would understand it well. We all agreed that you knew this but it would be good for you to see that you had understood it for yourself. We want you to believe in yourself and your ideas which you *have* worked out for yourself. It is important that you know this about yourself so that you do not think that all your knowledge is from us. We have been sent to expand your knowledge. You have been learning by yourself but now what we wish you to know is fundamental to the tasks ahead. We will channel your 'knowing' with our knowledge to make it strong and help you. Our visitor will come again and is pleased that you heard a different voice - yes – you queried it from the beginning but trusted the truth within the words and as always stayed with it – no it is not to test you but you can always learn from the awareness you have had to hold on to. Always when your ideas are 'voiced' differently (the 'ideas' I mooted being those already known to them of course) they gain impact from being heard anew. – yes, it is your 'visitor' again. I will come again when you need me. This was by way of an introduction so now that you have 'met' me you will recognise me. Now rest with love from our hearts to yours. Thank you for believing in my words even though you were perplexed by the change in tone. You are learning well and we are happy with your happiness for that is your name and it is your treasure. You will learn more about me if it is your wish but that will come later when certain things have been accomplished on your behalf. – we will guard you so refrain from worry. You do not have to apologise to us. We understand your dilemma. We would rather you questioned than accepted blindly. You must rest now.'

As you see, it is the perfect illustration of my querying a new voice. Also, it shows my early doubts that perhaps I was not really a part of their thinking as I believed when we had these soaring conversations. And it shows the loving way they understood me, which was such a good feeling. To be known without having to explain oneself is so comfortable!

This next extract I wish to share with you is a beautiful example of the purity and loving intention of these dearly beloved Guides. It is described so perfectly that my own words can only be inadequate.

'.....time is non-linear here dear so patience is irrelevant here. We are filled with love and joy and bliss and this is enhanced and strengthened by the same that flowers within those on the earth plane. Any expansion of these however small adds to ours. We have complete awareness of all negativity dear but we refrain from encompassing it because we have learned to release all traces from our essence in these Dimensions – it aids our knowledge and understanding of the situations and condition of our precious charges so that we know what is happening and what is being experienced by them individually and collectively – all joy and love is sung of in the Singing Time and this sharing nourishes us also – this brings us joy and increases our bliss.'

Here they speak of the Singing Time. They spoke of this frequently. It is when Guides and those of the network they share, gather to 'nourish' themselves with their collective love, joy and bliss. Any *goodness, truth, lovingness* from *any* source on the Earth plane is sung of and shared in the Singing Time.

Obviously, this includes healing of any sort, and naturally energy healing through spiritual conscious awareness. This is much loved and sung of with great joy. *They* gain strength from this from *us* on this plane.

This was a new concept for me too, that *we* can contribute, that we *do* contribute. That is a precious and vital thought and one I try to be conscious of. This showed me how essential it is to work in this way, to shed negativity and reveal the lovingness within that we all have – yet do our best to hide, suppress and negate from fear of some sort.

It was beautiful to realise that even down to the smallest act of kindness, a smile, a gesture of friendship or just being nice is part of a whole positive energy vibration that flows around the world and between the planes of the Dimensions. Not one jot is wasted or lost. From the greatest to the minutest all goodness and lovingness works for us all, Earth plane and Dimensions. Powerful indeed as a collective energy, especially when you know that it is strengthened by the unconditional and boundless love from the Dimensional Beings and God no matter what awfulness Man does to Man.

This was not conjecture on my part or me being fanciful. Through our wonderful 'togetherness' on the various topics and concepts we shared in our usual beautiful way, their words say far more than mine could.

I see from the date that this next extract was in the summer of 2002 so we had been 'together' for nearly two years when I took this down. Although a way along the path of my experiences I am using it here as it perfectly illustrates the exquisite 'oneness' of clairaudience and the reality of these wonderful Beings.

'Thank you for comprehending our connections dear one. Our sharing was beautiful and full of love. It is a most enduring contact and greatly beneficial to the spirit within. It is a lovely thing to have this with you because it is reciprocated. This is a joyous thing for us. We feel your joy and that adds to ours increasing it unendingly. We love you dearly for your reciprocity and giving us this experience. It is most lovely and good.'

They also spoke of their times of being together. This was a most amazing and intensely beautiful sharing.

'There is much to tell. There are many Halls of Learning and temples where we meet and hold discourses and discussions, meet teachers and Masters. We also have open air places but these are for less scholarly pursuits. They are for being together for music-making, for listening, for the sacred dancing that is a delight and a true coming together. We can travel very swiftly but do so at need for there is much work in one's appointed place. We do not have a firmament as you have but we can 'see' yours because the veil between us and yours is thin. We inhabit a dimension, a part of many which are all inter-connected by inter-relationships. These are vibrational and it is along these vibrations that we communicate. It is both complex and simple at the same time because it is vast but with no barriers, only levels and planes. We do not eat in the human sense but we need nourishment and rest which we take also through vibrations but this is hard to convey in a physical way. There is order and orderliness but not under any form of control or obedience to law as on Earth – it is just reasoned and sensible for the greatest achievement of all activity. There is an inter-connecting mutual vibration that is a part of us all, for there is no negativity to disturb it. All keep their identities and individuality, but there is no negativity to disturb the harmony that all here move in. Our tasks and activities whether for learning or pleasure are all fulfilling and satisfying and undertaken to the utmost so there is much going on at all times. This is the 'voice' of many guides and essences dear dear one who are all happy to explain our dimension to you. There is much happiness in this talking to you. We are all happy with what you have perceived while we were describing our time here. One day when you are really refreshed and strong, we will take you on a journey. We will arrange protection and support and instruct you carefully beforehand. We know that you will follow these and we will know when it is safe and possible.'

'...All is one dear Felicity, Earth plane learning is from experience yes, via the senses, memory – Dimensional learning is from the understanding gained, yes, from the Halls of Learning where all is kept for reference and expansion of our consciousness for those we guide. Indeed. That expansion is also allied to the chosen task, yes, teaching, healing, the sciences, – yes, *all* fields and aspects, indeed, through the principles. Yes dear - infinite also!'

How wonderful this sounded. Oneness and a unity of purpose with a sharing and joy in it all.

Chapter 11

I did 'visit' the Halls of Learning. The perception that emerged was of lovely semi-circular rooms leading off one another with shelves loaded with scrolls between high columns reaching up into the air. There was no ceiling only a soft sort of luminous 'daylight'.

There were people there engrossed in the scrolls or removing one or replacing some. It was very quiet, but a peaceful quiet, that of those enjoying their studies. There was a distinct feeling too to these beautiful open rooms that enticed one to stay; what wonders could one learn here? It was a very potent sensation.

As I thanked the dear Beings who had brought me, soft waves of powerful yet gentle energy flowed out like ripples encompassing me and them and then out as far as I could see in this extraordinary sense of Oneness that was intensely sweet.

I 'knew' they wished me to have a sense of the vibrational lovingness, their experience of Oneness, they were part of. It lasted for quite a few minutes and I was reluctant for it to end. It was truly beautiful. That they let me share in the love they feel - for they are patently Beings of Love – that pours from them was wonderful. It infused my whole being. It stayed with me for a little while after I had 'returned'. Recalling it now, I can still feel the sense of wonder I had then.

The expansion in my heart chakra when in communion with them naturally gave and gives them reciprocal love. What an extraordinary privilege this was – and still is. Because they allowed me to share their precious knowledge, I sent them mental pictures of anything beautiful on the earth plane. Things I saw, like sunsets, a loving exchange, a child's face, delicate colours, spring flowers, trees, blossoms, music – you name it, I shared it with all the lovely Dimensional

Beings and especially the network I'm connected to. I still do and work as much as possible to deal with and release any negativity for their sakes.

They never fail to thank me either. If I get somewhat negative at times, they always assure me that they understand and that there is no criticism or judgement so to refrain from feeling guilt. Therefore, how can I feel less than honour-bound to do what I can to release it? I try to stay consciously aware.

As I've been going through my books and choosing excerpts to share with you, I have become freshly aware of all the assurances and encouragement to clear current negativity running as a thread through them. It has certainly shown the constancy of the efforts needed. They were always there with the right help.

'When you feel the hollow space within, refrain from thinking of sadness. Think of it as a valuable space that can be filled with love and joy - where else are they to find a 'home' if not within the very self? Rejoice in it being there for it is a measure of the work that has been done. – indeed – but only empty if you perceive it so – it is merely a space within. – yes dear Felicity make use of it.'

'the Moon is the body that rules water, its shallows and deeps and its movement. It is very potent as it moves and draws your spring tides and this always plays its part. The swelling of the bodies of water with the swelling of the buds and roots within the good earth are all heralds to change and development and fresh beauty. Let all these good things dwell in your thinking dear dear one. Think of the patient oxen ploughing the spring furrows making all ready for the new seed – all will come in the fullness of time. Each furrow has to be completed before the next is run dear girl. So it is with all things. Let each day be a steady furrow - a loving preparation for the new seeds so that they fall as they should and grow into strong crops.'

Clearing major stuff from the past achieves a great deal, yes, but there are so many facets to those events and experiences that there are still all the little threads that mean attachments to niggle at one. It is definitely an on-going task!

Something I found that helped me with this constant 'traffic' of everyday negativity is the loving Hawaiian Ho'oponopono mantra which my friend Sheila introduced me to. I use it therefore as often as I can.

She told me to look up 'Zero Limits' on the internet to read up about it. Looking it up is very worthwhile if you do not know of it. A blessing indeed

There are always negative thoughts, feelings or judgements that I realise I am carelessly sending out into the Universe. I do try to remember to use it rather than add to the 'cloud' that is being emitted everywhere.

Conscious awareness is sometimes elusive. Nevertheless, we really do need to understand that every living thing on the planet shares the same energy.

What we emit as individuals of whatever quality are part of the ether of our world, our Universe. Every human being contributes his and her thoughts, emotions and desires both positive and negative to the cumulative energy of our world. We are all responsible for its quality. Hence the value of the Ho'oponopono.

On a personal level I also find it helps dispel whatever I might distress or stress myself with in the given moment. I am so grateful to my friend for this valuable tip. We really do need to do what we can. It is so good to have another way to increase lovingness for ourselves and the planet.

The mantra is beautiful and simple. It has many uses and it can be used in any given moment to bring the mind quickly back to positivity, which is so good. Saying it within your mind from your heart is very powerful and loving. And it certainly serves those beloved Beings who have such constant loving interest and care for us.

~.~

My development was being very thorough. My beloved Guides were with me for certain aspects. Ja-San, Tibetan Grandmother and Eyes-of-a-Doe were with me to develop my spiritual and metaphysical understanding of all energy and vibration and that within myself. Dr Ying Po naturally helped with this in relation to the spiritual philosophy of the body, to guide my thinking when I was considering *any* aspects of the body in fact.

These dear Guides had come to help me understand the principles of healing and best use of focus, balance and bringing my thinking into my heart energy rather than follow a thought for the sake of it.

Naturally at the very beginning they had been concentrating on my understanding of all the necessary aspects of energy and its significance in healing.

They had taught me that a gentle flow of Rei-ki energy from the heart where one felt the love of the channelling and the willing intention creates a 'harmonious link for the Rei-ki to vibrate along' for the needs of the body receiving it.

Their guidance and teaching were for me to understand my own energy and how I used it or wasted it and how to make better use of it, especially my mental energy.

We discussed the significance and nature of vibration, frequency and momentum. They explained and guided me to understand the energy in my hands and the importance of balancing and re-energising the chakras to enable the energy to flow and help the correct physical condition of the body's organs and tissues. How to listen within during a healing and how to feel the energy changes. How to pull back my thinking and not project it forward and anticipate but learn realisation in the now.

It was hard work trying not to think forward to the next step and make judgements and seek conclusions. That works in decision making but is irrelevant when answering someone's needs in healing. The body under your hands tells you through the energy exchanged where healing energy needs to be applied. Following the flow of that energy is the focus.

'We have come with knowledge beyond your own to give to you to add to yours. You do not have to strive for answers as you always have done. At last teachers have come to you.

We will weave the knowledge together. Rest in this way of learning. This learning comes from truths. There is no battle to glean knowledge through ego and subjectivity. We give you our knowledge for the task. That is what a teacher is for – to bring the missing dimension to the pupil. This is what your teaching will be.'

They also spoke to me of the approach to need in people.

'your development will move on when you refrain from concern over the needs of others…..the tenderness of your heart needs to metamorphose into a strong vibration of love and lovingness…tenderness is good. – direct it towards their need rather than solving it…..love will strengthen you from within for that is what you will receive in response rather than their Will to either have the problem or solve it – and when they are ready and even willing. Accept their problems as theirs dear dear one as you accept your own …….their needs are not only theirs but ones they need to hear……by leaving that energy field others may enter it as of necessity but it will not be available to them until you do. This is to answer need.'

This rang bells, I can assure you! As always, straight to the heart of the matter.

They saw everything! This was timely as I was so eager to help people. Also, one's instinct is to seek a solution for people who tell you their problems rather than just listen and learn what was really needed. This also subtly reminded me that to present one's idea of a solution was actually to impose one's Will. Hmm! As they added later.

'..you can only breathe for yourself – to breathe for another is inconceivable.'

I did discover that metaphorically that was often what people do. Also, there were those who expect it of others. Also, others who demand it manipulatively of others.

You can understand that I felt immensely blessed by their insights, wisdom and attention to the most salient detail. Yet I had to grasp the subtle difference between feeling humble and unworthiness, which was self-criticism.

They taught me about all aspects of negative energy, illusion and delusion and how to recognise it and deal with it for myself. Always this was for the purpose. The purpose of the intention, the goal, the project or the task, however simple. Significantly however was the understanding of the Will. We discussed this frequently; the use and misuse of the Will and its purpose. It plays a crucial part in our lives.

'.....the Will is also a source of active energy dear Pupil as well as an instrument of control that you perceive it - its capabilities in its capacity for 'intent' – indeed that which brings the conscious down to conscious awareness and holds the focus for the purpose. This is the inner Will – the outer Will is that which you have explored in your 'studies' of the imposition of Will – it is the outer Will that is subjected to negative energy. This is what creates distortions. If the inner will becomes distorted by dense Root negativity it is turned upon the Self. If the inner Will is connected to the Divine within the heart chakra, it can benefit the Self by focus and as a source of refined energy can be a useful tool for what is determined as needful for the purpose.'

Indeed, we need that positive Will to achieve. It gives us purpose for needful action, to do what is best for ourselves and our life in general and naturally the people in it. Keeping it nourished by the heart chakra is the important thing! And it is hard work, as it is so easy to slip into using the Will against oneself and letting the Ego run off with one's intentions!

Our lives are in our own hands after all as Amanda, my friend's dear Guide said after a healing session working together for her precious charge.

'Hello dear Felicity. the path of each is created by the personality and the Soul journey of each individual dear friend – wherever life takes them therefore is from the ideas and aspirations and opportunities that are a part of the whole person and their physical template. yes dear friend. - Where it leads is always before them and will unravel from their own energy and actions.'

Chapter 12

The many ramifications of power and control also came into our synchronous discussions. Unsurprisingly, what emerged were the many uses Man puts his negative Will to - and these always, in some way or another, ultimately, works against himself.

'.....there is a fork in the path one way or another for some, that is greatly determined by Man's Will which can distort a Soul's original purpose – but that purpose will eventually be returned to for that *is* determined – the following of Man's Will and all its complexities and deviations is part of the knowledge acquired and until *all* that knowledge is acquired dear Girl, Man's Will will not be resolved to its proper form....'

It was good to know that Man's negative Will was not the be all and end all!

Although the Will is 'seated' in the Solar Plexus where its energy lies from all positive and negative Will, it was the development of the cerebrum and the *Mind* in Man's evolution that enabled man to *interpret, define, analyse and explore* his *emotions* from the primitive limbic brain.

The brain can store and calculate but the Mind has that amazing abstract quality, imagination. Negative thinking and beliefs conjured by the imagination then began to distort perception and associations attached to our innate survival device, 'fear.'

Man became 'Self' conscious. He needed to be. He needed to know he was 'created'. And to know moral right from wrong. How else could he develop? Sophisticated negative thinking however, prompted natures' own Selfishness further which thus exacerbated the negative Will.

Luckily this was offset to a degree as society developed and people became more Self-aware and reasoned against selfishness. Thus, *how* the Will is used is the issue. It certainly seems to determine the quality of life.

Viewing this now in metaphysical terms gave me a better understanding of something we rarely think of in particular. We talk of will-power, being self-willed, wilfulness etc: but it is attached to the incident or event so we are busy with that rather than seeing it in terms of 'how' and 'why,' 'cause and effect.'

'...gather the energy from within the whole body and direct it from the heart chakra rather than sending out a mental vibration from desire and the Will. This is to impose the Will upon the need. To use the unity of the chakra energy and allow it to stream from the heart is to allow the Will to be used as focus and the mental concept is then manifested more wisely and is more acceptable to the ether in this form. For it is beamed energy from loving need rather than a vibration pushed by the Will where the Will directs/imposes the momentum which changes its nature.'

Thus the will is all about choice. Realising this aspect clarified it beautifully. Being consciously aware of this, however, certainly requires effort. But our Will serves us better if we do. How often the Will goes ahead from negative promptings. And how readily we accommodate negative Will.

How beautifully my dear Guides always showed the way for me and yet always lovingly understood the demands and distraction of everyday life and especially my own dilatoriness and procrastination.

I had also to guard against berating myself for this and for allowing my worries and concerns to dominate my thoughts. Their loving understanding and wisdom were balm to me. They always put things back into perspective. In moments everything was right side up. Immensely reassuring.

'......rest all thoughts of a troublesome nature in the Divine within for this is where God's heart resides and He soothes and addresses all things with His love and understanding. Rest there gently dear one and refrain from anxiety concern or negative emotions and thoughts. The now is *good*. Place the names of all whom you love there too. All will be resolved by God's love and understanding.'

Would that everyone knew these things and gained solace from such knowledge. This wish is part of why I am writing this book and sharing some of my dear Guides' wisdom and affirmation of God, the Loving Being.

Their constant encouragement was such a blessing. It kept me focussed on method while ordinary life was naturally a distraction from metaphysical and spiritual thinking. They reminded me that preparation and preparedness were important for such work. Aligning my chakras and disenabling negativity were important 'disciplines' too.

'.....Establish a pattern dear one and gather the threads together as a guideline for steadiness. Accomplish this first and see what follows dear one. Go gently forward and take consideration of all things to create a tranquil pool. The reflection below will mirror that which is above and be like one image. In this stillness clarity will come. Ripples will even distort Happiness - still waters reveal...Even so - even that which is unseen. In this gentleness you will gain much also.'

This analogy was presented to me most vividly one evening when I was out for a walk.

It was a beautiful calm evening and a delicate sunset was just staining the clouds. I was walking along a path which curved round by the creek and there, the water was utterly still, not a single ripple disturbed its surface.

To my absolute delight it was tinted by the colours of the setting sun, gold and apricot, and turquoise and pastel blue from the sky. It had a dream-like quality that was exquisite for the lovely tints and softly massed clouds were reflected perfectly as in a mirror as if there was a wonderful city beneath.

I leaned over the bridge spanning the water and gazed at it enchanted. And the more I looked the deeper this city beneath appeared to be, holding mystery and beauty that was so calming, expanding some mysterious place deep inside me.

I knew also in that moment that my Dear Ones were part of this experience too, sharing it and at the same time, enabling that expansion. As it began to subtly change as the sun set, reluctantly I left it but wishing also to hold the exact images in my mind in the colours I had seen.

For both Dr Ying Po and Ja-San, water held great significance in their cultures. Its importance was deeply recognised in spiritual terms and was frequently used as a metaphor. We are 70% water ourselves and water carries energy as we know. And all energy is connected to, indeed one with the Universe.

Thus, we were talking of aspects of water one evening. We perceived it starting as a spring bubbling up from the ground and gaining momentum until it flowed in full force to supply nourishment and life all along its course but this naturally segued into its metaphysical affinity with Divine love.

'...water is powerful even when still and gently flowing for it nourishes cleanses and protects (the earth) by its constant presence and flow...(ah..simultaneously, as does the love of God -) yes, Jalal is here – that made him smile with warm eyes – he is pleased that you 'see' this - Yes, you felt our unity of smiling!'

Dear Jalal, my friend the delightful Indian Guide, was always interested in our illumined 'thinkings' together as well as any anatomical studies. As we 'thought' together on this theme he said,

'....I liked it very much – It is the two poles of the physical and the spiritual but one cannot survive without the other in the physical world – or the spiritual world dear friend – for the physical world gives function to the spiritual – indeed water can – but it goes nowhere and is wasted without function..yes, it (**the spiritual**) nourishes and carries nourishment from the physical plane through all 7 planes –thus, being *part* of the physical, gives it function. How entwined are the two! – but without the heart there is no love, no divine light to illumine the truths of the physical and spiritual planes. Thus are we linked to the physical to awaken the Divine spark within, to succour and nourish love in our precious charges. We are the bridge connecting the two! Yes indeed dear friend just as the (physical) heart is where all nourishment flows from it and that needing more, more flows into it, so it is with the Divine. – I do enjoy taking these journeys with you! They gladden my heart and stimulate my mind! Yes indeed! The Life Force! For true love is living in the knowledge of the truth and letting it flow through your being to nourish the Self and diffuse love and healing out to those around you. It is *good*! Oh this is the so good part of the thinking work you do dear friend...I can hear his lovely soft Indian accent as I write his words down! - it is the connections you make with the physical reality! – rooting it in those facts so dear to modern men! For this is another truth after all! All is rooted in the physical – it is a reflection of the Divine because it contains the Divine within it and is a reflection of the spiritual because that is merely the highest extension of it, a refinement but still a part of the whole. There you have it again dear friend! Bringing the Heavenly chi down to earth, in both senses! Ah yes! This is good indeed!'

My lovely personal Guides then came forward into my 'hearing'. We were 'climbing the shining mountain' as I call it, continuing the exploration of these concepts and thinking them together, our minds soaring together into a profound union that was so exhilarating that my hand skipped across the page as I wrote at the same moment of hearing.

'...the Divine love was seen as for the chosen few - it was elevated into the spiritual at the expense of the physical which became associated only with blood and punishment and death and the scapegoat was the senses which were deemed only physical for they appeared to be the strongest element that abused the body and Soul. But finer feeling could not escape from the taint of what was deemed base and the bondage of guilt obscured many truths. The spiritual was pushed further and further away to escape that which was deemed tainted and polarity was the result instead of unity. Value has to be returned to the physical both in Man and the Planet Earth and all its creatures. There is much that is enlightened - much change has taken place but man is losing sight of the spiritual as if it has no place in this awareness of the finer aspects of the physical, the knowledge that it is part of the whole, part of the cycle of life, love, goodness, truth and knowledge, the Divine and God, so that the physical is refined in order to develop. For this he needs the Divine within and the connection with the spiritual for the unity and oneness that is truly Man and God.'

It is this divide that has grown with our more secular and mechanistic times. So, we have come to denigrate the physical, both ourselves and our precious planet *and* spiritual comfort and wisdom. Does this seem to be progress for Mankind? These also make it a rather large task for those who offer the complementary approach to the body and its ills with the awareness of the unity of Mind Body and Spirit.

'....it would be wiser for Man to move to the sweeter and kinder level of healing for the body. This would lead to a better understanding of spiritual things because all things of the heart lead there. The energy from all things inner and spiritual is bright and good and strengthens all things good and increases the light that Man needs to show him the way to goodness and this leads to God because God is good and so love is fulfilled and the Will used for goodness and love.'

The rapid expansion of the variety of such healing and therapeutic approaches being offered and sought by many in our very urbanised world is hardly coincidental.

We are being moved forward through the guidance from within even though it is largely unknown and many people are unaware of acting on it. The time has been cosmically right for the reawakening of contact with these beloved Dimensional Beings to help us.

'Man is beginning to see healing not just as one man to another but as bringing the Cosmic Divine through the inner Divine to enable love and healing.' These wise words of all the dear ones of the Network are very heartening.

Yet there needs to be a concerted change in mainstream thinking towards the real wholeness of the body if we are to truly progress towards better health and mental, emotional well-being; offering conventional healing with love and wisdom as part of its *concept*, not just Medical and scientific knowledge under Newtonian and Reductionist principles. Such knowledge needs to be brought back into the heart.

At least though there is an amazing amount of movement happening outside of the mainstream to help this planet's spiritual development. So many people in so many ways are in conscious awareness of spiritual connection and awakening and work for that even on a daily basis. The worldwide network being created by all the dedicated Lightworkers is growing all the time,

'...Lightworkers who work with the loving lovingness create a network of love to encompass Man in his struggles with the dark side – all who play their part in that sustain it and strengthen it for all – it is this that moves Man and the planet on and this era is a new phase in that evolution.'

'...by clearing the 'core' the Divine, entering through the crown connects with the Divine within the heart chakra and brings the Divine down to the Root Plane. Therefore those that work on the core are doing this for the Universal/Planetary Root plane to enhance and disable the very low frequency that enables negative energy to become trapped. This connects with the vibrational consciousness working at that level spiritually. So any work on bringing the Divine through the core and the root are influencing that frequency......'

Their devoted work must hearten the Dear Ones in the Dimensions who 'see' everything that is happening in our earthly plane.

As my Guides said so beautifully,

'..the power of giving is immeasurable. The Life Force of the planet is from the fountain of light that shines from our Souls to illumine our hearts with love and giving and sharing for the benefit of all. Those who turn their faces from the light are sad and lonely Souls who are lost in a sea of darkness with no compass to guide them. But they are only lost not abandoned. Love is always within reach, they have just forgotten it because they believe love is just a passionate exchange and without that they are nothing. But love is on the inside of us all. We beam it out to the world without regard for receiving goodness from others then they will understand that love grows by being held within the heart as a precious gift for giving out into the ether to encompass-all of Mankind. Only then will they feel loved for they are filled with love itself for that is goodness and truth.'

This awakening in so many people of all the aspects of spiritual awareness and expanding Lightwork is surely *for the purpose* of raising and strengthening the 'feminine' energy vibration needed at these times.

Hopefully this will enable a better balance in the energy of both Men and Women and away from dominance and a consciousness of dominance.

Chapter 13

My own experiences and working with peoples' energy through Rei-ki had revealed the effects its condition has on the entire body; a view I had not had before.

This realisation was very important to the work and the purpose for which my Guides had become known to me. It was easy now to understand what an influence our energy has.

I was also finding that people became quickly satisfied and continue in a state of reduced physical wellbeing as long as it is bearable, as long as the focal point is reduced to a level where it does not interfere with life's duties or invade the mind's full consciousness.

Even then palliatives are more readily sought than causes. And people are afraid or unwilling to seek those causes. Frequently because subconsciously, they feel they will reveal emotional pain best left buried.

Their reluctance is understandable. It was – still is - quite difficult to help people understand that this can be dealt with *without* re-visiting past traumas and problems, which could readily be done with the very effective releasing techniques I had been developing, as well as helped with energy healing.

My use of these with the Rei-ki healing energy was of great help and appreciated by all the Guides.

'...much has been released and their respective guides are very happy – yes indeed very happy to help with the visualisations which have such happy results. Yes, it is good when those who are willing to receive are also willing to take part and work with you. This is an excellent partnership for healing dear dear one. The network rejoices at such things and all help is sent to aid you.'

Clearing, or disenabling negative energy as my dear Guides called it was so important to the Dimensions: less fuel for the dark side. As Dr Ying Po said,

'Being positive with the Mind is not enough – only when it comes from within does it unravel before one and find the right response.'

I'd learnt how essential that was. It spurred me on to help as many others as I could, especially knowing it helped the Dimensional Beings and made them happy too.

Overcoming both reluctance and the 'that'll do' attitude are real obstacles in the world of energy healing especially because it is an intangible.

And talking of obstacles, my dear Guides had perfect insights into those also!

'...obstacles are to be made use of – to give us time to assess things – re-assess things in order to see clearly how to find a way around them, past them......It is however unwise to put obstacles in our own path – but if we do we need to ask why and what they are trying to tell us...'

'....bring the conscious awareness on to the obstacle to consider its validity or how it has come into being.'

'The path for Man has many stones, rocks and obstacles so that he learns thoroughly all that is needed – these are not negative aspects dear one, merely the way to learning all facets of each aspect of the Will and the Will of God – yes, every hindrance is a positive because learning comes from everyone – that is of little matter dear - as the learning has to be complete rather than skipped over – yes! The path of best resistance – yes we like this, this is *good*.....'

'But the choice has to be with the individual person otherwise it is back to that imposition of Will, which is undesirable especially from the healer. So, it is down to the individual's Will in effect.

And according to my dear Guides,

'....this is the choice dear One – the dissolving of the negativity – each person's responsibility to him/herself for ultimately only he or she can let it go, for it is held within and covers the Divine. Love waits patiently, endlessly for the negativity to dissolve and disperse....when knowledge of choice is known in the heart then the Will can direct the choice....'

Oh, that we made choices from the heart not the Will! But we humans are very fallible indeed!

In circumstances where there is a reluctance to work on poor health or well-being it is hard to explain to people that negative will-power inhibits momentum therefore any change for improved health and happiness. And indeed, personal growth and progress. For although it is obvious that it is positive will-power from within that gives intention for actively achieving results we tend to ignore that fact.

'...it is the negative Will that obscures the inner voice which is the Soul's guidance,...yes, the barriers we spoke of yesterday created by fears anxieties doubts and confusion – Just so dear one - these do act as a shield to the inner voice and prevent the true core energy from vibrating positive energy and flowing through the core to refresh and harmonise it. The inner voice is often ignored as the lower chakra energy is allowed to dominate.'

Realising that hanging on to the fear of something perpetuates the situation and emits a 'fearful' vibration at the same time helped me to clear mine. I had no desire to go on attracting further negativity either. Naturally I was keen to clear this for others.

I was also realising that energy must, by its nature entail activity. Positive energy expands. Negative energy's activity is contraction; it intensifies, moves within by being under pressure from its own stasis.

It is actually crucial to identify the determination behind the Will if one wishes to change things because static Will is controlled by the negativity behind it of course. That is the problem. Negativity is a pressure. Positive energy isn't. I was keen for others to understand this of course.

There needs to be a very real change in thinking in general.

As my Guides say, 'harmony of mind is essential for maintaining health,' an important maxim in healing.

My Guides and I had been reflecting on this subject and how little thought, if any, is given to the varying degrees of emotional turmoil in relation to what is happening to the body. And especially the conflicts and denial of the inner being that occurs because of it and the way the body in general, is viewed.

'In the physical world, the physical is not only the most apparent but the area of human life most active - as perceived by human beings. It is therefore the most common yardstick for the concept of wellbeing as it has the full range of experiences of feeling and emotion to focus the mind on its condition. Any upset, any setback, suffering or disease is invariably attributable only to the body's well-being in the minds of men if this well-being, in other words, the physical, is not being well-served — though the blame is invariably attached to and directed against the unseen, unknown deity(ies) or Dimensions that man perceives or conceives shape his destiny. Man, bound up in the high value he places on the physical and his physical activities, does not by nature look to see the emotional fault or cause in what he values highest (the body enabling his active life). — equally, he is manipulated through negativity to harm that which is most valued by him through the three mediums of body mind and spirit.'

'Thus, dear one, he accepts negativity with which he harms himself, others and separates himself from the help available from Guides and ultimately from God's love which is God. Were Man to look at and be aware of the physical as a source of that which afflicts him, then learn what it is he does to himself, his perception might be able to be changed so that he could help himself.'

'*All things that enter the consciousness manifests in the physical dear dear one/pupil.* (my emphasis) It is in the physical plane where observation and comprehension are needed to read the physical world. There is an acceptance of suffering that obscures the clues and messages and sources of information that are available to read from the human form. There is much being done to bring it to notice but once again until it becomes part of the consciousness – a clear way of thinking rather than something to read about – progress will be slow.'

How I wished that this *physical connection with the emotions* I have emphasised in italics was being widely discussed. And I mean among the unconverted, the sceptics and the fields of secular science and education.

It was so succinct, so clear an understanding and statement of how we should be looking at the whole human condition in the modern world where so much of society is now even ultra-secular. It is these, the secular and ultra-secular that wholly endorses the mechanistic Newtonian view.

However, many do indeed recognise that there is so much more to the body than its organic parts, but the power of negativity needs to be known and taken on board.

On one occasion when I had been working on some negativity from some worry, annoyance or other, Ja-San said to me,

'...yes dear Happiness, clearing the undergrowth of old burdens so that new tender shoots can feel the warmth of the sun of enlightenment and the space of clarity to grow in. You can see more clearly now. Without burdensome baggage you can travel more smoothly and cover the ground more pleasantly dear one. Speed is not really necessary dear Happiness/pupil – swiftness is for the arrow or the sword - you are neither dear Happiness/pupil. You are a traveller on a path to a destination. The journey is accomplished better with fewer stones underfoot and unburdened. In this way all that is to be seen is seen and brings joy and knowledge once the mind is freed from the feeling of the burdens upon the body – we use them to slow ourselves down, to distract us from the good, to make things difficult for the physical body so that our thoughts are turned towards the body in the hope that we will look enough, focus enough, to comprehend what we need to deal with – both to comprehend the physical world and bring into our vision and consciousness all that we are distracted from - through the comprehension of the physical we learn of the physical and through the physical of the plane itself. – the Soul then uses the knowledge to comprehend those things that are of the ether and the spirit for they work through the physical for growth and development of the spirit.'

Such beautiful consoling guidance. So beautifully expressed and gifted to me.

On an occasion when I was trying too hard over something, Ja-San advised,

'.....Having so much on your plate that is indigestible is unwise. To chew on indigestible food wastes energy – leave what you cannot 'eat' and be happy with what is easy to deal with.'

Dear Jalal made me laugh with, 'an overladen donkey will fall down and give no useful service.'

Dear wise Guides. Our synchronous thinking was always exciting and satisfying. To them it was a pleasure and a joy. My comprehension was deepening all the time – that was the satisfying part.

'....Knowledge without comprehension is static and cannot develop. Your comprehension sweeps away the dam in the river dear Happiness, releasing the knowledge into the water, whose energy carries it to nourish and make growth begin.'

There were so many nuances, so many delicate facets to all the aspects we discussed. This always made it so interesting and fresh.

'External pressure is for learning from, not necessarily for making decisions to act. Action is best when directed from the knowing within. External knowledge is a tool to learn of external things so that comprehension can be made use of for proper action. Comprehension is created within. Once linked to the Divine within guidance for good action is assured. Indeed conscious awareness applied to the knowledge will determine comprehension in the face of doubt and confusion - these can be overcome in this way if the problem is a large one. But doubt and confusion are also those things used to steer you off course so can indicate that the course is a good one and just needs positive support to *stay* on course. Patience and stillness within are a good way to overcome the place of confusion. Then it will pass and the course will carry you forward. This saves much hard thinking and mental energy dear one. Doubt and confusion are to disturb thinking. Conscious awareness is better used for the realities around one to create comprehension for taking action. So you see dear one these are different concepts. One is to avoid speculation the other is to view real things that could influence what you think and do. In this way rightness is achieved from within in both cases.'

The 'knowing' they spoke of was familiar to me so they knew I understood this. The calling up of an intuitive certainty of the knowledge of something deeper than a conviction was the root of my 'knowing' of God all my life.

It is as if one has carried whatever the 'knowing' is in some obscure part of one's inner being. It then surfaces to let you 'know' it is an absolute.

Through our synchronous communication my Guides were bringing these 'knowings' to the surface for me for they were touching on insights that seemed very familiar yet had not been touched on in my consciousness before. Thus, the word 'know' was truly that of knowledge.

Expanding on our discussion on facts and comprehension one day, they said,

' yes - it is a feature of the essence of facts, they are the surface of knowledge – depth comes from comprehension and comprehension gives flexibility and therefore room for change in the thinking - thus the strength of a conviction based upon the 'factual' evidence' effectively holds the issue as a nail is held to the magnet. Its very aspect of unyeildingness creates the stasis.'

Clearly a fact is a starting point but rarely the answer. This struck a note regarding the modern trend of reliance on facts for knowledge, whereas they are actually just for information hence my Guides interest in, and stress upon, comprehension.

No matter what the 'discussion' was on, and we covered a broad range of subjects, their metaphysical view was always stimulating and certainly thought-provoking so they kept my mind very busy in the most exhilarating way. Their insights were always such intriguing prompts that my thoughts and ideas kept bounding along with them.

It was plain however that these were all relevant. There were no digressions into cosmic matters that were not germane to the theme of progress for the individual. This concept for the individual was significant to all that I was being guided to learn. This was not for a wide message of 'hope for humankind' aimed at the collective of Humanity.

How much better for each individual to realise that by concentrating on their own comprehension and dealing with their own negativity they are also playing their part for everyone else. So, this is no selfish progression.

With the cosmic law of reciprocity this in turn means that each person benefits further from their own efforts and those they love too of course. How much then can each person achieve for the many?

What I always found wonderful, was that what my beloved helpmeets had to say to me always came neatly to an end in the time I had available. Their synchronicity was perfect. And always they ended with a blessing and sometimes a sweet assurance. I've copied out a few from the many for you to appreciate them too. They are so beautiful.

'Rest sweetly in our loving care and the arms of God who loves all.'

'Rest safely in our guiding love ….. God's love enfolds us all and all is *good* dear one. You are safe and protected and loved.'

'God's loving arms tenderly embrace you with His eternal love and goodness.'

'Rest sweetly. God's loving arms hold you and keep you safe as does our loving guidance – we will talk again when you are refreshed – we love you dearly – all is well – all is *good*. Sweet slumbers dear one.'

'God's loving arms enfold you to a sweet and refreshing rest – we are with you always.'

'We serve love with lovingness in these Dimensions of which there are many.'

'All choices if shaped by lovingness are greatly enhanced dear Felicity. Lovingness always bestows a blessing. Connectedness to lovingness is Man's hope and comfort and strengthener and that is our choice in these Dimensions to vibrate a loving connection with Man in whatever condition he may be in or path he is on. This is the guiding truth of these Dimensions dear friend.'

Such beautiful words of support were intensely moving and reassuring, especially after a difficult time or frustrating day, and especially if I felt I'd been rather dilatory in my 'best use of energy'. How lucky I was to hear them, to know of such lovingness and touch on the profound love that is ours at all times. It is certainly there for us all.

Chapter 14

After such profound thoughts and revelations, this chapter will be about the Guides of others. How could I leave them out when they were all part of the marvels and wonderful experiences enriching my life?

Over the years I have spoken to many Guides so choosing was difficult. I have selected just a few, however, who illustrate certain aspects of being a Guide or are particularly apt to my book.

They were so interesting and happy. All the Guides who came to 'speak' with me when I asked if they would like to after a healing session were delighted to do so. I feel it is important to convey their 'reality.'

This can readily be realised through the obvious 'personalities' that are revealed in the talks I had with these lovely Guides.

These dear Souls have chosen to become our Guides and enlighten and guide us from within, even though the personality is quite unaware of them or even their existence.

I didn't hear them clairaudiently during a healing session; I did not know whether they were male or female. I had no voice to go on. They gave me clear and precise sentences to work with instead.

This was, in effect, very efficient, as listening to a spoken aspect could easily be interfered with. Working together was so good and so effective that it was no wonder I was eager to discover their identity.

These Guides I worked with were so good, introducing themselves and talking to me of the progress of their precious charge which always made them happy of course. They were also perfectly willing to satisfy my curiosity about who they were and what they did! They found it a great novelty as this was such a change from their usual vibrational communication.

As they spoke, I always perceived them and the events they spoke of. It was like looking into history and meeting a new friend there. Marvellous! I loved it. The whole network took delight in it. When I revealed their Guide and their conversation to the person, great was the joy from coming into the conscious awareness of their precious charge.

My Guides had told me very early on,

'A conscious channel is always the best and strongest method for us in our guidance dear one as it brightens the vibration and this gives the task the focus needed to work well together.'

It followed therefore, that knowing of their Guides gave a stronger link for those who now knew of them and was a help to their dear Guides too. I found that so many of these dear ones were really pleased to talk to me and glad of an opportunity to speak of the progress of their precious charge. It was lovely to know that this made them so happy too.

Sometimes they just sent a message to me when I next spoke to my Guides that they 'rejoiced in the peace which was flowing in their precious charge and that this strengthened them too.' Sometimes they only spoke just briefly of the healing......'your work was very helpful to both my charge and to me – working together is good. These thoughts warm my heart dear friend. Kindness is beauty and beauty is joy. To put her thoughts towards life is *good*.'

It was lovely to know that this made them so happy too. Here is a lovely example,

'Hello I'm E's Guide– how nice to be speaking to you – I have not done this before and it is a real treat. And rather exciting too! It will be lovely to have my precious charge know my name and speak directly to me. How lovely!.........this has been such immense fun and to form a picture in E's mind and an identity for her to talk to is a lovely thing. Goodbye dear Felicity...much will be shared in the Singing Time.'

It was so heart-warming to know of this beautiful reciprocity that was flowing between the Earth plane and the healing Dimensions. My Guides also called it 'the sacred circle.'

Happily, those Guides I talked with and took down their story, were pleased to 'communicate' with me. I always asked the Guide who had obviously been working with me if they would like to talk to me. I was never ignored, they really enjoyed talking to the Earth plane.

Naturally all Guides who talked with me spoke of their times positively because there is no negative emotion in the Dimensions.

It is hard however, for me to convey that when we were in that togetherness, subtle depths, glimpses of the reality behind their words of how it was, came to me with the perception. The only way I can express it is like a split second of being there and 'knowing' for them.

This is the extraordinary reality of clairaudience. It is not just simply hearing. This is what enthralled me in talking with these wonderful souls and why I am so eager to share them with you.

I would love to share them all as they were all so lovely, but here are a few of the Guides, lovingly willing to talk with me about the work we did together for their precious charge and only too happy to tell me a little of their lives and which illustrated their personalities so well. Sharing them with you is such a pleasure.

'...yes – my name is Alexander. – I have been A's Guide since his birth – he has been my precious charge for some time now and I love him dearly... - yes I was a Greek physician and studied in Persia and Arabia. Yes I taught in the schools and worked in the hospitals in many cities for travelling and learning were urgent with me as much as practicing and imparting the skills that I acquired. -I had a great love for the work I did and was always eager that my pupils felt as I did, for this love I believed imbued what I did with the extra element that tipped the balance towards success in both treatment and imparting knowledge. Without the love of the subject and the learning, I believed that the intellect was arid and could not then grow and develop fully without the energy from the heart. Thus the combined energy of the heart and mind were the tools to heal the body and in so doing touch a spark within the heart and mind of the patient to aid healing from within. These concepts were my aim and my joy dear friend……..'

He spoke further of his precious charge but these words were so exactly right to the healing path I was now on that they struck a lovely chord in me that I wanted to share with you. What a wonderful and enlightened approach to the healing arts. That was several hundred years BC. More than two thousand years on, do we have this approach in the mainstream medical world?

I was making one of my periodic visits to the Cotswolds and had some very interesting conversations with a Guide of someone I was giving healing to. It is such a beautiful part of the country. I was very absorbed by it and giving a lot of thought to the natural energies there.

'…….Man may yet learn the value fully of Nature for he looks to it now for a source of Spiritual energy rather than a nourishing breast as he did before when the Earth was 'worshipped' for that purpose.'

I was however struck by the sad fact that young people born there and who love it, and wish to live there near their families who have roots there, cannot now afford to in so many cases. Incomers despite appreciation for its beauties cannot have that particularly deep 'connection' that those born there have and which nourishes the land at a deep subtle level.

Because we are seemingly near a crisis point in the care of our planet, I thought that what this Guide had to say was relevant.

It transpired that this dear Guide, John, had lived in this very area in the 17th century, owned land and loved it too.

'...this is indeed sacred land and has very ancient connections with the spiritual and the vernal rites that gave the land rebirth and renewed its glory both in nature and the sacred............ Deep in the heart of this land is laid a secret yearning for life and an awakening to the glory of the sacred – but as part of a whole, not as an object of separate worship............ The light within was within those who were part of this beautiful earth. They loved it from within therefore it flourished and was rich in what it yielded both in nourishing viands and the sacred ways of our life here......it needs to be loved and cherished by men who love and cherish their real selves to preserve all aspects of it for the future as well as the present and maintain its sacred links and sacred life.'

His observations clearly showed his deep connectedness to and care for the land and revealed his vital personality. It was a very interesting insight into his times for I received perceptions of him there as we spoke.

There was certainly a feeling for nature that was very deep in those centuries. I received a strong perception that in those times the consciousness of nature was a fundamental force that was both personal and cultural. This had a profound effect on me and gave me a whole new way of thinking of Man and Nature working as one in harmony and connectedness. It was a beautiful and powerful concept.

John was much taken with our working together with my particular approach so our talks segued readily into energy and nature which added further insights to my learning which I enjoyed very much.

It is no wonder many spiritual people are drawn to the Cotswolds; the energies there are potent indeed. It must have a collected vibration from its past harmonies. It is obviously being served now by their love and appreciation. It has certainly retained its lush, calm beauty. so, unsurprisingly, draws many people to visit it too.

A very different view of nature than that largely held in our urbanised secular society. We do seem to have become separated from these understandings and from nature's truths in our modern machine world. Such a pity, when we are so dependent on Nature as well as an irrevocable part of it.

Do Urbanites even realise, or care, that it is the natural world that actually provides for all their wants in the life they are immersed in? But city life is so internalised that it is sadly understandable that it has become disconnected from Nature and the natural order of things. A sad separation.

What a pleasure it was that so many Guides talked eagerly and happily to me. Nice to know too that giving me these priceless glimpses into their times and lives and their always interesting personalities was a novelty *they* enjoyed.

Communication was their whole *raison d'etre* after all. Within these conversations I always learned some point or insight, aspects and mores of their times so they were always of subtle benefit to my understanding.

You can imagine my huge delight in 'meeting' lovely people like these guides. I feel so lucky.

In this beautiful way I 'met' nurses from the Crimean war and both the First and Second World wars and who lost their lives during their war service. One Guide, a lovely Australian girl who worked with the Flying Doctors in the 1940's lost hers too in this service. They all loved their work and were immensely fulfilled through it.

I was much struck that quite a few Guides had been members of the healing professions. I would love to share all their fascinating experiences with you. (I'd need another book!) They were all so happy to talk to me and sharing them was beautiful.

I would however love to share this particular glimpse of a nurse in the Crimea. It is most poignant.

'Hello dear, my name is Veronica – yes dear I was a nurse in the Crimea at Scutari. I caught the typhus which raged through our poor poor soldiers – but I had been with them a year so I was able to be with them and help them in their travails and suffering before I was carried off too. The comforting hand and presence of a woman was felt to be as much of a blessing as any nursing care we gave them. The poor dears. They were less afraid. Most of them bore up manfully but those that did not were piteous souls so it was altogether a sad time, although uplifting and enlightening at the same time – so *very* different from our safe English country life! Yes, I was a squire's daughter and much fired by the new thinking of our dear Florence Nightingale and other women who wished to do something with their lives other than marry and have babies. Dear me! There was so little choice! To stay at home with Mama and Papa seemed a terrible fate! One is so idealistic when one is young and buried in the country! A very safe life but quite without incident. Well I certainly had plenty in Scutari when I answered the call to *that* adventure. And it was, you know. A tremendous adventure. I felt that I was doing something with my life at last and doing it for God as well as our poor men. But I was no longer idealistic – that *could* not last. But we will not dwell on the horrors of war – there was a great deal of love and compassion and true true heroism in amongst all the truly dreadful things there which is the best part to dwell upon. I was 30 when I took up *my* call to arms – just enough sense to be of some use but young enough to be strong in body at least! Oh yes! And Will! I was very determined! It needed a lot of determination as you can imagine! Papa was *not* pleased but I think Mama was a little proud and envious too which was nice. It was not spoken of but I saw it in her eyes and dear face though she kept her thoughts and feelings to herself.'

    She was so pleased that her precious charge wanted to know her, that it would be very nice for her to 'talk' to her. Her story like all the others flowed so beautifully to me, that her personality came through as if we were together in the flesh as well as the mind.

    I did 'meet' another Guide from the Second World War, Adam, a rear-gunner in the RAF who got killed coming back from France.

    Another brave young lass had been killed parachuting into France in the Second World War. Riveting stuff! All, in life, were full of life and vitality and eager to do 'something worthwhile' with their lives.

All, without exception spoke positively of their demise; it was a transition to the joy of their choice to become guides. No remorse or pain. That had all gone.

I was much struck that independence of spirit was very much a feature of the Guides of both sexes. Independence was certainly a priority to those dear female Guides from the mid-18th Century up to the last war.

They all wanted their lives to have meaning out in the world. Strength of character was definitely a feature as well as a loving heart in them all. Even those who found satisfaction in being wives and mothers showed that. Unsurprising, for wishing and choosing to have a meaningful 'life' for others it followed that becoming a Guide was the perfect next step. It is definitely the very essence of being a Guide.

Another dear Guide I worked with a lot was Sebastian.

'Yes I am French and a monk and young but I do not speak English. Like you, it is translated as I hear it. I was the herbalist at my monastery. Yes, I learnt form a small child and took to it with much naturalness and affinity. I learned from a good and holy man whom I loved as a father. He imbued me with much love for all things in nature and how nature is the source of all healing. Yes, I wrote poetry about trees and flowers and nature and feelings and how I loved things. Yes my herbalist tutor Tutor Fra Buono insisted that I knew and was able to write all the Latin names for the plants we used and knew all the ancient writings about them. Yes, I took notes of all he spoke to me and read and re-read them till I knew them thoroughly. Lives were often at stake dear friend. Thorough knowledge is essential.'

We talked together often regards the healing we were doing together on his precious charge. He called me his 'little chicken'.

I can share their words with you but it is not possible for me to convey the perceptions I had which gave me a sort of rounded 'view' of these dear guides and their moment in time. It is such a lovely subtle partaking of the events and situations going on then. When I recount these amazing 'conversations', I feel the essence of them inside my heart chakra and the 'reality' of the speaker again.

Every single one of these dear Guides that I met this way were naturally interesting people albeit that they all led the lives of ordinary people like the rest of us.

The special quality they all have obviously played its part in them choosing to becomes Guides. The timbre of their voices was always warm and of course loving. Their 'vitality' was also always apparent! What a joy. Copying out these few 'lives' for you gives me a lovely flavour of them and an expansion in my heart chakra all over again.

It is so good to realise that such loving Souls devote their sweet energy to guide us here even though they are largely unknown and unacknowledged. This is immaterial to them. The love and guidance are subtly 'known' to the essence of the personality receiving their blessing.

~.~

My connection to this network of beloved Beings, however, meant that if I was really interested in and on a tangent from a new subject, someone was always happy to come to talk with me. For example, I found an entry in the November of 2013 when just such a blessing came to me.

So, I include this as an example of the true connectivity of the way the network comes into play.

I had been giving a great deal of thought to our cellular fluid and memory in relation to all that I had been working on by that time, on the body. This was after I had been reading Masaru Emoto's book and others about water memory and their experiments. *

That evening a dear Guide, picking up my interest through the network, came unbidden to speak with me. I was delighted. He had been a scientist and he found my concept very interesting as he had studied molecular substances in their fluid environments in his own scientific researches on the body during his incarnation.

'...the study of molecular substances such as proteins in their fluid environment was part of my field of course as all my studies were biased to the human structure rather than that of the Universe – there were plenty of Scientists eagerly embracing this new aspect as we entered the age of Space and its matter/non-matter – the human body and living particles was more my area of interest as yours is. I am very interested in your conceptual theory...' We went on to have a fascinating discussion opening my mind as we covered all manner of aspects of human, animal and plant life in regards to fluids and fluid environments in relation to my work with the body.

'....'life' is a fascinating subject in *all* its aspects and moving the scientific thinking to encompassing the metaphysical is the challenge for the scientific world to take up and bring into realisation over this new age, yes my dear, raising their consciousness, for their cerebral activity is a very strong component of the planetary energy! - I must return now to my tasks my dear. Trust and believe in your comprehension and at all times you may call upon me or any others for assurance and confirmation. It has been a good experience to be a part of your thinking and 'talking' with you....it will be sung of in the Singing Time.'

It was so lovely to be sharing this mental journey with someone whose particular field I had touched on. My concept and interest had drawn him forward and he was so happy and eager to help expand my thinking through this synchronous mind-sharing. Naturally it brought joy to the Dear Ones of the network... '...we are all filled with joy at all that is being accomplished so go with God. Love is all' Such reciprocity and loving exchanges are so enriching.

*I met a lovely Italian lady later who took samples from all over the world, and photographed her experiments of the water quality, so found out for myself how water responds. Most revealing!

Chapter 15

In the course of working with the guidance from my own lovely Guides, there was an aspect I was keen to make sure of. I was anxious that I use my ego properly as much as possible. I was always concerned about the fine line between selfishness and self-interest, and self-awareness and self-love. They helped me deal with doubt and the way for the Self so that I could determine for myself what was Ego and selfishness and to understand the value the Self should have.

'This is the Self we wish you to know is not a place of selfishness that you are so concerned about. The true Self needs to be cared for and loved in order to come into true being. And that these subconscious vibrations do not attack you, focus your mind into your heart chakra if you feel that negative thoughts are forming in your mind. In this way you will not attract what is not good for you. This is the understanding of Universal Love. It gives outwards and protects at the same time and therefore is in existence - it is not directed or striven for it is just in being - within the Divine. The reality of truth is its simplicity. We make life complex with working from our minds too much and not believing in the power of the heart. The mind is a tool for knowledge of the physical. The heart is the place for knowledge of God and Man and Love. The principle of three. Yes it is part of the plan that Man loves Man but not as God but because of God who loves Man. As Man we grow in learning. Yes the learning is then taken inward to the Soul itself. You asked for learning of many different kinds. You have always asked, what do I learn from this? Your path has been one of learning for your Soul and the path you are now on is to learn about the Self and love. Your Self is within the Divine. You do not doubt the Divine so it follows you cannot now doubt the Self.'

As you can see this is a gentle and loving 'voice', the syntax is pure and clear and concise and is not mine. They also say so much within their concise syntax.

As I wrote out that extract, I felt such an expansion in my heart chakra, for their power was re-awakened in me as I brought them into being on this page.

They make me feel so humble and so honoured to have been given words such as these to expand my understanding. The most potent sentence in that paragraph I highlighted in my writing at the time so I would like to bring it to your attention again.

'..that *Man loves Man, but not as God, but because of God, who loves Man.*'

How simple and truthful, how pure and absolute is that statement.

Still on the subject of the Self, this is a tricky one for *so many* people. The prominent factor in the Rei-ki and clearing sessions I have done with people over the years, is that of negative self-worth, or self concept.

As my Guides said, wisdom

'Worthiness /unworthiness is Man's Judgement through lack of comprehension of Love.'

We are so vulnerable to criticism and put-downs. We are so eager to believe things against ourselves, believing ourselves unworthy, inadequate, feeble or of little or no consequence. We accept criticism and judgements almost as if we deserve them. The dark side has been feeding off Man's negativity by encouraging and endorsing it so that *we* create more negative energy *for them* to thrive on. Indeed, exist on.

For they *use* energy. This has been aided and abetted by the moral conditioning from nearly 2,000 years of being made to believe that we are born sinful, are unworthy sinners with a multitude of sins to be guilty of and must atone for. Thus, we must judge ourselves but also need to strive constantly to be good or we will be judged and punished.

Judgement therefore, is a major negative element. I have encountered lack of self-confidence, worth, value, regard and all nuances thereof i.e. judgement against the self, in virtually everyone whether they come for healing or not.

And this state of mind leads to many other negative consequences. The phrase *self-sabotage* has now become a virtual buzz-word these days but it has real significance.

Buzz-words however, always put something into a box that acts as an explanation so thoughts about 'why' fail to come into it. *Why* is the most important aspect. We all know *what* it is. We need to grasp that negativity against the Self has become a perpetual cycle that equally, needs to be broken.

It is a pattern that perpetuates in a subtle way so that we are barely aware we are in it. The social conditioning that plays so strong a part in it, is a pattern too. And a subtly subversive one at that. The increase of peer-pressure through social-media these days is really hard – often brutally so, - especially on our young people.

I was taught that one does not put oneself first, consideration for others' needs is paramount. An accepted social more of the time and generally the value deemed correct. Now this is admirable – but up to a point!

In amongst the events and needs of others I had encountered, somehow I lost the idea that I owed something to myself. My darling mother would be horrified to learn this. She loved me unconditionally for a start which kept me strong, always taught me 'personal pride but never vanity,' never questioned that I did my best and she believed in me completely. And yet....! I discovered several areas where I felt and believed myself to be not good enough, even inferior. But also, that going for what *I* wanted, was selfish.

It took me years to learn that frequently the acceding I did to other's needs was invariably to the detriment of myself. I'd wake up to it now and then but feel guilty and selfish even while what I was actually doing was working towards self-preservation.

It was also years before I cottoned on to the fact that as I acceded to the wishes and suggestions of others I was actually 'doing as I was told' and that it was really to suit them or even serving someone else's Will rather than the right thing to do or right for me. I acceded to the judgement of others deeming it better!

There is no question in my mind of the need for consideration for others. That is essential. But discernment and balance are definitely needed so that you save some consideration for yourself, *and* without guilt. I was too busy worrying about being selfish. One thing I have always been clear about however is that self-pity *is* selfish!

As I have been going through my notebooks, I have come across the most comprehensive statement on selfishness one could hope for. This is from my dear sweet Tibetan Grandmother who always spoke directly and to the point!

'To be wise to the Self is not to be selfish. – selfish is to do careless things for self and others. To not value what is good within is to be selfish – to hurt the self within is to be selfish. To allow bad things is to be selfish - if bad things are for the self this is more selfish. With this selfishness others around you will feel the dark energy and inner pain. Not good for others also.'

I think this should be written up somewhere. I'll put a copy of it in my kitchen to remind myself!

Working against ourselves therefore is assuredly being mastered by our own negative Will. 'Being' ourselves is the positive way. All Guides and Dimensional Beings want this for us too.

In the course of my 'visualising-style tie-cutting' I did eventually discover the source of my particular 'Self-worth' issue. I was so used to it that I didn't give it any particular thought or grant it any significance in relation to my view of myself. It was only because the memory eventually asserted itself that I came to realise its significance.

It came from one of my siblings and in the stoic way of children, I accepted it, neither did I query it. On the whole, I was, in fact and always have been, self-confident and that thanks to the total sense of security that my Mama's sweet, strong, calm, loving personality and presence imbued in me.

Consequently, I never doubted her belief in me or her love. She was my anchor. And yet, this situation regards my sister created an insidious need in me to 'prove myself.'

This seems like a contradiction to being self-confident but how subtle are the little worms of negative belief. This new comprehension was a potent lesson on the effects from childhood on *our view of ourselves.*

I'd like to also stress those words, 'insidious need'. It is something we should learn to recognise, for it determines so much negativity without our knowing it.

Over the years this need to prove myself had been acting as a magnet to anything else that was associated with my 'worth' I discovered. But the subtle cultural conditioning of 'having to prove oneself worthy' I realise, helped it along nicely!

Everything stuck. Because it had naturally built up over time, unravelling the subtle threads has been hard work. Also, finding the attachments that glued themselves to the original problem takes time! I'm sure there are several remaining as there are little slips now and then, so I do try to keep a watch on my attitude to myself. I just wish I'd known years ago and saved myself a lot of nonsense. As Ja-San said to me, 'Be gentle with yourself. Be like melting snow on quiet water Happiness.'

It was a while before I made the connection to the initial cause. Having lived with the pressures of unworthiness myself how much easier was it for me to understand for others who lived with this and its consequences. Moreover, from dealing with it myself I could help other people to do the same and come out from under it for it came up frequently in my healing experiences. All unknowingly, my sister had played her part in this for me. What part had I played for her I wonder? Reciprocity and the purpose once again.

Having looked into selfishness and its subtleties, I came to realise that there was a great deal to it. It ranged so much between a certain amount of egotism which is natural, and often actually needed and the extreme of 'self-consciousness' where everything is directed at the Self and is of paramount importance and frequently at the expense of others. Being Self-aware is harder but a much better way to be - as long as one doesn't then go in for self-criticism! Perspective is everything! That's what my dear Guides helped me to realise.

My Guides helped me enormously in my 'comprehension' bless them. Their understanding and loving encouragement helped me to comprehend some of the complexities of the Ego and the Will.

I had to learn quickly and undo a lot if I was to get moving along this new pathway I now found myself on.

Little did I know then I had a task ahead of me that required very real understanding of many things from my life-experiences.

I also came to learn that each and every one had played its part in teaching me what I was very much required to understand for that task and to accomplish it.

'...thank you for seeking our help dear one – our task is the path you are on. We will do all we can……..the stillness within will strengthen you Happiness – speak what is in your thoughts and strengthen your Self – in this way clarity of thought and purpose will be served. Prepare the foot, Happiness – stay with the plan for the journey dear one/pupil/Happiness for the work is the journey and requires careful attention for reaching each stage. Steadfast to the purpose dear pupil – remaining on course will achieve much.'

Chapter 16

One day I was told someone had come to speak with me. To my delight this was another Guide come to help me; his name was Anthony. He was a lovely surprise to me as I was hardly expecting another Guide. But as always, he came for a purpose! When he introduced himself, immediately I perceived him, and to my astonishment, I was viewing his waistline! I knew this because I saw a rope-like belt around his body before me. He was wearing a darkish garment and it took a while to travel up his body to his face! I realised then that he was immensely tall. He told me he was 7 foot 2 inches! He was of large build but sturdy, not fleshy.

He had a beautiful gentle stillness about him and came across as about early middle age. Once again, the features were indistinct yet the impression of his face was broad with kind eyes. He was a monk from the 13th century and worked with, tended and loved the large farm animals in the monastery he belonged to.

'But I also worked with the sick in the Sanitorium and with the herbalist. I was very close to nature and all its beauties and fascinations -but also its dramas and the wild side of the elements. These things were part of everyone's life in those days. My ancestors were Celtic and Viking. My mother was tall and majestic, my father very big and strong. A mighty warrior and man at arms. I had more peaceful inclinations.'

His father earned a living from making bows and arrows, 'for he put all his skill and love into each one – he chose the wood himself and prepared each piece according to its qualities – all his feathers were hand-picked set in and trimmed according to the weight of the wood also – he tuned his strings till they sang the note of the bow and kept the sound in his head for restringing – he said it was his way to serve God even though his arrows were to kill or wound. He believed that to defend is to honour life and this enabled him to follow his craft – yes – at first it was hard (Anthony choosing the Monastery) but it turned him away from killing with the bow himself except for food. ....He was a *good* man. My mother loved him and his skills were above reproach so there was no room for judgement. If there is love in the purpose all is *good*. The skills we have are for the purpose and are put to good use, goodness results. This is the way of God and the Angels and Man is wise to follow them.'

His father had been called upon by his liege lord as an archer whenever his skill was needed for war. Anthony was naturally taught by his father from a child and had great proficiency. His increasing height and arm length were a decided asset. However, Anthony could not bring himself to shoot his arrows to kill anything. So, he chose the Monastic life. Anthony was truly a gentle giant. Strong with a beautiful Soul.

He had come to help ground me. This was no surprise as I was functioning metaphysically on the mental plane and the ether; I needed to be kept in touch with the planet's energy too. I called him my Rock and he loved that. He worked with me to encourage me in connecting the energies of my chakras from the root up to the crown.

He helped me make good use of my root chakra, and the energy in my feet and to gain Conscious Awareness of the energy from the Earth, right down to the magma. Also, that of all the living things of the plant-world, trees, plants, grass, even the earth that they drew their life force from; that all these aspects of the planet were part of the Universal Life Force channelled in Rei-ki and of course, of our own human energy. Conscious awareness of including the Earth plane in metaphysical comprehension was essential and a reminder that our love and respect for the Earth we live upon was greatly needed.

He always seemed to come to speak with me when I was feeling a bit washed out after work, giving me some physical strength to keep on with the inner strength work. This was always very reassuring. In his lifetime, he was a man totally at one with his beloved natural world. He carried this in his essence as a Guide.

We were speaking of the work ahead of me...

'Yes dear girl – hand to the plough. It is always calming and gentles the mind and spirit exceedingly. (a perception came to me of him ploughing with oxen out in a slightly misty countryside so I asked him about them.) yes dear girl, for their rhythm becomes one with the man and the good earth is ploughed with love and tender care for its fruitfulness. The song of the earth, the song in the hearts of the beasts, the song of the air and the steady hoofbeats, the following steps of the ploughman and the combined beating of their hearts was the sacred dance also. So the Sacred was returned to the earth after her gifts of food were harvested, given up by Mother Earth from the goodness within to those who lived upon her bosom and her bounty. The true rhythm of life dear girl. I carry all this within my heart chakra and sustain you with it when those things of the physical plane beset you or have something to guide you to understanding. You chose a good name for me dear girl (my Rock) – most apt. I like that dear girl – it is *good*.'

As he spoke these words to me, the poetry of them and his deep gentle voice was truly beautiful to experience. I seemed to be part of the serenity and lovingness as I could 'perceive' the vision he conjured and the reverence he had for his every part of it. Sharing it with you allows me to regain some of the flavour in copying it out for this book. A joy indeed.

Anthony was such a dear lovely Guide. He had such a poetic way of expressing his view of 'being'.

'If the land is loved, all growing things thrive, if the body is loved growth for the Soul is enabled – the Soul is planted in the body in order to grow and develop fully all aspects of love and goodness within the body to love the land and the glory of natures' abundance and beauty. Then the Soul can sing within the heart and be one with God and the Earth. This is the glory of the physical plane......there is always life whenever there is the tiniest source of nourishment for something to grow – so it is with Man -that even in the darkest hearts there is a place for something to grow into beauty and love – it is this natural Law that holds Man in Universal love. For love is the greatest nourishment of all. All things grow from it, with it, for it, because of it and so it will always prevail.'

What a truly beautiful concept. A profound belief and understanding we need to grasp and hold on to.

Another time we were speaking together of the beauties and magical qualities of nature, landscapes and trees. I liked mentally sharing images of our lovely countryside and trees with him whenever I saw a beautiful view or place,

'I do thank you for all the lovely country scenes, the woods and trees and changing deepening colours with the touches of bright gold – these sweet pictures are joy to me for the bounties of nature were so much a part of my happy life. I can smell the earth and fallen leaves and thank you for the scent of water from the rivers and streams – a lovely thought to arouse my memories – these things are sweet to share. My heart is filled with joy and gladness at our sharing.'

So, he spoke to me again of his time at working on the earth.

'...the spirit Dimensions were very close to those who lived on the land in rhythm with the seasons and the changes in the earth's vibrations as the year turned - our attunement was so much a part of our lives that we took it for granted – it was the way to live and receive the Earth's bounties – there seemed no other way so we did not question it but thanked God and the Earth through our way of living – those I spent my life with lived in this way with gratitude. The way of the fighting man and men of war was not for me though I often saw the results of it and was heartily glad not to be part of it as they were. My turning from my father's skills did change his – in his later years he fashioned bows and arrows and taught the skills instead of using them against others for which my heart rejoiced. – there was always great love and respect between my father, mother and myself – yes! They dreamed of a mighty warrior son! They had such hopes as I grew and grew! No, the land called me, - yes, lacking the ways of pursuing money and not having the need to own what to me was free the Christian church was my answer and a blessed life it was dear girl. It gave me shelter while I worked out my purpose – it was *good.*'

Another time he spoke to me of:-

'....when the things of the land were simple and the love of the land and its fruitfulness was deep in the Souls of simple men.'

These glimpses into the values and mores of different ages were so interesting to me. I'm sure that is why so many Guides were happy to talk with me about their lives as they all felt the keenness of my interest and enthusiasm.

I was very taken with the fact that my Guides frequently used metaphor in their guidance to me.

A lovely example came about when I was 'talking' to Ja-San about Japanese archery I had come across in an article.

'..thank you for your loving thoughts and wishes for Japanese perception and sharing these things of my country with me. The true flight of the arrow is like the vibration from the heart chakra dear Happiness/pupil – yes dear pupil Dr Ying Po also. – for the arrow to fly truly there must be a harmonious stillness of the practitioner which finds the finite point from which to release the arrow for the purpose. The energy from the stillness flows into the bow to aid the arrow so that all is one in the moment of release. This is the fulfilment – the release of the energy through oneness of mind body spirit. This will enable the arrow which carries the energy forward to find the target. The loving craftsmanship finds reciprocity in the archer and archer from both craftsmanship and craftsman – one is part of the other's purpose - good connection dear Happiness/pupil – a loving circle which re-creates itself in the act of 'being' and of action for the purpose, a triad, yes dear Happiness/pupil. The energy is created by the coming together in the moment of focus – good connection dear Happiness/pupil – All are distilled into oneness.'

How beautifully put. I loved this kind of philosophical 'conversation'.

Coincidently I have always been drawn to metaphor – my eldest sister and I share this and remark upon it in the delight of sharing it. That my Guides used it to illustrate something seemed most natural and delightful too. An instance of the affinity between one and one's appointed Guide! And in my instance, Guides.

'..look for tranquillity in pool, not fish rising!' Tibetan Grandmother.

'….A stream's beginning bubbles up from the ground. It must set its own course. Once found it gathers momentum and carries the abundance it finds on its travels to where it is needed most.' Dear Jalal loved metaphor too.

Ja-San:-'……..Create a tranquil pool. The reflection below will mirror that which is above and be like one image. In this stillness, clarity will come. – ripples will distort – still waters reveal, even that which is unseen.'

'….walk slowly, savour the journey, and see much otherwise dust will obscure what is vital to progress.'

'let the mind unravel the ball of silk itself. It is infinitely able to follow it unaided before the consciousness picks up the threads from the pathways explored. The clever part is to recognise them and follow them in the full consciousness of seeking conclusions and knowledge…' **Dr Ying Po and Ja-San together!**

'your thoughts may dart like little fish but we can catch them in the net of our understanding.'

'…Knowledge spreads like the opening of the lotus petals in the sun.' **Dr Ying Po.**

'…comprehension sweeps away the dam in the river releasing the energy from the knowledge into the water whose energy carries it to nourish and make growth begin.'

'Do not run on ahead into the shadows that are not there.'

'….Leave insecure and negative thoughts untended and they cannot then grow. They will be left on the road behind your footsteps which are in the light.'

'....Use all knowledge and comprehension to negate negativity dear dear one, not nourish it. Refrain from turning it into a spear to thrust at your own heart dear dear one. Better a new vibration to uncover truth and reveal the light. This in turn will illumine the path ahead. A slow-burning lamp uses dark substances for they create the densest energy. This is the way to make use of it for the light is always above the darkness leading one towards the true light dear dear one.'

'Dr Ying Po is glad to have been one with your thinking...he likes working with your mind......He enjoys it very much....you cast your net and brought in the right fishes dear pupil, that is what matters. A full net is not necessary dear pupil - the few fish can be considered for their worthiness! - Good!'

'.....this is time better spent than pursuing dark shadows along a rocky path that hurts the feet. Stumbling is not helpful to the journey! Shadows are not for catching! Anxieties and perplexities are shadows only! All illusion to beckon you towards negativity so that you enter the shadow and are blocked from the light dear Granddaughter.'

'I am glad that you are keeping the thread of our project going. Holding the tail of the kite keeps it flying dear pupil, and in sight – most important! We will pull the strings together dear pupil and guide its flight at the proper time when you are refreshed and your mind is supple and rested.....when the pathway is clear, proceed.'

The images they thus created not only made their speech lyrical but their wise messages - always profoundly to the point! - memorable also. The joy I felt when we spoke together was so lovely an experience: the images they conveyed through their metaphors was an added delight. There is a depth of feeling with this way of communication that is hard to describe but it warms one in such a beautiful way. Those of you who are clairaudient and channel the wisdom of cosmic Beings will know how this feels.

Chapter 17

Having started along this new path, the significance and beauty of crystals had come into my life quite early on. Specialist shops were now catering to this newly awakened awareness of these amazing treasures from within our planet.

However, I had so much to study and occupy me that I did not make a really in-depth study of these beautiful creations. Their properties are a vast field.

When aligning my chakras, however, and sending my energy down into the planet I always connect with the beautiful crystal layer. It is a very powerful part of the Earth's energy. What an astonishing creation they are within our planet.

Tibetan grandmother told me that,

'....they bring the tranquillity of the dear Earth into conscious awareness for focus and their vibration therefore is gentle – use this for serenity through conscious awareness Granddaughter.'

I loved 'talking' with Tibetan Grandmother; she was so much attuned to crystal energy and its ancient use. Although this crystal connection with her seemed to be just another facet of her wisdom, it was in fact a grounding for a future aspect of crystal potency ahead of me. I should have realised that of course, everything had a purpose. This was not just some delightful insights into a subject that was an extra to my growing healing knowledge.

One time when we were exploring crystals, a dear Guide Piotre Vassily, who had been a geologist in his lifetime, came to join with us. He obviously loved this beautiful part of our planet.

'...it is the time of preparedness of the Earth, for spiritual enlightenment will bring balm to the planet for it is in great need. So it is that the rebirth of crystal and mineral awareness has come in to this time. The re-connecting with the network will bring the 'spirit' to the earth for true oneness, for healing and reawakening that which has been dormant for so long.'

Learning of this connectedness, this oneness of healing for the planet as well as Man was another perspective of the importance of the times we are living in. Also, the part that those in the fields of healing and light work were very much playing their part for us all.

~.~

After about a year, I had been advised by my Guides to become attuned to Rei-ki II. This was no surprise for as I was full of enthusiasm I had been gradually advancing along that particular path. After this beautiful attunement, I was advised to go to the Temple by my Guides.

The same sequence followed, crystal chamber, Angel of the Light. I always waited with a clear mind for events to unfold, just holding the focus of where I was.

Once again two Beings came forward. Once again, they carried me aloft. As we landed, I recognised the chamber where I had been robed in the white and violet gown. I was made aware then that I was actually wearing it as I stood there. This time another gossamer garment was passed over my head on top of the one I was wearing. It too was purest white but had a deep hem of golden yellow. I was suddenly put in mind of amethyst and citrine points which are white quartz but tipped with colour. The Being before me told me these garments together made a vibration that enhanced the Rei-ki energy and I was to use them together now.

Another stage had been reached which again made me marvel and even more aware of the responsibility of using healing energy and learning the metaphysical and spiritual way.

It was some time later that I learned that Uriel's 'colours' are amethyst and gold. He had been the first and 'busiest' Archangel for me, always protecting the channel to and from the mental plane which was essential for me for quite a few years. He always comes to mind first and comes immediately when I need him too. This cannot be just coincidence. There is always a connection in this work and for a purpose.

It wasn't long however after Dr Ying Po had come to add his voice and guidance, that a new Guide's voice came to me. This voice had a quite different quality. It belonged to Samuel. He told me that he had waited to bring his voice to me because the first need was for my knowledge to expand in relation to the understanding of energy through Rei-ki channelling that had been developing in me. As my Guides and I explored spiritual concepts in our synchronous thinking his voice was added and he also contributed separately – as they all did from time to time – to what was being said to me. Everything to the purpose, for the purpose. Timing is everything I discovered.

In one discussion we were having Samuel came forward.

'Yes, Samuel here, yes, use the negative to think of changing to the positive. In this way the positive energy is added to by the changed negative energy. But the impact of the negative energy has to be felt in order for the change to be set in motion. Yes - this brings the positive thought into existence. It is the pain that begins the learning to find the cure – also the desire for the cure or the end of the pain. Pain is not to 'teach' – it is to set the learning and the positive energy in motion. If this is comprehended then the pain is not held on to but is a beginning of change – which is a positive thought in itself. Unfortunately, the comprehension of pain was misunderstood and its negative energy has been allowed to grow. That is why so much healing is now needed for the growth and development of Man. Pain is a consequence not a concept. It has been created into a concept in the minds of men.'

We called this 'turning the coin over'. It proved a very handy device for quickly dealing with any negative thoughts that came up! I need to remember this from time to time.

Tibetan Grandmother gave me an excellent saying to hold on to.

'Now is the beginning of all things.'

How neat, how concise and helpful is that.

I soon realised that Samuel had come forward at this point to add his particular guidance during my studies. These I had undertaken to learn about the body, more of which I will come to. He had a clarity of style that I discovered was part of his search for learning, his love of the scholarly. He brought an extra dimension to our wonderful discussions.

When my time with the Open University ended, I had had serious 'withdrawal symptoms'! I missed my studies and the challenge of the TMA's so much.

I toyed with the idea of a Post Grad course but I knew that that would only be to satisfy the void I was feeling; it didn't really seem an answer. The urge to study something was very strong. I wasted time and energy over this for a good while looking for a solution; a real 'ought to' moment! Realising this, my dear Guide Samuel advised,

'...no burden is of benefit, the pressure of what you feel you must accomplish is the burden. This disturbs you on an instinctive level and you must trust this. If it tells you strongly that something is out of balance then negativity will prevail. The negativity has revealed that you must look for change. The negativity itself must direct that change. Reverse it upon itself to positive energy. Dissolve the negativity behind you so that you do not carry it forward....'

There was no doubt that the metaphysical aspects of my life held far more interest and moreover where I'd far rather give my attention. There was so much more to learn from my beloved Guides. Listening and learning from them was an unmatched joy. There was so much ahead of me, all new and all to stretch my mind.

Looking through my early books of dictation of around that time I found this which seems so appropriate. I have to say, I was frequently 'striving' over something!

'Your essence which is *within* will be strengthened by the stillness you acquire from refraining from striving. Acceptance is helpful dear Pupil (**Dr Ying Po**). Be gentle with yourself and observe without demanding so much of yourself. Spread thinly is to waste your strength and substance. Follow requirement dear girl (**Anthony**) and gather your strength as you would the harvest, to use as nourishment for new growth. This will occur as a natural consequence so allow this dear one without searching and striving.'

How lovingly and gently supported they made me feel.

Whenever I could I was doing Rei-ki healing with friends, a couple of willing relatives and more especially, people who came to me through recommendation. Thus, I was able to put what my Guides were advising into practice. I loved it. The realisation that one was enabling a warm loving energy to flow into another person was a beautiful thing. Without doubt it soothed and relaxed the recipient.

This was but a part of it, but that it encouraged and stimulated the body's healing resources was wonderful. To also reduce or remove pain for example, or to rapidly inhibit a cold's symptoms, or clear negative emotional energy, for I invariably included guided tie-cutting, meant that *change* occurred.

Change is the key word. And change towards improvement is the essence, the whole point, of healing. I would have been happy to have a constant stream of people under my hands!

Change however, is what so many people find difficult, and understanding and accepting that is all part of undertaking the offering of healing to other people. This is so well-illustrated by my Guides of course.

'....and negative disharmony from the cerebrum which we feel your friend is holding on to from much uncertainty and fear of change which is allowing all negative exchanges that have become habitual to find a core to become attached to. All of the issues now are becoming on one hand a prop to forestall change and a familiar pattern which clouds the real issue which is to let go and move forward but also creates the belief that their seeming persistence makes them seem insurmountable which adds to the negativity and also prevents moving forward both from within and without.'

This idea of it being insurmountable was a definite factor, I found. People couldn't believe that the simple effortless visualisation methods such as mine could clear anything, let alone that an invisible energy like Rei-ki could either.

Fear of change and an underlying agenda not to change are really quite strong in people I discovered. It didn't take much to realise that some feared, even shrank from being able to cope with it and some used it against the Self as a form of punishment for being either unworthy or worthless, (their own belief!). Sometimes they used it to punish or control others.

In the course of my healing experiences, I discovered every nuance of this wish, desire or determination not to change. And how close it was to control! And this from a wish to believe in their own weakness. A perfect example of illusion which always comes from negativity.

For those who had poor health generally, being unwell was so much a part of the dynamics of their life and relationships that they were unwilling to give it up. Thus, their ill-health controlled their lives *and* their family.

For some it was an agenda, a control cycle. Being hunkered down into ill-health certainly inhibits change. However, some people wanted to be unwell for a short spell as a way to take a break or opt out for a while. A choice that I realised I had to accept as well.

'Letting go' has become such a buzz word these days. Most people think the problem or concern can be dropped from the thinking, putting it behind one. Through my visualisation work I found that it merely becomes suppressed or buried in the subconscious and retains its negative vibration and therefore perpetuates itself. It needs to be cleared thoroughly for change to happen.

Thoroughness is definitely the key! It is certainly more than either dismissal or a view to dropping something, I discovered.

~ . ~

At that time Rei-ki and energy healing was not really being taken seriously, often being viewed with either scepticism or indifference and sometimes recoiled from. It was not easy to get across that only willingness was a requirement; scepticism was then countered easily by the results.

Believing in it or believing that it will work is irrelevant. So many people think that is essential, – that it only works if you do believe in it or believe that it will work.

Belief does not make the energy flow. The *need in the body* draws it through the healers' channel. She or he doesn't 'give' Rei-ki or 'will' it, or direct it to flow. The body receives the energy *it* requires, therefore Rei-ki will work on the body's energy, revitalise it and stimulate its healing capabilities. The only thing that prevents that flow is a negative Will to resist it. Ergo, just willingness to allow it is needed.

Reluctance and dismissal however, have to be accepted without resentment or feelings of rejection or that they devalue what was being offered.

It is important certainly to allow all choices freely. In my enthusiasm I offered it as soon as an opportunity presented itself. My Guides patiently and lovingly advised me to learn to wait to be asked from the need and choice of the person. That was hard I have to admit. I was champing at the bit!

There was one delightful occasion when visiting a friend. She in fact, was lying stretched out on the sofa as she was feeling the effects of a bad cold. Her lovely boxer dog was lying in his basket looking very woebegone as he had just come back from the vets after being neutered.

I knelt down at the end of the sofa and placed my hands on either side of my friend's throat to channel some Reiki for relief. The dog then came over and hitched himself onto my root chakra! There he stayed for over half an hour without once moving! (I got very hot!) Now, there's a sensible dog! He helped himself to a nice Rei-ki flow on his afflicted parts.

After that he was his usual cheerful self as he bounded around her son who came in from school shortly after. I could say an undoubted success for Rei-ki healing! My poor friend found some relief but the cold had a good hold and we had to part for other demands intruded.

There is a great deal more awareness of Rei-ki now and many people 'practice' it. There is however, still a great deal of scepticism and dismissal of it as a healing method. Many think it just relaxes you, that it is for pampering. This has been somewhat aided by the fact that many practitioners can only get rooms or salons in Hairdressers' and beauty treatment premises. Renting a single room is costly. For a stand-alone complementary therapist the need is to offer a variety of therapies to increase the client base: Rei-ki being just one of them means that it rather loses its prominence. But attitudes are improving.

It is understandable that it is difficult for people to believe that an invisible 'energy' can improve or even affect a person's equally invisible energy. This energy seems unexplained; so much is taken on trust because there is no real explanation offered. Thus, it is either trusted and experienced and found efficacious, or rejected.

Often there is an expectation of a miracle, that one or perhaps two treatments fixes the problem. Alas the body invariably needs more attention than that to right itself. In many cases, Rei-ki is often a *last resort*.

By the time the Rei-ki practitioner is approached the condition has got a good hold. With the accumulation of negativity added from being unwell, plus either distress or frustration at not getting better, the body has by then a lot to contend with which can't be given a quick fix. Rei-ki, however, does enable the body itself to work efficiently by re-vitalising and improving the energy. That is the key.

Rei-ki energy settles the physical stresses caused by the emotions so that even at molecular level vital equilibrium can be improved, even restored. The principle of quantum physics. That's why it feels relaxing.

Then the clever and efficient body can sort out its proper functioning and repair, replenish and heal itself. And at a very fundamental level.

But energy healing is doing so much more than that. The skill of the Rei-ki channeller and the use of the symbols can clear negative energy blockages from those emotional sources and from both physical and mental pain that are disturbing the bodily particles.

It follows that holding on to the emotional traumas, stresses and distresses is going to keep our protons and electrons jiggling about and inhibiting all their efforts to re-adjust themselves. So, they *keep trying*. Now you know what going against the flow really means!

This is how we waste energy! Playing our part helps the energy *around us* as well. For importantly, quantum physics tells us that every electron, proton and even smaller particles in proximity, is also having to readjust its equilibrium too, all the way into infinity.

Therefore, enabling this equilibrium with energy healing methods will change it. Thus, one invisible energy does indeed affect and change the invisible personal energy it is in contact with. And truly releasing those negative experiences and concerns buried in the psyche, with those tie-cutting visualisations I had been introduced to as well, was invaluable to maintaining those changes.

Up to now, I had taken Rei-ki energy and its effects on trust myself. I didn't question it because I had experienced it and found it good. It was quite a while before I understood the quantum physics of Rei-ki. It wasn't taught to me unfortunately. I discovered it as I developed my knowledge of the body and understood the nature and variety of vibration.

Didn't Einstein tell us that all matter is vibration and form was vibration at a very low level? I found all this a fascinating new view of things.

Chapter 18

Then one day in June, I was told that there was a 'visitor' to talk to me.

'Hello Felicity - my name is Illych T.... Yes, I was a Russian pianist and I became a Guide. – yes, in an air raid while studying in London – yes….. I did not embrace the new regime and left in good time with my family – 2 children – yes a good life for all, although war came to your country soon after. But now they are without the horror of war since they have grown to adulthood, thanks be to God. – ………… It was a good place to come to find a new life – much variety and new things to learn! It gave me renewed energy after the despair and destruction in my Mother Country. Leaving tore at my heart – this is very Russian you understand – but what was happening there tore at my Soul so I had no choice for my family so it was a good move!!.........the life I led them to was good even though I left them. It is important now that we talk together for I have come for a special purpose.'

He then went on to explain that I was to be attuned to Rei-ki III, Master energy, having received my certificates for both Rei-ki 1 and Rei-ki II. He was to help me in my preparation and to teach me the new symbols and how to use them and one in particular.

'Once you are attuned to Master energy, your own vibration will be raised for the connection with other Rei-ki Masters…yes – a pathway which their vibration can and will travel to you. When the Master's energy itself is needed you will be guided……..the Masters will always help you and protect the Rei-ki for you at all times. You will receive all the knowledge and guidance for gentle learning dear Felicity. Once the attunement has been accomplished all will unravel, clarity will come. Once the attunement has been accomplished I will be the one to help you. All the symbols when used by you will have a brighter vibration – this is helpful to us because the change within strengthens us for the network connections we work with. As you have been learning and experiencing channelling Rei-ki so this vibration has developed its *pitch* so believe dear Felicity that your comprehension of your experiences has accomplished this. Our guidance enables you to focus and be open to learning – your comprehension is the essential part for the reciprocity in the Physical plane.'

Over the next several days Illych advised and guided my preparation and understanding for this new third level.

'All is going well and the alignments are coming into place. You will know when it is time. When the time comes you will be fully protected so you will be able to clear your thoughts of all concerns. – we are telling you this beforehand so that you can be focussed and keep a steady vibration because this is the point of change and will attract unwelcome attention which needs to be quickly negated to dissolve the illusion.'

Just after the Summer Solstice, on the day appointed for my attunement, Illych came to me. He advised me how to be very focussed and align my chakras with particular care using the combined *chi*, finishing at the Soul point.

'– the Soul point is an area for holding energy and then sending it to the Soul-template for connection to us.'

Being grounded and balanced would direct my energy efficiently to strengthen and stabilise the higher vibration I was to be attuned to.

The attunement itself was a very profound experience and after it I was required to go straight to the Temple by my Guides. Then I had the most, - again I have to use the same words here as they are the best ones - profound experience so far. I was taken to a room where there were several Beings.

One, the Master of the Third Degree, came towards me and set a 'heavy' intricately embroidered cloak around me. I couldn't feel the weight, only perceive it and that it was beautifully and richly embroidered and intricately embellished. It fell to my feet and closed down the front of its own accord. I automatically straightened my shoulders and felt that this was ceremonial in some way.

I was then escorted to another place where, what I was told was a coronel, was placed gently on my head. This was an openwork 'crown' type of object which had fine, silvery rod-like structures of differing lengths rising from it. I could feel it encircling my head quite distinctly and was conscious also of my crown chakra. This coronel, I was told, I was also to wear when I was channelling healing energy and was to connect me directly to the Master of the Third Degree; it was 'one with my substance for recognition when needed.'

The cloak was then taken gently from my shoulders and I realised I was wearing the two-tiered amethyst and golden-yellow edged garments. Then I was smilingly told I could now return and call upon the Master of the Third Degree for assistance at any time.

When I 'returned' to my present surroundings I sat there in a semi-stunned reverie. If I hadn't felt the coronel still upon my head I would have believed I had imagined this. Yet I knew that that was nonsense and that it *was* completely real.

As soon as I was fully myself, I went straight for my notebook and pen to talk with my Guides about this. I felt it would also be good to be absolutely sure that this had happened! I was elated by Ja-San's assurance that it had and was indeed an enabler for connecting my raised vibration directly to the healing Masters and thus enhance the healing I channel.

'It is part of the beautiful process of reciprocity dear Happiness/dear One. That was placed upon your crown chakra to contain the energy of the symbol for recognition when it is needed. You are a Rei-ki Master dear Felicity/dear dear one. Indeed it is so Happiness! Dear Pupil your thoughts are like fireflies but we catch them! -extra love for the levels you have gained for us and the task we are all part of. Our hearts are full too dear precious charge. God's blessings be with you for all you achieved.' Rest now in tranquillity – safe in the love of all here and God's gentleness. We will speak again soon.'

What a beautiful ending to a marvellous day.

From then on, I found I could readily bring the coronel into conscious awareness and 'feel' it upon my head whenever I did a healing and I still can; I can bring it into my consciousness very easily, plus I can feel tingling energy in my crown chakra.

Very soon after I had a 'visitor', the Master of the 3rd Degree.

'My dear pupil – it is needful for you to know that the way is clear to the Master levels for any help you may need - use the vibration through the coronel at every healing from now on – you are entering the spiritual healing in your era in your life from the solstice as your preparation time moves you to this higher level, for your apprenticeship draws to a close – you have achieved much in comprehension dear pupil in the short time and been faithful to your source. We at the Masters level now ask for your application to the coronel so that your learning and abilities deepen. Open the way consciously and allow what is needful to enter without seeking it – with practice this will become easier and more will be revealed as you progress. The method you have chosen is most timely for the network and our work will oversee it. All is part of a reciprocal cycle dear one – the body's need is part of that cycle with Guide and energy, vehicles and karma all part of it and when you as channeller and clairaudient are drawn into that cycle new momentum is created and the energy increased for the healing purpose. All is 'one' in answer to the need for the release from negative energy which you have chosen to do with conscious awareness on the psychic-emotional plane. This is a great enabler for the Guides dear pupil Felicity who rejoice in the brightening of the vibration. The aspect of the way chosen by you is therefore significant to the work you have been called to for you were chosen for the Rei-ki because of its re-awakening across the world and its recognition by many and in this way more ears will hear as the need calls for an answer. The seeking for answers and help is a clamour of many needy voices. To release the love within is to open the way for the Divine and this is the purpose. We will speak again dear pupil. Your Guides are here to guide you to your rest. Value yourself for you are part of what we do – God's love and blessings keep thee safe.'

As you can imagine I felt very blessed by this visit.

Not long after that I was instructed to use the symbol Illych had taught me to use for focussing the energy for karmic issues creating an enhanced energy to clear them. And he would be working with me.

I was to use the symbol for focus so that the dimensional Masters would deal with it. As usual I followed the guidance I was being given, happy to know I was playing my part as required.

Now I had been helped to yet another level of development and I was very happy that I was making progress. Towards what, was on a need-to-know basis as always!

~.~

My esoteric knowledge was slowly being gleaned from my Guides. I realised however that this knowledge was given in response to, and to clarify my own queries and the concepts arising in my own mind. I was not being offered a treatise on esoteric knowledge per se. Also, my knowledge of chakras from the very outset was very small.

Thinking of it now, I didn't raise the question about chakras to them; I had so many other things to think of and talk with them about and the subject itself never seemed to arise. Whatever work they gave me to do I just did, happy in the knowledge that they knew all about it so all was taken care of.

Although Reiki energy was directed towards the chakras to clear and re-align them - I'd heard enough to know that lining them up was important, they didn't puzzle me at that stage. It also seemed that the endocrine system was involved. It was spoken of in the Rei-ki books in conjunction with the chakras.

There was no indication in the books as to why the glands and chakras were significant to each other, only that the chakras were about certain things.

I knew of the endocrine glands in general from my nursing days but from what I read in the Rei-ki books I couldn't for the life of me connect what the chakras were to the glands at all. For example, I couldn't see what the Solar Plexus had to do with the Intellect Will and Ego or the adrenals on top of the kidneys had to do with the Root in the area around the base of the spine. Knowing so little, I thought I had better read some books on chakras themselves as questions about everything were popping into my head.

I couldn't just blindly accept that a) that's what one worked on, and b) that was the associated chakra for that gland and c) these issues belong to this chakra. I needed to know why. I felt profoundly ignorant.

So, I went in search of an appropriate book. At the specialised shop I found, I asked to see books on Chakras. To my amazement and horror, the shelf that was indicated was half the length of the shop! So many? Where do I start?

I took one out at random.

The language and illustrations were not alas in my style. I tried another. It was somewhat the same. I had to admit I recognised none of it. None of it either resonated, or even appealed to me; rather it dismayed me and made me feel even more ignorant.

However, though daunted, I didn't want to give up, so, I thought; - I'll go and study the Endocrine system and get that under my belt first. It's much more in my line for the present. I can cope with that as I remember some of it and medical facts don't unnerve me. By the time I've got to grips with that and learnt it I could well be further along into the spiritual so more capable of grasping this chakra knowledge. I'll get back to it later. After this bracing chat to myself, I left the shop feeling as if I had a goal at least.

Chapter 19

My Guides of course heard my doubts about tackling such books. Thus, the next time we talked they fully understood my querying the necessity of reading these esoteric books on metaphysics that were so abundant and popular, even though they had not drawn me at all.

'You are a fresh page dear dear one with no concepts to colour or over-shadow what you do. – your instincts and methods are your own – not pre-conceived but a natural progression from your own learning and comprehension. It is the thread you wove and are following dear dear one.'

So, I was a 'clean slate' for the purpose of my learning all that they wished to guide me to. Consequently, this pleased them. It was now quite clear that these books were best left unread so that I did not inadvertently draw on their information at all. Everything had to be *my own* discovery and comprehension.

Somewhat relieved and ready to investigate the Endocrine system I set about acquiring some good quality detailed books on the body. At last, something I could physically study! I was quite excited at the prospect.

I was really delighted to have found another aspect of my ongoing learning about energy healing and one that I believed I could get my teeth into. At last, something to fulfil that urge to study something again.

As a result of my determination to really understand the endocrine system I ended up with seven books on Anatomy, Physiology and even one on Histology. I intended to glean everything there was to be gleaned from all seven on each and every gland.

Some of the books were really large and heavy. The only place I could deal with them and have them spread out around me for cross-referencing was on my double bed. So, propped up against my pillows, a tray across my lap for my note pad and surrounded by a veritable sea of books I got started.

As I delved into them to get an overview of hormones and endocrinology as such, I was pleased to find that this was familiar and happy territory. What I had learned in my nursing training in the 60's made things a lot easier than starting from nothing at all. Medical and anatomical terminology also had great familiarity to me.

I was certainly not daunted in the least by the task I'd decided on. Far from it. I was totally involved from the beginning. And it came quite naturally to me since I have a medical family background as well as my own nursing.

In proper style, I took down all the relevant features of Endocrinology itself. Then, starting with the tiny little Pineal gland, I planned to tackle each of the glands themselves, their structure, function and processes from each and every book.

I was fascinated right from the start. I couldn't wait to get back to my books and notes as soon as I'd had supper at the end of the day. Even though I was in full-time work, I was still fresh and eager to get into those books.

Having grasped the concept of the hormonal system as a whole and then discovered all the details of the Pineal gland and its intricacies, such as were known, things were beginning to fall into place. I found I was readily able to connect up these function and processes. This was greatly enhanced by reading about the same gland in all seven books.

I discovered things in snippets as one book recorded something another hadn't. I found it very absorbing and exciting to delve into this world within an organ and see what it was doing in regards to the body.

Once I'd done my 'collecting' on each and every detail of the anatomy, functions and processes I could find on the Pineal, I naturally went back over all my detailed notes to date to see what they all amounted to. This tiny pea-sized gland was incredibly active; its two main known functions so potent.

Then the light came on in my head! I re-read the notes to check my understanding. Yes! Now I could see as clear as day why this gland was associated with and influenced the crown chakra. Not only that, but I could now grasp the actual *nature* of the crown chakra.

My hand flew across the page as I made notes, outlined the cause and effect and recorded the salient facts alongside and in the same manner as the scientific ones. The connections seemed clearer the more I wrote. I was so excited I couldn't wait to study the next endocrine gland.

I realised it was also time to get myself a laptop. There was going to be a whole lot of writing up of notes!

I was now even more eager to explore the anatomy and physiology of these highly active glands to see what they too would reveal regards the other six chakras.

That was the beginning. Over the next two years between my daytime job and all the ramifications of everyday life, I studied, collected and collated all the data on the whole endocrine system and the main organs associated ineluctably with them.

At the same time, I discovered and recorded all the causes and effects and nature of each chakra *through* that data and the connections within it. There was no guessing or surmising. I was diligent to stay only with the facts, the logic and the revealed nature.

The more I explored each gland organically and the organs closely connected to them in the light of metaphysics, the more I discovered. I looked only at the structure and function, the anatomy and the physiology, the causes and effects.

Once well into my studies I found myself wishing most heartily that when *I* had first learnt about Rei-ki and decided to understand the energy healing approach, that I had had *one complete book,* one that told me about the entire inter-penetrative relationship between the physical body, the emotions and the chakras. How helpful knowing how and why would have been! The holistic in a holistic volume no less.

There were Anatomy and Physiology books aplenty. There were books on the metaphysical and esoterical view by the hundreds. Never did they meet. Never did they overlap. Never did they seem to explain, merely enumerated 'what was what'. They were even in quite different sections of bookshops and libraries. But also in people's minds. Never did one really connect to or with the other, - even in the books on Rei-ki.

I decided a truly holistic book on the body was crying out to be written. Then I had the dazzling vision of being able to take it all down in dictation from my Guides! Though I hadn't read them, I had heard recently of the Alice Bailey books which were the channelled writings of a Tibetan Guide. Aha! *I* could have a book published from the channelled writings of *my* Guides on the body and chakras! How wonderful that would be! I was in a glow of anticipation.

Alas! My hopes were soundly dashed. Instantly following my promotion of the idea, came Samuel's voice. *'You* are the Writer Felicity., so the voice needs to be yours.' Ah!

'...trust and believe in your abilities to write for others to absorb and comprehend. Yes, Samuel, – you are our writer. We guide and give you necessary knowledge for the purpose - ours is not to dictate our thinking for you to pass on for us. You have been chosen to use your thinking processes for the purpose from the knowledge we can give you dear dear Felicity– because you have developed your thinking and are among human beings and the negativity that surrounds them oppresses and baffles them. A human voice with its overtones of human frailty is the 'voice' for the purpose dear one. Too gentle a voice may not be 'heard'. A little pragmatism and a practical tone is what we feel is required to keep the concepts grounded for those who find the esoteric to be either unacceptable or something to fear or despise.'

I was made to understand that this had to be *all my own* work, everything was to come from my brain, my analysis, my comprehension from what I had discovered and the connections that had been revealed from the actual anatomy and physiology. Naturally they had been following all my thought processes during my studies!

'the diligence with which you worked was a great enabler dear friend. Yes Khatumi, we prefer that your mind works out these concepts freely from the anatomy and your inner knowing without influence from external philosophies.'

A clean slate indeed!

This was to be metaphysics rooted in *science*; logical and precise. It was to be a bridge between the scientific Newtonian view and the holistic and metaphysical concepts of the body, mind and health. Dr Ying Po in particular made this very clear to me.

So, I felt I must put my best efforts into writing this book. Once I realised that it behoved me to do this, I was quite excited. Oh, sweet ambition!

Could I do this? I felt a bubble of anticipation rising in me; I knew I just had to see if I could really come up with such a book.

I decided that mine would present a totally fresh perspective on the body and the chakras, and naturally, its health. Not only that, it would be about the 'How' and 'Why' of every aspect and every connection I had discovered. That was paramount. Certainly not just about *'What.'*

'What' had, by its nature, a full stop after it. I wanted to prompt the reader's own thinking. Such a book was *needing* to be written, I thought.

Dear Anthony, who always came to give me strength certainly did when he came to speak with me about it.

'...to plough rough dead ground to let in the light and air to make it become fertile and useful is the purpose of the plough – as much as it is to renew. – This requires patience and persistence – both qualities in the oxen who drew my plough dear girl. I learned this walking behind them for I was but the guide to the work, theirs was the labour and between us the tool for the purpose – indeed a triad dear girl – retain your faith and belief for these are patient and persistent and will draw your work, your book – the tool for the purpose, on to break the ground – yes new ground dear dear one but hard and stony from becoming compacted by negative energy and neglect from fear of change...'

Although I was beavering away, rationalising all my notes and studies to form a cohesive theme doubts still assailed me. The actual making such a commitment, a firm decision to really write a book to be published therefore to be read by others, daunted me anew. Even though a book I deemed important, this suddenly seemed presumptuous.

As always my dear Guides were ever ready to encourage me:-

'It seems clear to us, that a new door has opened and we wish you to know that we are here to guide you through it for the next stage of your task. Yes we will help you to write what is needful, but we wish *your* voice to be heard. You will find it will become easier as you get into your stride over what is to be written. Remember, *you are the writer!* It will become clearer to you as you progress so do not concern yourself until the time comes – we will guide you to know what to do *when* the time comes. Yes, this has all been leading up to this. Yes, you were given this gift (clairaudience) for that but that is only a part of why, not the whole picture. We wanted to be in contact with you for your *Self,* your healing and your own knowledge and growth but now we can apply this *with* you for a wider purpose yes, being a writer but of something special and meaningful in this world of words and 'communication.'

With such endorsements how could I still cling on to my doubts and fears? It would be unworthy of their loving guidance and teaching. Clearly a definite pathway seemed to be before me and beckoning me to go down it.

This just seemed a natural progression from all that I had learned and was learning from my Guides. I have to admit, I was increasingly excited at the prospect, for the connections revealed to me through my work fascinated me no end. My dear Guides endorsed my theme and intentions for my book,

'...for knowledge and truth for the beginning of healing and how to think differently. We are happy that you have come to this realisation.'

I was, therefore, very eager to make this book come into shape and form. As I really got into the writing, the whole concept and graphics began to take shape from the way I felt it should be presented and as a natural consequence of the perspective I was presenting. This actually helped enormously in the writing because I felt from the start it should not be just page after page of text as books covering the subject matter usually are.

It took a while to work out the book and page size, the actual layout and to make use of shapes and choose colours that were most appropriate. I had to use what was available to me in Word on my home pc software but it was important to select those shapes and colours that had the right vibration. Both these forms have their own energy.

Energies from colour, layout, especially geometric shapes and the written word have a subconscious effect on the viewer and reader so my choice was hopefully to attract a recognition by whoever opened the book and went on to read it.

Although I had done a Clait course at college in the late 90's, I had only really used a computer properly since 2001 thanks to the admin job I was doing. I was having to learn how to achieve what I visualised by trial and error. But the graphics and layout in actual fact, surprisingly, came together nicely as I worked through from the introduction of the endocrine system and then on to the Pineal gland and the crown chakra and on down the endocrine system itself.

It all seemed pretty satisfactory to me but of course being human, I needed some human reassurance that what and how I was writing was valid. I believed in it. Would other people?

I had the perfect person in mind to ask an opinion of: my friend Sheila who told me of quantum physics. I had met her through a friend I had made at work who felt we would be sure to get on with one another. We certainly did, as soon as we met.

We had a lot in common from the beginning! Both Pisceans, both Scottish and Scottish-born, her roots in Aberdeen as were my father's, both trained as nurses under the same system, both with Australian experiences and both into complementary healing! Quite extraordinary! But aside from that there was an inner affinity that was very strong. And on top of that she had a positive library of esoteric, spiritual and self-development books which she had certainly read and imbibed so knew this field very well indeed. She had a foot in both camps; the medical world and the complementary therapy world. Perfect!

I sent her the first three chapters for her appraisal.

Amazing woman that she is, she recognised immediately, exactly what the intention of the book was. She had not a single doubt of its importance, especially she felt, to the medical profession, both doctors and nurses. She was still working as an NHS sister at that time both on the wards and concerned with training and nursing methods.

I can honestly say that her recognition, her grasp of its content and her faith in both it and my ability were an incredible tonic and fantastic endorsement, *and* now from the 'Human' reader's point of view. They kept me to the sticking point.

We hadn't known each other long so I knew she wasn't influenced by any sense of loyalty or consideration of encouraging a well-known friend of long-standing. She was judging it on its merits only. That was the beauty and value of her appraisal.

Because I was working full-time, progress was slow but I continued writing and working on the layout and presentation when I could between all the other demands and requirements of my life of course.

I found I was editing what I had written and correcting typos and punctuation each time before and after whatever I had actually set down. Thus, I discovered that there was considerable work involved in creating a well-written book.

Then there was manipulating and fitting all the different-sized boxes of information and creating spaces for future illustrations on the chosen page size. I had set myself a task alright!

Chapter 20

I took my initial chapters to show my daughter Caroline who lived in Australia on my next annual visit. She now lives there with her lovely son Josh. I always took opportunities to stay with them for as long as I could.

I was greatly supported by her appraisal and encouragement too. This was not her field but she fully grasped what I was aiming for and the way I was presenting it. I was truly convinced now that I could achieve this; that I could get it published, that it was worthwhile, not just a dream I had.

Although not chronologically correct to the life I am unfolding to you, it seems best to continue with what happened regarding my book rather than fit it between the descriptions of the other events I moved through successively between my on-going writing. Having to fit it in to my work routine and the various happenings in my life and claims on my attention, as you'd expect, my writing had become a somewhat sporadic experience.

So, to round my 'task' off to a certain point, I will continue.

I was close to retirement age by this time so I decided that I would leave work then and get on with my book. I had an idea to train for animal healing too. I definitely wanted more of the spiritual metaphysical side of my life.

As soon as I did retire, I couldn't wait to make a nice long visit to my daughter and grandson. It was also a perfect opportunity I thought, to work on my book in all that lovely warm sunshine.

So naturally I booked a flight as soon as I could. This time for 12 whole weeks. I set off full of enthusiasm taking my laptop with my first efforts and with all my data and connection notes on it with me. I couldn't wait to get going in earnest.

There was a lovely shady balcony on my daughter's house with large cushioned settles and a view over a semi-tropical garden. Blue skies, warm sun and birds singing! A perfect spot for a lap-top and myself.

My daughter was working full-time and away early, so between the time I dropped my grandson off to school and collected him afterwards, I sat out on that balcony and wrote.

Everything flowed and connected up in the most exciting way. Scientific fact flowed logically into the cause and effect regarding the chakras and the fascinating organs and Endocrine system.

As I worked through the glands and their appropriate chakras, revealing each and every connection, I discovered through the actual writing process itself how much more there was to these energy centres. This aspect really excited me.

The illustrations I'd seen of chakras showed them as being patterned circles on the body that beamed out light. This hadn't meant much to me I admit, but I took them on trust as being there and didn't really question this deeming myself ignorant of esoterics.

Now they were revealed to me as a reality indeed through the endocrine glands themselves; they were vortices of real energy.

The actual function and processes of the glands were revealing the *distinct nature* of the chakras. I think that is what interested and satisfied me the most. There was no getting away from the interplay between the functions of both endocrine and chakra systems, each influencing the other in total connectedness. Once more a light came on in my head! A very bright light!

But most importantly I discovered that the chakras were an essential part of a whole *system* in itself, an energy system that recharged and refreshed itself through its constant movement, vitalising and re-vitalising the whole body.

And that it was into this energy system that our negative energy settled and disturbed, blocked and impeded and needed to be removed. It was this system we look into to see what the mind has manifested from our negative thoughts, beliefs, biases and experiences.

The more I wrote the clearer everything became. It evolved entirely through writing about each gland and associated organ's functions and processes.

The incontrovertible emotional interpenetration from these unravelled with such clarity, and entirely as I wrote. How I loved that! It was most exciting as each aspect revealed itself. I felt as if my whole being were alight. The anticipation and delight at what I might discover next made me so eager to start each day's work.

So dedicated to it was I, that I actually finished the main body of the book, covering the entire endocrine and chakra systems in the time. By the time I got home I felt my book was virtually written and was practically in finished shape and form.

Naturally I was in contact with my Guides throughout who encouraged me and helped me stay focussed with constant gentle and loving reminders to work within the heart chakra and of making correct use of the Will and Ego for the purpose. And to keep my Ego from the driving seat and strictly behind the purpose.

This kept me grounded and helped me to be precise in the logical connections which I felt were vital. It was important to reveal the emotional metaphysical only through the *science* of the physical.

I so wanted to show that the energy system not only existed but was totally relevant to health and healing. It would follow too that those who quite naturally worked with the energy system in complementary therapies were working not only truly holistically, but that these methods were completely valid.

I felt it was time that holistic healing approaches were properly appreciated rather than looked on with a patronising, indulgent or dismissive eye; that the oneness of the complete body and every emotion experienced by the individual needed to be recognised, acknowledged and acted upon in the whole world of healing.

Such was my ambition! It was certainly my passionate resolve for everyone who read my book. There was no turning back now. I had total belief in what I had written.

As my dear Guide Samuel said encouragingly of my book and its intentions,

'....we are seeking change are we not? Change in the reader, change in the attitudes to spiritual awareness, change in attitudes and comprehension of the complementary approaches to healing and the relief of suffering. Awareness is essential if the seeds are to be sown. If the ground is stony dear Felicity then time will effect change but to get even a little seed into a crack in dry earth or between stones is worth the sowing......but sowing seeds to inspire, thinking will come from the words themselves and this is what you have been working on - for this we rejoice and the network is strengthened.'

My dear friend, the lovely Jalal, was always interested in my work on all the aspects of the anatomy of the body, so often came to me when I was working on it.

'Oh yes, this is most stimulating thinking! Working with you on this will be most interesting – oh it is very good work! The heart is made bright because of it! And yes! Always the light shines from your heart chakra when your mind is flying! Oh yes! Mine too! Mine too! Sun energy for the very bright aspects. Yes this is good synchronous thinking!'

What a beautiful encouragement as I explored and discovered everything as I wrote.

I knew that Jalal had lived in ancient times in northern India and had had a stall in the shade of a tree and dispensed herbal remedies. These were to heal both the body and the spirit for this was their obvious, natural and only way to healing. The understanding of the intricacies of the body, mind and Soul had been so much a part of the approach to healing for countless centuries in India and the East: the metaphysical view came naturally to them.

One day in the course of our delightful synchronous togetherness while discussing our favourite subject, Jalal said, '...many good things will come to pass for the healing and the love of healing and the love of those who need healing – I too am free in open spaces and in the hot sunlight where all can be seen, even to the smallest leaf and tiniest insect which are a part of this wondrous earth. This is where there is growth. Beneath and above the earth and growth is needed of the spirit and the mind in harmony with the beautiful energy of the planet and of the shining sun. This is good harmony dear friend for beautiful growth in the heart which is the centre of all things....'

These beautiful conversations certainly warmed my heart. The loving personality shining through gave a depth of interest to everything we 'spoke' of.

Jalal was always interested in my work because there was no exploration of the physiology of anatomy in his day and he always found it 'most stimulating!' Dr Ying Po was very knowledgeable about the body and endorsed my thinking on the internal workings and happily discussed the organ or gland I had just been writing on, pleased to endorse my metaphysical revelations and often adding some cosmic aspect. These I couldn't include but were always fascinating. It was very encouraging to say the least.

Chapter 21

Of course, on my return from Australia, there was still work to be done on my book. It had a life of its own I discovered. But that happens when you really start writing.

Very soon I was searching for a title and eventually after much cogitation, it came to me, '*Essential Connections*'. I felt that was nicely appropriate. Had I not made every connection that revealed itself through the wondrous workings and the very essence of the body? Certainly, it was about everything and every aspect being connected, not to say interconnected.

Because of the gulf in the literature and most importantly, thinking on the body between the scientific, Newtonian view and the other end of the spectrum of the metaphysical aspects of the human condition, I felt my way was clear. I was writing to fill that gulf. There were many and a many people who were seeking answers to their health and quality of life who would not look to either end for those answers.

As a consequence, I made a real effort to steer right down the middle with my book. Although showing and exploring the physical body, it was altogether about energy; physical, mental and above all emotional energy as this is the strongest and most potent.

In the course of exploring *negative* energy, its power and influence and the value of clearing it from our psyche and energy system, there was a constant connection to '*love*'. I wrote to show that our negativity was all that stood between our innate lovingness, its being able to flow freely and in the process, attract much love and lovingness to us. Change that and love was there.

'...lovingness needs to be learnt between human beings for advancement towards inner development,' Khatumi said during one of our conversations. And of course, my dear Guides assured me that,

'...love is the strongest of all. it remains even though obscured by shadows and even darkness. It remains unchanged for it is 'in being' and therefore 'is'. Nothing can dissolve it, only weigh it down, darken it's beingness or obscure it but it remains, even though hidden, for as you have perceived, darkness absorbs light, but the light is still there, in existence, not extinguished, only seeming so. Thus hope can never be lost for love and hope go hand in hand dear precious one. Hope keeps the vibration bright for that dissolves the darkness of negativity.'

'...love constantly renews itself and creates more energy. Partaking of love together is the best way.' And of course, partaking of love with my Guides was sublime.

Be assured dear reader, simply with the conscious awareness of all the dear Beings in the loving Dimensions, whenever we wish we can always go within and partake of the sublime love that is there in abundance.

'...stillness is breathing within to explore the infinity of the Divine – this is a boundless place, whereas inertia is the beginning of enclosing the eternal and narrowing the channel to the Divine. – this is the Will used by the dark side to inhibit contact with the Divine – yes dear dear one all is drawn to the centre, all is connected to the centre just as you have drawn all attention to the midline of the body. Yes dear dear one! Some use inertia as a stabilizer when fearing chaos. This is the illusion used by the dark side – indeed, drawn to the root and rooted in their place of being which is inert. Therefore, no growth or development. Thus the Will allied to fear serves the dark side. There is the illusion of safety – yes, God and the Masters make use of this to show others the way – a working surface, yes, for others to learn to refrain from inertia. Nothing is wasted. All is *good*. The still centre therefore draws knowledge and understanding to the 'knowing' which is the real stabilizer for *there* is certainty and this holds the centre point. The dark side use *much* energy to interfere with this dear dear one.....thus we can discern inertia from stillness and use the Will to be ready for change towards development and disenable negative energy and the dark side.'

It was so clear now, without so much as a single doubt, that the greatest inhibiter to all that is good in life was negative emotional energy. Everything I had been involved in on this new Millennial path and so much of the work that my dear Guides and I had done synchronously together had undoubtedly been to help me fully comprehend the nature of our negativity here on Earth. Unsurprising because we function so much within it. It is the hardest thing to combat.

It took me a while to realise completely that everything that I'd learned was leading up to, had led up to, presenting the case in book form as well as I possibly could on the importance of dealing properly with this weighty and detrimental energy we accept so readily. Releasing ourselves to lovingness was as apparent as I could make it.

That's what they want us to know.

All the wonderful loving Beings so want us to understand that the love they have for us is so very available to us. They gain strength and joy from our realising of the lovingness we all have within *us*. They long for us to grasp the sharing of love between us and the higher Dimensions which is unconditional and of an abundance we cannot grasp. It is after all a reflection of the Divine Love of God.

Yet I had had to steer clear of this precept in my book. Would my work actually succeed in conveying the essential message about love, I wondered, because I'd had to be secular in my approach?

Now, with *The Purpose Is Love,* hopefully I can show how much it means to them that we know of their immense love and that it is only our own creations and lack of knowledge of them that prevents our awareness of it. For it is there! All that is lacking is the conscious sharing between us which nourishes them too.

~.~

When I had completed all the work on '*Essential Connections*' and covered all aspects of negative energy that I could, I hoped I'd shown that really releasing negativity was possible. It was fundamental to all I had been learning from my Guides.

Positive energy cannot be removed because it 'is', it is 'in existence'. It does not need to be sustained or maintained, only allowed to 'be.' This is the marvellous thing about it.

Steering that middle course so diligently had meant that I had to steer clear of references to any spiritual or religious views on love per se. I'd kept metaphysical to be meta, = *above,* physical in the strictest sense, careful not to stray into the esoteric view of metaphysics. I did wish however that my book would give people an enlightened view of the metaphysical when all was said and done. As Samuel said,

'A key to unlock closed minds for the need is with the present climate of mixed opinion in the minds of those who both seek answers and wish to hold on to the old as a form of security. Into this chink a key can fit and be turned for this is part of the purpose dear dear girl.'

Keeping any reference to the Divine within was quite hard because naturally all my connections with my Guides were absolutely to do with that, the love of God, the unconditional love that abounds in the Dimensions where love, truth and goodness are the guiding triad. My belief is that one cannot separate God and love. This belief is an innate part of my substance.

But my work, my book did have a specific purpose and 'target reader' and so I gave all my effort and intention to those ends. I certainly poured love and my love into it. In my introduction I ended with the true purpose of it;

Be yourself
Yourself is within
Treasure it as the place where knowledge 'is'
'will come to'
And will expand the true self into a loving human being.

This therefore, was my full intention through understanding the body fully and writing of it so that others could help themselves and find the way to the love within.

My Guides and I spoke together regards my non-spiritual approach. They fully understood this dilemma of mine.

'all is understood dear dear one – those that need to comprehend to bring them towards the light need a pragmatic approach to encourage them forward. The denial of the spiritual has blocked their ears and their minds – if the way towards their enlightenment is based upon facts that they can accept more easily then barriers will begin to be removed and the concepts of healing more widely understood. It is those in the dark that need to be shown the light – for even a glimmer will serve a purpose -if only to reveal the darkness itself. There is much being written and offered to those who seek spiritual answers but even those need insights into practical matters of the workings of the mind and body dear dear one. Comprehension is that which casts the light upon the facts of knowledge dear dear one. With light other aspects are revealed but those are the responsibility of the reader…..unless these things are clarified and conscious thought focussed upon them the journey cannot begin dear dear one……….doors leading to further exploration will be revealed – so believe in your perceptions of the task - a bridge does need to be built between the non-spiritual and the spiritual in the way that will encourage and interest those who turn aside from an approach they feel uncomfortable with or even feel is irrelevant….this can only be good and lead to loving goodness.'

Such unified thinking was very supportive. It was good that they understood that I felt it wisest to refrain from including the spiritual and God. They were always so understanding. Clarifying things so neatly was very helpful in reassuring me that I was on the right path with this book of mine.

Along the way they had already told me that all my writing for the book itself had created its own vibration by being 'in existence'. This is so with everything in fact; thoughts, ideas, concepts and actions.

Once realised in the mind or body they are 'in existence' and therefore have a vibration. This is what is carried forward through the ether. (Thus everything, everything we conjure in our minds and hearts, good, bad or indifferent is carried forward to any connection it encounters and in turn connects us to the energy of all on the planet. We all contribute.)

The quality and strength of all vibrations and vibrational fields are 'read' by the outer Dimensions. As to my book, all the connections I had made were also now 'in existence.'

What was so encouraging to me was that all the work I was doing on them refined the pitch of the whole vibration which strengthened it and increased its impact. Naturally this is especially so with books written on the spiritual or esoteric. A lovely thought.

I had learned that Pitch and Frequency are highly significant to all vibration. And everything is vibrational.

'A vibration can be made effective in this way by fine-tuning it's note when it has gone off-pitch and cannot therefore reach its destination correctly. Its momentum is slowed and the timing that is essential cannot be met without the polarity to correct the pitch necessary for its fulfilment.'

'the correct pitch and tension of the vibration enables the message to travel quickly and correctly.'

Of course, this had come up in discussions on negative vibration and the importance of emotional equilibrium I was writing about in such detail in *'Essential Connections'*. Polarity was already very familiar to me and I had long understood its use so our synchronous discussion was very apt.

'Neutral is the point of 'holding' where there is no tension applied to the vibration. This then allows for free momentum set up at the point of existence......It is the conscious awareness dear Felicity that fine-tunes as you grasped. – the Will therefore has no place in this – it is the triad of the conscious mind with the intuitive instinct with the Divine within the heart. The heart and ajner are the elements of awareness …. This is the tuning instrument but it cannot be used fully unless from the heart which is the centre and connected with the passive and active, upper and lower, spiritual and physical to unify the whole into one purpose of knowledge and revealed truths…..clarity will create the tension necessary for polarity.'

I also had very interesting discussions about pitch and the human body with my dear friend Illych. Being a musician, this was his forté. That is why he chose to come to inform and help me to refine mine regards the Master energy for Rei-ki healing.

To his delight, whenever I was listening to music and a particular piece appealed especially to me I 'shared' it with him. Fine-tuning my mind was certainly all part of the reason for these momentous exchanges with these wonderful and eagerly helpful Guides. And fine tuning my 'energies' was the work involved in whatever I was doing and certainly while compiling and writing my book. The intention creates the consequences.

Despite not being able to express any spirituality per se, I was pleased with the chapters I had written on the metaphysical subjects of energy itself and negative energy in particular. I found that part of my writing very satisfying and was eager to let my friend Sheila read what I'd done for her informed assessment.

She was so widely read and knowledgeable whereas I still had not read those esoteric books. I was just relying on my belief in what I had revealed in my writing logically through the physical body itself, the perspective I had discovered *and* its uniqueness.

On my return from Australia, I had put my 'book' as it was on to a disc and sent it off to Sheila, now living over 200 miles away. She was really happy to get it and read all that I had written. I'm happy to say she was even more full of praise and encouragement and averred that it was a unique and absorbing approach. Not only that, very easy to read. She loved the presentation and style too. I was both relieved and mightily encouraged. Her disinterested, yet informed view was so important to me.

Of course, I knew that there would come more polishing and editing. I soon realised what a critical part of writing this was. Both proved to be ongoing tasks and in fact, led to expanding on certain aspects that was very satisfying. Fresh aspects from new experiences kept coming up as well.

There was always some little titbit to discover from people and even small incidents. The book was in fact, to my surprise, still in its growing stage! This pleased me hugely. I wanted it to be the best possible I could achieve.

Now I shall get back to my narrative and tell you more of what was happening in the metaphysical 'level' I was sharing with my everyday life.

Chapter 22

Naturally, during the two years I had been studying, collating and working out energy concepts for my book, I was experiencing other metaphysical developments. Nothing stayed still. Once on this new road I had found myself on, forward motion was determined. I had been given conscious awareness; there was no way back from that either.

Whatever sort of scales are on your eyes, once they were off you can't put them back on. Also, it seemed that whatever timing had been right for me to be manoeuvred in this direction meant that there was no impediment, as this road was untraveled; there were no patterns on it for me to be repeating. And I was having to get a move on!

So, I was working full-time, doing all that I could regards my Rei-ki experience and knowledge, learning through talking with my Guides, engaged in healings and enjoying chats with other Guides. Life was busy and continuing to be full of interest.

Then one evening I was going into the stillness within when I saw a dazzling golden light with something in the centre that looked like a geometric shape.

It was like looking into a fiery furnace it was so dazzling and the symbol seemed to be glowing and radiating energy. I was puzzled. The light was so bright that the shape wasn't very precisely defined. Then it seemed as if it was in my heart chakra and I was surrounded by the golden energy of the light. I was told that this symbol was connected to my healing and that I would be advised further about it.

Once the light had subsided, I could see it more clearly. I could see a base and some triangular shapes lying out flat within my chest. I was then asked to focus my mind on raising the sides from the base. This took a lot of concentrated effort, I assure you. I didn't recognise the shape it created however.

Once I had mastered this, I was told to visualise this symbol when channelling Rei-ki healing and 'realise' it as part of the energy being channelled.

It was not long before I discovered one in my throat and brow chakras. These just appeared there. It was then that I was asked to 'see' a replica lower half of this shape.

Once visualised, I was told to practice rotating the whole symbol so that it produced an energy field around it and then activate them all like that before my healing sessions. It was really hard work.

The next stage was to learn to turn them over so that energy from the chakra could be directed forward through the symbol to any chosen area that needed healing. This action of course was to be done under guidance from my Guides. Again, this took considerable concentration till I mastered these stages.

Sometime after that I discovered one in the crown chakra. By this time, having quickly got over that initial astonishment I just blithely accepted what was in fact a remarkable phenomenon.

Writing about it now makes this more apparent. I wish I could convey the sublime acceptance I felt of these really momentous progressions. They seemed such a natural progression and that on the whole I don't recall feeling that this was in any way out of the ordinary. I always felt this willingness to go along with whatever transpired.

Something rather out of the ordinary did occur on one occasion. This was when I was staying for the week end with my sister Grace who knew of my clairaudience. We had barely finished lunch when a symbol popped up in my solar plexus! I was quite taken aback! There was no doubt! There it was! Now I had four to spin and turn. That time I did think, 'Whatever next?'

I worked with these for a long time and then found one in the sacral and root chakras. The symbols were all built now so I perceived them as complete and three-dimensional, and a shape I guessed as octahedrons.

When lining up my chakras, having to spin all seven of them took a great deal of concentration. Thank heaven I only needed to turn one over at any given time if I was guided to in a healing!

As time went on, I learned gradually about their significance, but as everything was always on a 'need to know' basis, this transpired as the appropriate situation occurred. But this was as far as things had developed by this time.

When I look back, I marvel at this unquestioned acceptance of these quite extraordinary happenings. Also, not discussing them with anyone perhaps led me to assume this was happening to Rei-ki healers as part of the healing path. I don't know if this is so. I just did as guided and requested.

I was of course, taking constant 'dictation' in my growing pile of writing pads. It was always such a joy to be in oneness with them and hear their gentle voices and words of wisdom, reassurance and encouragement. They were a perfect balance to the intricate science of anatomy and physiology I was involved in in such depth.

I noticed that when Samuel spoke with me it was most often to do with my studies. I presumed he'd come to me for that purpose for he had a scholarly mind. I loved our 'explorations'. I had perceived him as quite tall and slender and in a long dark gown. His features as such, like all my Guides, were indistinct, but I was aware of dark hair and a certain quality about the eyes.

He had been part of my guidance with my Guides for a little time when I discovered that actually he was my Life Guide. This was a surprise as I hadn't considered such a rôle. Samuel told me this on one occasion when we had been 'talking' together, synchronously exchanging thoughts and discussing my studies.

He explained that now I had reached this point in my learning of metaphysics and energy and he was encouraging these particular studies it was now appropriate that he revealed that he was my Life Guide.

He had become this when I was 12 years old. My Life Guide up until then was a very wise lady who had been a Guide for many aeons. It seems that her time had come to go to the Halls of Preparation to begin the transition to reincarnate again, so Samuel had come to work with her so that he could then take over as my Life Guide. He had done so fully when I was 12 as this was her time to move on.

'.....it brings me joy in the sharing of this knowledge with you. I connect with the vibration (used by my Guides) with you in this thinking so our vibration is synchronous from the triad of vibrational sources stimulated by this area of learning. – yes indeed dear Felicity for the ability for conceptual thinking is inherent and was why I became your Guide at puberty when I took over from your childhood's Guide who was ready for re-incarnation at that time. Yes, she was a very wise and experienced Guide who was chosen for you. She was incarnated in those (ancient) cultures before becoming a Guide and was chosen because of those links for you with those times – these were necessary for the ability to comprehend ancient knowledge even though you were a new Soul-part. She was your echo to the past to help you with the task but you needed the cerebral vibration from my energy to stimulate that area in you for your conceptual thinking to develop and blossom. It was necessary that you achieved 'life experience' as an enabler for the conscious cerebral development to give your present personality the knowledge. This has now been brought to you from both your childhood's Guide and myself and the dear Guides who have come to expand your consciousness and impart the knowledge you need for the task. You can see the complexities that make up the links to the Akashic records and the network.'

As you can imagine I found this very satisfying. It certainly explained my interest in, not to say love of, all ancient history.

Naturally, with my usual curiosity, I was keen to know something of Samuel's life. Before I copy out Samuel's story about himself however, I'd like to tell you of something when I was about 12-13.

In our RE (Religious Education) lessons I was absolutely fascinated by the city of Babylon. The whole concept for it, its city planning and architecture and its libraries and literary culture really fired my mind.

So much so that I started writing a story about a Hebrew boy call Mikail who with his family was captured and taken to Babylon with all his people as slaves. I can still remember my opening paragraphs. I even remember the pale green exercise book I started writing it in. Sadly, I didn't get any further with the enterprise. Probably because it was too ambitious, also School life was really full and became quite demanding so my intention faded away.

How appropriate was this when Samuel described his Earthly life.

'Now I can tell you. I was a Hebrew scholar and writer of the history of my people who came from Ur, but it was in Babylon that I wrote our story in poems and prose to hold our history not only in our hearts but for the generations to come so that they had some understanding of God and our people. Yes dear friend. I know this, yes it has always captured your imagination. You were chosen even then. I taught in open air schools. I taught the history of our people so that it would not be forgotten in that city of dreams. As I taught, I wrote – I learned all that I could of this craft in their great Bibliographical Libraries. There my mind soared as I learned the beauty and power – and I mean goodness and love – of words.' **My Guides'** collective voice said, 'Samuel is glad you read of those piecing together his people's history, that history he helped keep alive in Babylon. He loved his people's history, keeping the sacred past alive was his joy and showed him the way to learning and opening his mind to study.' 'Like you' **added Samuel**, 'I had a desire to know the essence of things and events and ideas that grew from this and threw back the horizon to a distant place leaving me a vast space to fill with 'knowing'.'

I was so bowled over by all this. How this resonated with me! What a perfect connection, reflection and cohesion of myself and my Life Guide!

On this occasion Samuel and my Guides were exploring nuances of knowledge and learning with me.

'Scientific thinking channelled 'thinking' into proving facts - just so - separating the two instead of uniting - keeping the thinking only in the intellect. But things are changing dear one/Felicity. Ideas are rising and penetrating stony corners for facts alone are stony things without life. Ideas give them life and cast light to reveal truths. Facts alone do not do this. It is the belief that they do that has narrowed men's knowledge when they believe it is expanding. Those that built and created those artefacts you have been reading of designed them from ideas not utility. That they continue to fascinate man is *good* – if only they would explore more of the ideas than the 'technology' then their comprehension would be very much better.'

Later Samuel spoke of his lifetime to me again. I had been reading of the history of the written word. I found it quite fascinating. Sumerian texts and cuneiform found in the Anatolian plain seemed to be where it originated.

'The knowledge of God came to my people in Ur and the valley of the Tigris and Euphrates, the Cradle of communication, writing and historical chronicling - the Anatolian plain, very significant dear dear one...ah yet another - (we were making connections together) - Threads in the unravelled ribbon, dear pupil - (talking of Babylon). - Yes I was born there. I was not among those who returned to Judea. I was 'visiting', - a life among strangers for my awareness of being Hebrew was central to my search for learning and my teaching of our laws and history to my people to keep it alive.'

No wonder I loved to study. It was so perfectly apt that Samuel was my Life Guide. I was always studying something at different stages of my life. In fact, I felt incomplete if I wasn't. I still do. Circumstances precluded me from really scholarly work but I sought what I could in the library.

I loved any, and all history, archaeology, any part of the ancient world and of course Egyptology. They all enthralled me, but I had to fit my sources and time into a busy family life with children. Later came total joy in joining the Open University which pushed my thinking further into other areas of study. I truly had withdrawal symptoms when my studies with them ended. I naturally leapt at the chance when I had Endocrinology to explore.

The added joy for me was the joy my dear Guides felt *with* me and that my enthusiasm and growing knowledge gave them much pleasure. I was in a different zone when I was studying, a cerebral zone which I found very satisfying as I researched and absorbed all the information in all those seven books on the body.

I've described a little of what making the metaphysical connections made me feel. They were more like mental jumps which is why I found them exciting. Some fact in the processes or functions would trigger these jumps and off I would go. I was in a world of my own.

Later, needing a break and always but always wishing to hear my dear Guides' voices I would come out of that highly-charged zone and enter the calm gentle zone that occurred as soon as I heard them and wrote as they talked synchronously with me. There were usually timely reminders to link my cerebral work with the heart chakra of course.

Sometimes, at any time during the day, I'd be triggered into making some connection or other by all sorts of things from reading something or encountering a particular trait or behaviour in someone. It was always on the fringes of my mind.

I always had a notebook to hand because I kept note books everywhere, especially by the bed and always in my handbag. I still do. My beloved Guides were always eager and ready to cover any aspect of my thinking, my need to know, guiding me into complex subjects etc. with their wisdom and support. The lovely thing was that whenever I made these conceptual connections they were sung of in the Singing Time and they enjoyed my delight and excitement too.

'....these things create interest and diversion where a set pattern would lack all challenges and all in the network like to work for the purpose – this brings interest to the Singing Time and any changes are stimulating also. Inertia is not part of the network – stillness and calm vibrations are part of our work but these are a gentle forward energy that accomplishes much. There is joy in all movement for the purpose. Beloved dear – connect with us in loving Oneness for this is great joy for us and a sharing of blissful love.'

Who would not want conscious awareness of their wonderful unconditional love if they but knew of it?

Chapter 23

I was well into things by 2003 when my notes tell me that I had obviously been pondering deeply on 'conscience', - that place where, as humans, we have the innate knowledge of right and wrong - so that it was brought up when I settled down to have some wonderful synchronous talking with my dear 'friends'.

'Dr Ying Po would like to work further on your analysis of 'conscience'. As you surmised dear pupil, guilt is a double-edged sword. Both against the self and for the Self and a powerful weapon in the hands of those who manipulate for power and social control. It needs to become a tool for the conscience but not as a negative feeling of guilt but as a conscious awareness of displacing good by certain actions for the Self within. To determine an action against another is to invite negativity which is not good for the Self but also binds one to the other through the negativity. Also that negativity awakened in the other by one's actions is not a good gift for it will rebound and bind and be passed on to others also. The 'oneness' you had ascertained so well is not served by giving negativity as a 'gift' for all will receive it.'

How I loved these subtleties of perspective that they gave me so succinctly.

I was made very much aware of the necessity of using the intellect through the heart.

'....reason is for facts – conscious awareness is for comprehension, for seeing with the inner eye, feeling with the inner being.'

The separation of the two was, and still is, definitely under observation by the upper Dimensions. The energy from the cerebrum is that of calculation, reasoning, analysis. These need the warmth from the heart for comprehension and wisdom plus intuition from the third eye, the inner eye in the brow. This is their territory so to speak.

Bringing the thinking into the heart is part of the purpose they hope to kindle in Man. So, for myself, while I was absorbed in all the study and science of the body, I tried to remember to make a conscious connection between them both to ensure that imagination and Ego didn't affect my work. It was a way of grounding me so I didn't live in my head too much.

When one dear Guide or another came forward with their own contribution it was so seamless that everything fitted perfectly together. This made our synchronous thinking so interesting. That they were all simultaneously involved in my thoughts and responses and answering everything perfectly is amazing to experience: a constant pleasure and a delight every time as well as wonderful guidance.

One important aspect they wished for us was, and is, that life should be made easier by using a more spiritual approach rather than staying in any darkness of mind or spirit or retaining underlying stresses. This naturally led to much synchronous thinking as this illustrates!

'Go lightly over stony ground dear Happiness/pupil. This way the feet are made less sore. The tenderness of the soles of the feet is both positive and negative, dear dear one as always. The positive aspect is that it is a place from which learning comes.....the discovery of the condition of the road. It is also a defence so that one can look for safe placement of the feet. Cool detachment is needed for this dear one. Conscious awareness at all times. the negative aspect is the vulnerability of the feet that can experience pain from hasty travelling and carelessly overlooking obstacles. Bring the conscious awareness on to the obstacle to consider its validity or how it has come into being. Use this time dear dear one/happiness/pupil to view the path with care but travel lightly with no burden of negativity to make you stumble and hurt your feet or make the treading deep upon the ground'. '

Dear Tibetan Grandmother added:

'Swifter passage on soft feet! Littlest effort is good thing Granddaughter. Wise old woman make little effort. All things come if patient and little effort used up! This way when something come you are ready and content. Energy then to enjoy! Don't waste energy on bad things Granddaughter. Save energy for love. Love is good, love needs little energy. Plenty energy then left over for good things! We love you very much too. We are happy indeed that our guidance helps to soothe your painful thoughts and bring peace to your heart chakra.'

This 'oneness' together made everything so clear. As we continued, I was pleased to hear that the work I was doing on releasing so much had helped *them* help *me*. This encouraged me in my wish to help others work with methods to enable this.

'With the tie-cutting also much negativity has been dispersed and disallowed dear one. You are working hard and doing well for us. – indeed! It makes our work much easier dear one for guiding vibrations benefit from no barriers – yes, especially of the upper chakras of intuition and spiritual connection, which is where we communicate from the mental plane. – yes indeed dear one – a good flow of energy benefits us immeasurably – yes dear one they do but any blockage overlays karmic imprint and both prevent it being dealt with on the physical plane and is hard for us to penetrate so that we can recognise all necessary aspects which we can guide our precious charges with in their thought processes. All things are connected and inter-connected dear one. This is the eternal circle.'

You can gather I had been making my contribution by 'thinking' questions! Always throughout my brain is absolutely fizzing Their connectedness as always was instantaneous; it was amazing! Conversation with them was truly seamless! Such a joy.

~.~

Then a new element to my healing work took me completely by surprise. In fact, it was both astonishing and illuminating for both me and my 'client'.

People would come to me quite randomly for Rei-ki for pain or emotional problems, through friends and family. I was only too happy and delighted to help and to channel this lovely loving energy.

One young lass asked for my help as she was in a lot of pain from an old injury that was interfering with her working life, in particular.

I had given her a couple of effective sessions, Rei-ki with visualisation releasing, with considerable improvement. The condition however was needing more work. We had been using the sentence clearing method which she took to very readily. It really suited her. She was a very willing and uncritical lass.

From the start she didn't know what to expect but was so taken with the effective results that she was quite happy to carry on and uncritically allow me free rein to bring up the needful sentences.

These came to my mind with great speed and clarity and always, but always, were totally recognised by my young client. I knew that I must be being 'given' them by her Guide as they were totally pertinent to her. Things were improving immensely so she was very happy.

One evening we had just started on another session and I was just channelling Rei-ki energy. Suddenly I 'saw' in my mind's eye, a picture of something that I 'knew' was from her childhood. Suddenly, a sentence popped into my head which I felt compelled to voice. Without question or hesitation, she cleared it. More sentences pertinent to this situation were given to me to give to her to clear.

Again, with no hesitation, as each one flowed one to the next she faithfully cleared them. Extraordinarily she quietly accepted each without so much as a query! I continued obediently with the sentences. It seemed obvious that they resonated totally with her subconscious for her acceptance and continued clearing without question was sublime.

What had been occurring is naturally confidential so suffice it to say we just continued seamlessly until the sentences came to a natural end. Simultaneously, a bright light appeared behind my lass's eyes.

In fact, she opened her eyes thinking I had turned the overhead light on. But of course, I hadn't. We knew then that it was all cleared.

Somewhat bemused I asked her about this. She told me in more detail about what had happened. We were both rather astonished by the accuracy and particularities of the whole session. I then asked her if she would like me to continue helping. She was only too pleased. I had by now told her of her guide and that the sentences were not from me.

This entire session quietly astonished me to say the least. And was totally unexpected. But I knew I was being guided so it seemed wise to see how this unfolded.

What transpired over the following weeks was where this new aspect came into my healing sessions.

We both discovered that this injury and the consequences were part of a pattern from past lives. This was entirely new to both of us. For myself I had heard of this but had no personal experience of it at all. My young client accepted what subsequently unfolded without fear or question because everything made sense and the results were always obvious in her present life in her continuing improvement both physically and at stress levels.

Now each week I perceived/saw a different person in a different time. The critical time of her life was always as a young woman. There were similar traits in her character too.

A pattern emerged: the events always led to the same conclusion and ran through every life that came up. Only the circumstances differed as did the situation and people involved. Bit by bit we cleared the critical moment from each life.

I never knew what would be revealed. I did not know if anything was going to be revealed. I can say with perfect honesty I was absolutely obedient to what I was given. For I was 'given' everything. I did not know psychically what had occurred in her past lives; I never tried to guess or invent. That would have been stupid and useless anyway.

Life by life we cleared the painful and traumatic occurrences. My lass never entered them, never experienced them at all. I just spoke the sentences her Guide gave me and she cleared each one thoroughly until eventually the sentences ceased and the 'light' came on as before.

I was never once permitted to experience her distress and sometimes terror in those lives that I was given a glimpse of. I was closed off from the emotions and protected by the Dimensional Beings and her Guide. The sentences were, as always, concise, and *moved seamlessly to the exact point of conclusion every time*. In all, we went back seven hundred years to the initial cause which explained everything.

It was a personal journey of lifetimes that belonged to her and are definitely not mine to describe. I can remember to this day every one and what the crisis was in each, but especially the initial one. It had been so bad that she had turned on herself and subjected her 'Self' to such bitter, negative anger and self-abnegation that it had become this pattern that repeated until God and her Soul determined it was to end.

Her dear Guide, who, it transpired, had been her brother in one of her incarnations was so good to work with. Although as he added,

'My girl's willingness opened a channel that I was able to work through which is why we worked so well together. Our work has been good! Love and the work are blessed things….there was no barrier….My joy is great for her. I thank you for your thoroughness and application to this task. She will now come into her own 'Being' at last - a fundamental and intrinsic innocence despite all those centuries of karma. She has not deviated from the pattern. The (**original**) Will was of incredible vibrational strength and it held its course with great determined purpose. However that karmic burden is much dissolved and the Soul template is bright as is the vibration. – the tension is nearly correct. Before it was under very strong tension from the karma which prevented its brightness travelling along it, as it was rigid with determined Will – because it was not dark karma as you have learned of, it was not made heavy – only rigid. This is what held it in place so that it did not deviate – that is for later discussion dear friend …… this Oneness is *good*! There has been a bursting of light because of it. Love is good. We will talk of other things again dear friend. I have now to go to the Singing Time and share this with the others.……Love and blessings dear dear friend - my heart is full…….'

That I had been called on as an instrument if you like to clear this terrible karmic burden from another, humbled me immensely. But I also felt a real inner joy.

Chapter 24

At the December Solstice that year I went to the Temple as I always do at each Solstice and Equinox. This time I was taken to a room full of soft golden light where there was a Being standing behind a very large open book. This was also imbued with this soft golden light. It seemed to be beautifully made with thick pages like vellum.

The Being said he was The Keeper of the Book. and I was to come forward. He pointed to the page and I saw the word 'Happiness' written on it in beautiful script. 'That is your name and it is now in the Book.' He smiled and nodded and I was returned to the inner temple.

When I opened my eyes, I most definitely needed confirmation for all that occurred. I couldn't wait to talk to my Guides about this mystifying event.

When I got out my notebook and pen ready to talk with them, after our initial greeting they said,

'Samuel wishes to speak with you – Hello dear Felicity.... your name is known – strength will be given to the connections you need to make. Your awareness will be sharpened and we ask that you give time to yourself to move towards the 'knowing' that will come. The Masters acknowledge you for you are willing and faithful. The Rei-ki will pour forth with renewed vigour. Align your consciousness to it through the stillness within and your touch will be sure for it and reveal all that is needful in the given moment with greater clarity. This will be read with greater ease by those Guides helping you and enable the release of layers of negativity with greater efficiency so that karma can be made clear on the template. This will be most helpful to the Guides – (a new voice) This is The Keeper of the Book dear Felicity..yes Happiness – We understand the obstacles which is why we have entered your name so that you receive focussed and direct help along the channelling vibration. For those circumstances stay within and the way will be shown you....Go gently towards this development – you have comprehended well. Go over the facets of this carefully and establish them well so that guidance can be swift and sure for you as you channel the precious healing energy. Much can be accomplished. (then my dear Guides) You are our good and faithful pupil dear dear one/ Happiness /Felicity.'

My beloved Guides were very happy with this new development for me. I too was *very* happy. That The Keeper of the Book had kindly came to endorse what had occurred was both humbling and elevating, as was the fact that the method that had developed was deemed good for the purpose and the Dimensions as well. Yes, I was happy.

I never knew when this 'seeing' other lives for people was going to happen. It always came as a surprise. I was just obedient to it. Each time however it included the sentence clearing technique as the person's Guide perceived it the effective way so gave me the exact pertinent and concise sentence for them to eliminate.

If another method was needed as well, I was always given to 'know' what to offer. Since every sentence and every method used worked with little or no resistance from the person I was helping, I knew that it was all guidance from the Dimensions, not my choice. I just 'knew' what to offer. There was no doubt we were working as one for it was so clear and flowed so easily.

Every time a pattern was revealed. Circumstances, era, environment, countries and nationalities even, and personalities differed but certain character traits and the pattern were constant. And always the initial trauma was where the personality turned on itself with deep anger, or anguish or most often an almost ferocious guilt and self-blame. And I mean a sense of guilt. Not *being* guilty of anything; only as perceived by the personality.

Each time my 'client' trusted me and what was required because they did not become emotionally 'involved', or, relive anything. The Guides and Dimensional Beings' intentions are to enable the karma clearing to be exercised simply and easily to remove pain, to remove any trauma. Reviving or evoking emotion is *not* the remit.

These visualisation-releasing methods I had developed fit this exactly. The Dimensions I had now learned, were very happy with this aspect. The synchronicity between the methods and receiving the Guides' exact information was wonderful. Their efficiency in reading what was to be cleared was immediate and precise and so easy to work with.

For those whom I worked with, the gender was the same as the client's throughout in all but one instance. This was a lady, but in each past life she was consistently a man. (in this lifetime she was a career woman, fiercely independent and ran her own life entirely.)

Since the trauma or circumstance was repeated it seems that the gender choice was consistent due to the intensity of the emotion when the personality turned against itself. This seemed yet another pattern. Only the Akashic records can reveal the reason for that choice.

I was not given the opportunity to clear the karma right back to the original trauma for all of these dear people.

For some it was one serious trauma that was revealed to me to clear for they came only once or perhaps twice with a problem. That it would have had a beneficial effect on their lives in the future in some way is extremely likely, especially given the seriousness of the trauma for each of them. I would not have been 'given' it, had it revealed to me, otherwise. I didn't seek either event. It was one less burden for them, that was certain.

For another 'client,' sessions are intermittent with months in between. Sometimes it is a present problem we deal with, sometimes a past life incident is revealed which we clear very thoroughly. It has been like taking off layers so that the pressure the karma has exerted is lessened each time.

This has to be what is necessary for her and is determined by the Dimensional Beings who direct this. (Her Guide or Guides must have become ensouled as I had no knowledge of them. (See p 194)) Little by little as it were, as was appropriate to her needs.

Almost from the beginning, each time I was immediately shown a particular, crucial and very emotionally painful moment in her lifetimes from centuries ago to the present day. Clearly this was the pattern we needed to resolve, and we have successfully worked to clear each one.

But there was an even more deeply traumatic and significant moment long before that, that actually triggered this pattern, which has taken a lot of work. Her past is a very long one and into very ancient times.

In the case of another, because the Karmic result was physical, painful and recurring, I was given a lot of small incidents to clear in each session until eventually the initial trauma was shown to me after a period of time.

After each session the pain ceased. There was a recurrence though with longer intervals but the 'cause' still needed to be unravelled further so the pain reappeared as a signal to clear another set of incidents. That the cumulative effects from the beginning until the original trauma and destructive self-blame was revealed and cleared meant that there is now no recurrence. What a difference it has made to their life.

For all these dear people, once again each 'life' showed a clearly recognisable pattern that had to have had a particular source because it was so singular. Because *I* am given the pertinent sentences or an image to clear means that the person is not involved emotionally in the incident. I do not describe the event. I just follow what comes into my head from the Guides to do and keep the person focused on the *action needed*. That I have never had a sentences or sentences queried, shows how truly pertinent they are.

Sometimes in a session dealing with pain I am shown a karmic incident as the initial cause. Instead of a sentence, I am given a perception of it so I use the visualisation technique I call 'using X-ray eyes.'

I ask them to imagine they have X-ray eyes and look into the painful area in their mind's eye. Sometimes it is fibrous knots, looks red or black and they might even find an arrow, or a bullet.

I get them to remove whatever they see and heal up the area. They feel no physical sensation and do not know what occurred to get it there. But if needed I am given to 'see' how and why it got there. It isn't necessary to tell them; sometimes they ask.

Frequently they see a red rawness or a deep wound which the person then watches being healed up in their mind's eye. Often this needs to be repeated to ensure complete healing of what they 'see.' It is extraordinary the types of wounds and objects that are revealed. It needs to be thorough since any wound indicates a recurring effect.

If you are interested and have a painful area of any sort, go into your mind's eye and look inside the place that hurts. Whatever you see could really surprise you but focus only on removing what you find and healing it by any means your imagination can find! And try it again to see if it is still there or not! If it is, keep going!

Regarding the sentences I am given, whatever the circumstances, the sentences are always recognisable to the client and they invariably seem to relate to something in their present lives. Even then, if they didn't particularly recognise it, the sentences always somehow made sense to them; they 'knew', so accepted them quite happily. That they were not simple to erase but did go, endorsed this.

Perhaps they resonated so clearly because the Soul is ready to allow the connection and subconsciously, they can accept the truth of it. Whatever the situation, I follow the guidance totally.

In every case, there has been either a noticeable change or a resolution of the problem from clearing these karmic patterns, depending on whether we have reached the initial cause.

For one client, during several sessions on one of his lives that had had a powerful impact on him, several North American Shamans came to help me. We worked well together in a deep harmony that was quite a singular experience. My perceptions on all those occasions were very clear and took in every detail. They enabled a lot of clearing that was very beneficial to my client.

Not long after this I was in my kitchen and preparing food when I knew I was being 'called'. Someone wanted to 'speak' to me. Intrigued and certainly not wanting to miss the opportunity, I went for notepad and pen.

'Someone is here to talk with you dear Felicity– hello, my name is 'Night Owl. I am of the Cree nation -my tribe was the Napawan and we suffered much at the time of the white man's coming to our sacred lands – many of us agreed to become the guides of our people for their return to the Earthly plane to work out their destiny and that of our nation – I was in the time of the early coming when we did not know the white man and his ways or his ways of death so all my knowledge is of the old ways and the long days of my people – these we carried to our people through our Guidance for they are the ways of truth for people of the Earth and all its bounties. We carry this love and this truth through time to all people who would listen in their hearts. Hear me dear Felicity– your words of truth and love should be taken to my land for there they will listen with ears that are ready for practical ways to better lovingness. Many listen but are unable to grasp the way forward. Idealism is taken up by those who think and some take action, but many cannot help themselves so their thoughts remain unused except for passing between themselves – this then is unhelpful for practical ways to change. Change needs to come to the inner mind where the darkest energies reside and bar the way for truth and love. The knowledge for releasing them gives space for the true knowledge of love and respect for all that lives on the Earth, land sea and air – all things that my people love but whose voices are not heard. The Shamans you have been working with are now connected with you and the work you do, so the pathway has already begun. Ways will be shown to you and knowing will enter your heart – this is the beginning and more will be revealed to you when it is necessary for you to know these things, so work to prepare for all things good - the Divine Light will guide you for we are all within the love of the Great Spirit who knows all things, we will speak again Little Feather for that is your name to us......all will be revealed when it is time. All is good dear Felicity- all is understood. These are truths for you dear friend.......rest gently in God's loving arms and our guidance. Love and blessings to you also dear Felicity/ Little Feather.'

I could feel the depth of feeling and the sensitivity in his voice at an extraordinary level within me. I was deeply moved by this dear Guide and somewhat reassured by Khatumi's last remark. I could feel the love he had for his people and the strength of his personality most clearly. I wished greatly that I could honour this wish, that it could be possible to go to Canada and perhaps do talks there but I could not see how that could be achieved. I felt honoured that he should come and speak with me.

Writing his words out and re-reading them moves me as deeply as when he spoke to me.

The guidance and help I received for this client gave us both extraordinary and profound experiences. Night Owl came to speak to me again.

'We have worked well together since you answered my call Little Feather. – you were wise to question and be sure that flights of imagination were the cause or not. You 'see' me, that is good. I speak with you for we work together as one and together for I carry the voice of the people as the truth and the love. We know of one another but our paths are different – each has a chosen one that he walks in a straight way which are the chosen trails of the people of my nation to guide and protect those on the Earth plane.'

The timbre of his voice was so potent with feeling. I thought of him often but he did not come again.

However, time being non-linear in the Dimensions maybe this union and work in Night Owl's country is for the future. I can only assume that this was due to the beautiful and intense connection made with the work done with him and the dear Shamans who came to help my client so well. I have included this dear Guide's words here because it is a unique insight into something important and meaningful so I wanted to share it with you.

Covering so many eras, I also learned aspects of war, society and belief systems that led to appalling circumstances among other things, from the 'lives' of my clients and those of their Guides too. Much of it was rooted in the mediæval period or dark ages which I had not studied, my interest having been in ancient history. It was all a revelation. Intriguing, riveting and extraordinary.

Chapter 25

Other than friends and relatives, I have never sought out people to channel Rei-ki to – and certainly not for clearing karma. These latter have only been those whose path was at the right point for clearing this. Those that do come, I know that God sent them to me. What was needed was deemed time for those dear people and I seemed to be assigned to the task because of my clairaudience and my own method with Rei-ki.

But I also learned a great deal about karma, the negative Will and Ego, the strange self-destructive element within us, courage and the endurance of people. So perhaps that is partly why God sent them to me to learn from. All is reciprocity after all.

The most important thing I have learned incidentally is that God *wastes nothing*! Everything has a purpose, is put to a purpose. Every negative act thought or belief has a consequence that enables something else, something necessary and important. 'the network uses all methods through reciprocity for the purpose thus receiver or activator (of negativity) will be determined by need for learning.'

We learn and develop because of adversity. Through this we discover our strengths and weaknesses, compassion, altruism, courage and endurance to rise above anything.

These make us grow in understanding of ourselves and others, and consequently, develops humanity. The human spirit needs something to overcome and has risen to amazing heights as a result.

A gentle sweet rather uneventful life can so easily mean a rut and nothing learned that has real consequence. Like the grit in the oyster that means the creation of the exquisite pearl, we need that bit of grit it seems. We are not yet ascended beings that we can live in that state of conscious awareness and spiritual accord. Not on this earth plane, where the root of survival is the elemental and vitally necessary one, fear.

Though we frequently bury them, we have a great capacity for nursing our fears, holding on to them, feeding them and following every negative thought prompted by them down a long dark road. (I refer to the everyday and the ordinary only.)

All we can do is change our own negativity to lessen ours and the global weight of it even in some small measure. And strengthen the Dimensional Beings which then lightens the burden throughout the planes as well. A good use of Free Will.

While going through my precious dictated notes I have come across a further conversation Dr Ying Po and I had that very apt, and as always very illuminating.

'.....it is this matter of choice that can add a further dimension to what the Soul has chosen as its path. It is this unpredictable quality of Free Will that can invite changes which come from the personality reacting to events and people along the way setting other events in motion which can make the road harder. Even then these which result in other events and encounters will always be put to good use for the learning of other Souls in this interlocking pattern of life upon our Earth dear pupil. God in his infinite patience wastes nothing so all is put to good account even though Man invites disaster upon himself by his choices directed by the imposition of his Will and his self-interest. The work of the Guides is to help with Man's choices and the consequences of them also. For this task we have to learn to have no negativity therefore no judgement or control of the Will or the minds of others. – thus being aware of these things and going within for comprehension, guidance will be found for learning rather than for punishment.'

Naturally karma cropped up and if it was incidental to the 'now' or when there was a point to be made, it just flowed into our discussion. It was very apparent that 'there is much to the whole intricate play that is karma.'

It seemed that many people see karma as a punishment for previous misdeeds so I did ask my Guides about it.

'...if the personality has enacted a power influence over others - yes, caught up in the acceptance power cycle - then exerting that negative Will is the issue – thus it will be brought up to the person through the experiences until the issue is released –there are many factors that affect the nuances of negative Will control dear dear one – yes indeed, - which chakra aspects are involved – these all contribute their nuances which is why it is a complex business dear dear one. The issue needing attention will be the cause as much as the aspect of exerting power and that too – yes, the desire for self-punishment also is a separate issue but that too will have its root in an initial cause – indeed – often the cause is revisited and this will be what will be brought up for attention – indeed dear dear one – many threads and all interconnected. The stronger the action of the negative Will the more it is pointing to the cause. Guidance for learning to release negative Will is a constant dear dear one so *all* participate in aiding others to this purpose and enact the rôle needed for the purpose. This is the work of the Karmic Lords who know the Akashic records and 'see' what is needed for the purpose to which all are willing to participate in for the hopeful release through the experiences they are willing to effect in a continual spiral journey towards the Divine.'

'...God does not burden us, but gives us tools for the chosen task and for the consequences of negativity. – if Man's knowledge of this was clearer he would gain so much from the tools he is given and the choices he could make but fear draws much negativity and is an ancient habit! Also a useful tool dear for God wastes nothing - Yes – keeping negative energy in creation (us) good connection dear dear one/Happiness/pupil/ girl – God maintains and sustains the light through 'Being' – He wastes nothing from knowing everything – every aspect of knowledge added to the 'knowing' enables this.'

'The oneness of the Soul with the chosen personality is complete during that lifetime but something remains afterwards in the karma that is carried forward - as history for the Soul, signposts, a reference and a guide – the source of knowledge gained from the experience……..releasing the negativity does indeed release it for its true purpose, that of learning and development and the more negativity is released the better for the Guide and the personality and the work that is done by them together for comprehension of the value of karma and the problems that can occur if negativity overlays and obscures karma preventing the personality from making use of it - a significant purpose of the negative forces.'

How appropriate 'misguided' is then when we use the word.

'….release from the physical plane changes the upper vibrations so that we can see more clearly what is to be done. Yes dear pupil – it is that which is buried in the body physical that gets the least attention! And this is the cause of many physical ailments. Yes indeed – the manifestation of karma – in order to work through the karma the Soul will choose the genetic plan most likely to make the karma physically manifest. All journeys are for the clearing of karma as the Soul learns from each new set of experiences - and this time is for the clearing of much karma as the time of Aquarius gathers momentum in order to settle into the vibration it is to follow. It is the establishment of this vibration that can only take place once the change-over is complete – Man's spiritual changes take the longest alas as he clings to his beliefs (they were speaking in general), which he feels will give him an anchor to the material changes that he presses for with all his physical and mental energy. The paradox is in the fear of, yet desire for change which no longer follows the rhythm of nature but Man's desire instead. This is what creates the distortion dear

Happiness/pupil – there has to be the cycle of life and death both physical and metaphysical, but Man's Will creates the discord that causes the disruption but it seems that learning comes best from this as Man needs challenges and tests to the spirit in order to move on to more development.'

All the subtle intricacies involved show that it is hardly a clear-cut issue of simply deed and consequence. Anyway, sin and retribution are concepts that have no place in the Dimensions for there is no judgement. That is Man's. Moreover, the Divine is Love.

I did ask my Guides about karma in relation to myself. My sister Grace had told me that I was a 'flown-inner' which I will come to later. Most people assumed that I had a karmic past but I was puzzled so I sought counsel of my Guides.

Naturally my Guides' own words tell you better than my paraphrasing. In this case Dr Ying Po spoke with me.

'Hello dear pupil, I will help you with this constant reference that puzzles you. This aspect in your chart that seems to reveal your karmic past is of the areas within your life's experiences in this personality that have the necessary connections for others willing to help you with your development by bringing their karmic issues to you to initiate those situations that you need, but such is the nature of reciprocity they themselves receive a learning experience as a result. –yes – yes – a co-operative enterprise! – Thus dear pupil what appears there, are those issues for development for you from necessary *external* karma provided for the purpose which are readily perceived in our planes and Dimensions but are being interpreted differently on your physical plane as being your past. You are a new Soul-part dear dear one/pupil/ Granddaughter/child/girl – the connectedness ensures sources of awareness and knowledge and allows for the loan of karma as we have described. This is for the learning to initiate knowledge therefore will remain that of those who help in this way..............each must carry its own karma for the 'learning towards knowing' – thus dear pupil consider that which appears to be 'karma' as books on loan from a library for the purpose of study and research!. The knowledge you have acquired will be your map, signposts, encyclopædia and history book for your Soul's journey and will be the beginnings of any necessary 'karma' for future lives for that knowledge will initiate experiences and responses that will contribute to its substance as the necessary tool we humans need. Yes dear pupil I am happy that this has been helpful to your understanding. –. We will speak again dear pupil when it is needful and helpful – it is *good* – rest sweetly in God's loving arms dear dear one – all is well! All is *good*. – Trust and believe as always – our love is with you as is that of the Masters and dear God and the Angels. Sleep well.'

Such sweet parting words. The word good always held emphasis. 'Good' to the Dimensions was something deep; it seemed to be far more than our interpretation. Thus, I felt that goodness was inherently part of lovingness and truth.

So, mine was a new incarnation, bringing no karma with me. I was to work *with* other people's karma, by being a working surface for them and for myself, for my learning of those things necessary for my own development. That made so much more sense to me. This knowledge, however, really only mattered to me. No doubt I've collected some in this lifetime for use next time round.

As to the term 'flown-inner' this was to denote people who have come into fresh karma-free incarnations. Some are new Souls and some are Souls that have completed their entire cycle at some stage; in other words, worked through all their karma. Some completed their cycle aeons ago and have been incarnated for specific purposes to do with humanity's development as we come into this fresh Aquarian age - for it has a quite different vibration and therefore nature, to the Piscean. This is because different energies are required now.

I did learn however, that I was 'loaned' for a purpose to Atlantis. I was sent to trigger something for two people there who are very advanced Beings working now, leading their separate lives.

I have naturally been connected with them in this lifetime as their being at this time is vital. Reciprocity is the constant element. All is working together for knowledge, comprehension and development.

Cycles and patterns are what karma is about and determined by both individual and collective beliefs. These beliefs hold karmic patterns in place very strongly indeed. Re-incarnation and the existence of karma and its repetitive nature itself, are about and subject to, the strength of beliefs as well as negative and insistent Will.

All incarnations are for a purpose and that is known to the Soul and God and the Souls of those involved in that incarnation. But all is part of the Divine Plan and that is God's.

Being a mite curious about this lifetime's ups and downs affecting my next time around I did ask about this, and one particular event especially.

'Hello dear pupil – this is a wise question – the Akashic record will hold the experience you had and will also hold the solution you apply to that experience. That you have faced and that you have applied your comprehension to that experience will balance the weight of that experience – and the result of that balance will also be held in the Akashic records and become part of your 'life-experience' template for your next incarnation – the balance and therefore harmonising of the experience will be the important aspect of anything you choose to learn about for have we not discussed the 'knowing' dear one? The amount of comprehension will determine the quality of the 'knowing' and once the 'knowing' is established that of course remains within the template as a task accomplished – any facets that should remain will be part of any future work dear pupil – which is very satisfactory for it works for the purpose....'

It was good to know that working to clear and resolve, and how much, was written into the records too.

It also seemed highly probable to me that karma was involved with illness. Simply by the accumulation of unresolved negativity, particularly over lifetimes. This seemed to me to be part of it. Certainly not as retribution or punishment.

'....yes dear pupil it is a very complex inter-woven state…..All karma is a working surface - for the self for working within to make use of what is brought on the journey and in an exchange to learn from and move forward – for all knowledge opens doors – to 'within' and to new experiences and levels of development…………releasing karma is the way of karma – binding to it is to invite inertia – the Soul is then on a harder journey to enlightenment and the body will manifest this collected energy from the Will and Ego. – this is the body's part………..**all things that need to enter the consciousness manifest in the physical dear dear one/pupil since it is the physical plane.** (my emphasis)– observation and comprehension are needed to read the physical world – indeed – they do but rather overlook Man and his physical state – there is an acceptance of suffering that obscures the clues and messages and sources of information that are available to read from the human form. There is much that is being done to bring it to notice but once again until it becomes a part of the consciousness – a clear way of thinking rather than something to read about – progress will be slow…….all is manifested in the physical – that is where it is all written so that concepts can be formed to enlighten…Man is given much information if he but makes use of his brain and senses to comprehend it. Yes dear Pupil, Man uses and changes his environment and carries his mistakes along with him to learn from – he needs now to read both himself and his environment and in doing that will take responsibility and develop his Beingness within – Conscious awareness only comes from the connection with the Divine within – only consciousness will enable him to read all that has been written for him by the hand of God...to understand that dear dear one/pupil is an accomplishment. The brain, the instinct and the heart – these together are the enabler............'

'....Guidance for learning to release negative Will is a constant, dear dear one so all participate in aiding others to this purpose and enact the rôle needed as determined for the purpose. This is the work of the Karmic Lords who 'know' the Akashic Records and 'see' what is needed for the purpose to which all are willing to participate in – yes, for the hopeful release through the experiences they are willing to effect in a continuous spiral journey towards the Divine. Many methods are tried and they will be much determined by cause and where it can be inter-related to the need of the willing participant. You are beginning to grasp the complexities dear dear one.'

As usual, my thoughts and mental comments were pinging up and becoming part of their exploration of my queries; another sublime experience of taking dictation in that instantaneous intermingling of minds.

It is noticeable that there is no criticism or judgement, but certainly any reference to what Man is seriously ignoring in these words is wise and full of understanding. Both aspects are why I wanted to share them with you.

Later, Tibetan Grandmother spoke to me when we were speaking of healing. Her words are so beautiful I naturally wish to share them with you.

'Disenable the darkness from those chakras necessary to the purpose – Ah! You comprehend dear Granddaughter, – it is *good*! Draw *within* and connect with the healing within and with us – all is well – all is *good*, the Universe has answered with that which is for the universal purpose. It has lain untouched and waiting for release to the purpose of healing into the keeping of those who have been chosen for the purpose – the Soul, - yes - the intellect and the heart vibrations in readiness for its future use of healing and knowledge. Trust and believe dear dear one/dear

Granddaughter. These things are to come to pass – draw from the well of the Divine within at all times of doubt and confusion for there is loving insight and all Divine Truths. – Rest now and live in joy for the purpose is love – in being – in our guidance and in God's protecting healing arms, so rest sweetly dear dear one – All is *good*.'

I have just come across this 'conversation' in one of my books today but I chose the title for my book weeks ago! Perfect!

So, you can see, a *great* deal was happening in my life and shaped my view of things in amazing ways.

Having discovered metaphysics, life became (and is) even more fascinating than ever. My life was wonderfully enriched by this as well by as by my beloved Guides. I seemed to be galloping through a great deal of new knowledge and understanding, comprehending things I never dreamed of.

That this had begun when I was nearly sixty and at this speed made me realise that I'd had to have had a good taste of life first because I came in as that clean slate. My life had indeed been full of frequent change in *all* theatres of my life so far. Settled it wasn't and never had been.

This made sense to me now. I'd obviously had a great deal to learn! Nothing was really coming as a surprise to me any more. Or so I thought.

~.~

I came across this entry on January 9th 2004. My lovely Guides and I had been talking of 'the nature of the Soul which is good and created from light which is love'.

Then into their collective voices a different voice came through and entered seamlessly,

'....for the 'knowing' which is God's, so all is used for the knowing, for God and Love are 'in beingness' without end....love is healing and healing is love and all things good for God is good and all that is with God. This is the beingness of all things and lovingness is the purpose and lovingness comes from the knowing within for *there* is the Divine who knows and is Love. All this is possible in the heart of Man if he believes in Love and goodness and knowing love for this is the source of light to light the way to the 'knowing' within for the 'knowing' is God and love for they are one. These things are true for within truth is the light and love and they are also one in the beingness of God. All is love and the way is love through the light which is the Divine within where you will find truth for all things. Dwell therein for all things good.'

The voice seemed to be coming from a very far off place. This voice was new and had a most singular vibrancy. I was held in a point of utter stillness inside throughout by the timbre of the voice and the beauty of the words.

It was an extraordinary moment. I had a feeling of something within me expanding even further than usual.

My Guides however, just continued, again seamlessly, on exploring the purpose of Man and the Soul with me. Who had spoken was not revealed.

'The 'knowing' will come because that is the purpose of the Soul– indeed, even in the 'knowing' the Will and the Ego will resist the knowing. It is this 'progress' that draws all 'knowing' into the consciousness because that is the purpose – denial and non-acceptance just delay the point of completion. Yes indeed, dear dear one, the 'knowing' is always 'known' and recognised within, for that also is the purpose of 'knowing' and this purpose *has* been fulfilled through God's infinite wisdom. It is this that brings all knowledge to the Will which is the purpose of Man, the human personality, the Soul's vehicle. The Way, the Truth and the Light - this is the journey dear dear one – the journey to all 'knowing' for all must 'be known' to accomplish the purpose for Creation. Indeed, each Soul must also attain all the 'knowing' for since we are all one this is completion for all to 'know' we are one.'

My Guides then continued with explaining the choices for Soul and personality. I found this very enlightening as always so wish to share this too with you dear reader.

'…..the spirit of the personality is an amalgam of all the essential traits of character acquired from the genetic line and the planetary influences which have a positive and a negative side to them and which will be part of the energy system that will attract the appropriate energy and influence for the Soul's journey. These are the tools for the journey that the Soul has chosen to enable the personality to find difficulties or development for the purpose and do indeed work unconsciously. This is where the question of choice resides dear dear one, to make of the experiences what it will. In enabling the psyche towards positivity, the Soul is enabled as guide for that which is to be 'known'. It is the element of the personality that attracts the karmic experience for the Soul's 'knowing ………The Soul is impenetrable dear dear one but the 'vehicles' are not, so absorb the negative energy that it needs to carry for the purpose…………….yes indeed dear dear one, the threads form an intricate network of great complexity – that is why the Masters are great Beings. – we are all one dear dear one – the difference is that here there is no negativity or Will but the vastness of the knowing is available to us so that all aid is given for the purpose. Yes, on a 'need to know' basis! That is good! Only 'all knowledge' belongs to God for this and His purpose. The Human Being is the seeker of this knowledge for God – we in these Dimensions hold our share for the purpose of guidance and aid and understanding of what is needful. For all is from the 'knowing', to the 'knowing' and for the 'knowing' dear dear one Rest sweetly in God's loving arms dear dear precious charge. All is well, all is understood. – The purpose will be fulfilled where there is love and willingness and faith in all things loving and good.'

Chapter 26

Energy has certainly been the main focus of all the new metaphysical experiences I was having, and a significant part of what was now a way of life for me.

It is no coincidence, - there go metaphysics again! – that for years the word on most people's lips from politicians to environmentalists to media coverage has been Energy! So frequently is it referred to it is almost like a neon sign!

It has been foremost in our thoughts yes, but in terms of all the many fuels for our modern needs and mechanistic way of life and travel. There has to be a reason for this emphasis. Everything that is reiterated time and again is a message if we had the wit to realise it. We are so used to the word however, that we have ceased to consider its significance.

Well, there is one energy resource that is overlooked. It is vital and free. Human Energy.

My Guides have certainly covered every metaphysical aspect of it with me. I seem to have been delving into every possible feature, and also written on it at length, ever since the Millennium. There has to be a purpose.

It cannot be just coincidence that 'energy healing' methods have been brought increasingly to our attention over the last twenty-odd years. It seems highly probable that it is because our *energy needs healing.*

It is undeniable that modern living has put it under intense pressures and stimulation at an increasing rate. These were unknown until the last century. The progression has been very swift and gained ever-increasing speed in the last fifty years. Well, we have been provided with the means to heal it.

The way I have been so singularly prepared and guided also seems appropriate. All is accounted for.

On the one hand the 'secular physical' has been accommodated from just releasing negative energy through simply looking into the system and clearing it.

Then on the other, the esoteric, the needs of the 'inner being,' accommodated through both the significance of and releasing of negativity, even karma, for enhancing our energy, as well as part of spiritual awakening, comprehension, and realisation of the loving self.

Both achieved by helping one's personal energy and both accommodated by energy healing. With the energy system being the comprehensive factor, it all connects. There is no escaping it. What is also clear is that it seems to have been overlooked as a component to be considered in any concern about our health.

Neither our energy system nor its vitality is a feature in conventional healthcare although its quality is fundamental to our health and well-being in every respect. How could it be otherwise when we are alive because of it? And it is a fully-functioning system like any other.

I have just come across this in my notebooks from 2009.

'Healing and energy are the words of the age. They need to become more than words dear friend. They need to be understood.'

There are scientists who have acknowledged our energy field as a fact and done research into what they now call the 'human biofield.' Its toroidal structure is constant throughout every structure in the Universe. Hence the way the energy flows through the chakra system. So, unsurprisingly, the human energy system works exactly as does all energy in the entire Cosmos. Tesla understood this principle of energy as a free resource. But perceiving how it could be free, Tesla alas was denied. But that's another story.

But what of the complexities of the components of our human energy system? And there are certainly complexities. The responses and reactions in our relationships and experiences are determining factors but there are also external vibrations that influence our energy system. Being the interesting and emotional creatures that we are, these will be coupled with emotional responses and reactions too. An example is in how we respond to music.

Illych, my Russian 'friend' and my Guides, having introduced me to pitch and frequency for their relevance to vibrational fields, were interested in the impact of sound on the human body. As always these were stimulating explorations. These definitely sharpened my thinking and gave me brand new perspectives because I was now realising many aspects I had not associated with health before.

Through exploring the energy and impact of sound with my Dear Ones I was discovering how *all* aspects of vibration involves the health of the body and the mind. The amount and variety of sound in our modern environment, is considerable, so it was naturally significant. All vibrational changes however, are of course visible to the Dimensions so they are aware of the impact on the tissues of our bodies by the changes in the energy field.

This was giving me a lot to think about. Through my writing and studies, I certainly now knew that energy goes to energy. And sound is definitely energy. Our bodies have a very efficient resonating chamber in our chest cavity – one can feel it when music is extremely loud after all! But we also have a very intricate nervous system that transmits energy.

Other than the sounds created by sound bowls and sources designed for either healing or prayer, their interest was in the modern sounds we live with, now of a totally different quality and even sources quite different from that of previous centuries.

Because every cell produces energy it follows that this must interact with the energy of every other cell since each has pitch and a frequency, so, will respond or react to various pitches of sound at a deep physical level, indeed, in all the tissues of our body.

All harsh, strident sounds; shouting, screaming, screeching etc from both humans and machinery, highly amplified music, - all being at various pitches of 'loud,' have a very strong frequency. This is bound to resonate at tissue level too from cellular energy absorption and through our hearing on unconscious and sub-conscious levels to our nervous system. All living tissue will resonate with its environment. There is proof that talking lovingly and gently to plants, is highly beneficial, because the pitch engages with their energy, for tests have proven that this encourages growth, and shouting and loud discord creates a chemical alarm reaction and inhibits growth. Is the human body less sensitive? Animals and man have a greater response to sound being physically complex creatures. Watch an animal react to any loud noise.

Society creates an incredible amount of noise and not all of it pleasant! Modern urban life is full of artificial stimulation and noise. City life particularly is full of artificial clamour and uproar, plus a great deal of human noise; the mind and body are all unknowingly and invisibly absorbing everything. They say that city life is the most stressful! It is certainly loud.

We don't really give much thought to the impact of quarrelling and shouting and even screaming between people and family members especially in confined areas. This is all being physically absorbed as well as at mental and emotional levels.

We all talk of 'being in harmony' or 'in tune' or even 'out of tune' with someone. Also 'discord' between ourselves, or 'striking a discordant note', something 'striking a chord within us.' We are so used to these phrases that we give them no thought. Yet we are mostly unaware of the impact of adverse sounds and especially constant harsh sounds and rackety even ugly noise.

However, it *all impinges on the nervous system;* you have only to consider, for example, strobe lighting and pounding music. The nervous system will both absorb and react immediately so together, they will have considerable impact, particularly after long hours of exposure and be absorbed by our delicate neurological tissue.

Yes, we need and enjoy stimulation but it would be helpful to be conscious and understand the impact of excess.

But modern life in all its technology and complexities has established itself. It's here to stay. It is certainly our 'now.'

We are both mostly inured to it and accommodate it. We also enjoy a great deal of it. Factoring it into considerations of our health, and appropriate healing approaches, would help enormously. The impact on our general state of health shouldn't be ignored.

It is not mere whim that complementary therapies are conducted in virtual silence or with perhaps soft sounds chosen to soothe. Also, there is much we can do through awareness to help ourselves, especially with human interactivity.

The modern world has made huge strides in medical knowledge and care. Doctors and hospitals are abundant and well-equipped and medical skills increasing all the time. We have plenty of good food, high standards of hygiene in all walks of life and yet - so many people are ill. *Ill*-health has a very high profile. Perhaps rather than solutions we should be asking 'why?' more often by looking deeper than just at the physical in Newtonian terms.

Chapter 27

I came across another lovely piece of guidance that so aptly fits all this garnering and growing of concepts from the knowledge I was accumulating.

'Many things requiring clarity will become clear in time dear dear one as each new thread needs to be revealed. The cord is only as strong as the threads that make it up – their quality and correct number will ensure the lasting quality. So it is with all connections and the ribbon of knowledge that unravels before you. Each stepping stone over uncertain ground is from knowledge revealed and comprehended. – yes, dear pupil it is that which draws them together for a smooth safe pathway! No danger of wetting the hem of the tunic through incautious proceeding – this enables focus and disables distractions so that travelling forward harmoniously is possible. The time taken for comprehending gives time for centreing and achieving balance before any necessary action dear pupil.'

Such lovely gentle wisdom; Staying focussed and conscientious is hard work.

'We all work together dear friend for the purpose and the love in 'being'. It is our true purpose dear, that of Beingness of Love, the Universal energy that is the accomplishment of all energy sources in all planes. It permeates all planes, all Dimensions from all levels of consciousness, thus the raising of consciousness is the 'beingness' of love, the Universal energy – thus infinity. This connects us all – the dark side merely block themselves from the light of this love and 'feed' their 'shield' with negative energy in the illusion that their existence is 'real'. Because being dark it differs from the light. God uses all dear friend as a force to be worked upon for consciousness to be raised and understanding and knowledge developed, for in this way, energy has meaning and purpose – yes, life, good, meanwhile the dark side work hard to maintain both their 'shield' and illusion to God's purpose. They merely exercise it and believe it exercises their power, but while it is a force it is always overcome by the power of love because love always grows and expands so therefore can always be greater and always has the potential for more. (me.. 'it doesn't use energy it is pure energy.') yes indeed dear one, it 'uses', that is the key word - Because it (negative energy) is a created energy they believe the illusion that they are creators, but the Creator and all that He has created are 'in existence' and remain so without the Creator's assistance whereas the dark side only exist through the effort of the dark ones. Once that effort is ended the dark ceases to exist, whereas Love remains in existence into infinity because God 'is.'

My mind was in a particularly profound oneness with them here, as usual, in that beautiful immediacy we had together. It expands my heart chakra anew as I copy out their precious words.

All along the way, everything I had been learning from my dear Guides and the Dimensional Beings who all help my understanding, became threaded in to all those subjects and interests, fragments of spiritual philosophy and belief I'd had all my life.

Everything seemed to be coming together and making my mind brim over and race along with fascinating thoughts and ideas. Such a happy result of the astonishing about-turns my life had made since that impact at the millennium.

That I had a medical background through my family, my nursing experience and my yet non-Newtonian view of the body was perfect. They were obviously the strong foundation for this fresh and intense perspective on every aspect of the holistic health of our amazing body.

I was off and running from the start, eager and hungry for all that rolled out before me. Following where it was leading me seemed absolutely right. I seemed to have gathered up all the divers threads from my life to find them completely relevant to what was developing in my book too. It was becoming clearer to me that here was a pattern for a purpose; everything connected.

~ . ~

My book meanwhile was speedily approaching completion. It had developed neatly into three sections and I was very happy with the way that they were yet interconnected and easily cross-referenced.

I had shown every possible connection through the anatomical functions and processes and all the elements of the energy system. This had very full coverage of course and included all the subtleties and nature of energy and its consequences that I could discover.

Naturally it was essential I include definitive ways of clearing negative energy (but without specific recommendations of complementary therapies). Since I'd found my visualisation methods to be so effective it seemed only fitting to offer them as the tools to do so. They were all fully within the capabilities and responsibilities of the reader.

This was my aim, to give people the choice and the ability to work on themselves in a field untouched by the scientific approach to health.

I had loved working on every part of my book. I felt an affinity with what I was writing because I believed in every aspect of it so completely. I was very eager to put it out there and genuinely help people to have some control over their health. And this without pressure to change their ways of life. Just their energy!

And most importantly, in doing that they would discover lovingness, the lovingness within and inviting love in too. Then the quality of their lives was theirs to choose as well.

Not least was what it meant to my Guides and the network. That is beautifully expressed here.

'...we all love you dearly for your love and faithfulness to the purpose dear dear one/Felicity– it has much meaning for us in the network – it is strength and brightness for us. All help will be given – the love you feel for the purpose is shared by us in the Singing Time and all rejoice. Willingness and faithfulness are treasured dear one/Felicity but conscious willingness for a task has an added lustre that benefits us all.'

I had long ago discovered that what we do from lovingness, commitment to our inner 'beingness' and that of others, raising of consciousness and all work that opened the heart was moreover, an added strengthener to the whole planet as well as a joy to those in the Dimensions.

Knowing this added something extra to my wondrous contact with them all. It would be so good if this was in the conscious awareness of people generally then they would understand how important being loving is to everyone on the planet, for we are one with the Universe in its entirety.

'....our guidance is with you always, for you are our precious charge and all that is helpful and *good* strengthens us.' How enlightening and good that is.

'....we are all one with the earth and its energy and our purpose is to bring the spiritual energy into balance with it for the benefit of all. The energy of the physical is precious and necessary for the experiences of the spiritual Dimensions - the reciprocity of development and experience are part of the 'regenerative' process of that upon the Earth for the rebirth of all living things – so it is for the spiritual Dimensions for their 'beingness' is nourished by knowledge and this comes from the experience of the physical – thus we are one in our regeneration and nourish one another.'

It would also be good for people to know that they too are guided and loved at all times. The love within the heart and the innermost understandings people have innately, are all one with their own Guide or even Guides who are part of the inner voice that is the Soul. They each have their own inner link to the Oneness of the cosmic Beings and the pure love of God. No one is alone.

Sadly, so many feel and fear that. In a secular unbelieving world this is hard, if not impossible for many to encompass. In many people's minds, it is all attached to religious dogma and doctrine and rejected as a result.

~.~

Happily, there are ever-increasing numbers of people connecting to their inner being and growing in understanding.

There are amazing people writing and speaking publicly about all the wonderful aspects of the cosmic Dimensions and God, quite outside the boundaries of institutional religion. I have only learned of them in the past few years thanks to being 'introduced' to such inspirational people as Bruce Lipton, Gregg Braden and Esther Hicks through my friend Sheila's DVD's.

She knew I was staying clear of the esoteric knowledge of others whose books she had, so this was well after I'd written my book and it was in the last stages of being published.

I have since learned that the internet has given people access to these interesting people and all the incredible information and experiences they have and the cosmic knowledge they have acquired.

I had access to the internet only a few years ago, but only recently discovered YouTube and the videos there of incredible channellers who make their work and abilities known there for all to see.

I was so heartened to find that there are so many of these Lightworkers happy to show this to the world. This did encourage me eventually to believe I could write *this* book without being thought I'd lost the plot. 'Hearing voices' has always been considered a sign of lunacy or at the least attention-seeking and allied to hysteria. Many such beliefs are fully entrenched to this day. Yes, there is a certain amount of acceptance but on the other hand, there is plenty of patent disbelief and being looked at askance. So, I have been most reluctant to be known publicly as clairaudient.

I digressed again!

But before all these more recent discoveries of mine on Lightworkers, I was tootling along in my somewhat small and private world albeit incredibly broadened and enriched by my clairaudience and satisfied by my writing and whatever healing work came my way.

On the practical level, I had been finishing off the illustrations that I felt were important to the book. The subjects I selected were merely to clarify and aid what I had written about of both the organic and chakra side of the work. Any more were unnecessary. There were fully illustrated books aplenty on anatomy for those who would need them.

It had taken a little while to get the title right but eventually it evolved into *'Essential Connections, the How & Why of Your Personal Energy.'* as that was exactly what it had developed into. I had also been making submissions to literary agents and publishers.

Needless to say, I approached quite a few. The instant query was always, *'Have you been published before?'* This, and that they didn't handle unpublished authors or their quota for new authors was full was a constant.

I knew about 'genres' in the publishing world but eventually I discovered alas that mine fell between two. It fitted neither the scientific anatomical sphere or the spiritual, esoteric, or metaphysical, despite being much to do with metaphysics and love.

Mine didn't fit, so I presume they thought it too risky for investment. Moreover, the cohesive subject that had emerged in my book was, as far as I knew, not currently a subject in itself. I presumed there was no genre for that either. It took me a few years to fully realise this important fact.

It proved to be a costly and time-wasting exercise alas. I seemed to be getting nowhere. Being patient was tougher than staying positive. I cared very much about both the rejections and the futility!

Naturally my dear Guides were reassuring me and full of loving wisdom. I, of all people was all too well aware by now of the pulling power of negative energy so I should know that staying positive about my book and holding to my belief in the importance of my subject was essential.

'...negative thoughts darken and distort perception. Clarity lies behind negative energy which shuts out the light to prevent clarity entering to conscious awareness and coming into being.' was well-known to me!

It was not hard to realise that negative energy's endeavour is to get you to give it mastery over you. Positive energy is the enabler but isn't it easy to think and believe negatively? But certainly, I was aware that when it is stuck in the subconscious it means that the psyche controls *you*. Illusion and delusion become believable. Doubt and shifting levels of frustration kept rearing their heads so I had to stay on my toes with my releasing techniques on myself.

'.....remain calm and still within where love and 'being' are to comfort you and provide balm for the little wounds of life so that they go quickly.'

'.....keep the concept clear dear friend and disallow all doubt and questions – intention is the key and that has already taken form dear Felicity.....stay with the intention and leave the details to manifest as occasion requires – in this way doubt and questions will be unnecessary. Leave those to God.'

'....the unknown is shrouded in shadow dear one – the light of clarity and knowledge resides in the now – to seek shadows is to find shadows only and possibly illusion and imagined shapes. ....the path is only strewn with the stones and boulders of our own making.'

And don't we all seek shadows. And expect them too!

~.~

Throughout all this 'to-ing and fro-ing and submissions of my 'manuscript', I was continuing my healing work. Most of the time I was of course including the visualisation methods. These were well developed and had become honed the more I had worked with them.

That they proved to be effective in combination with the Rei-ki channelling was definitely through the affinity of working with the Guides who could read everything so clearly and communicated with me so precisely. This ensured quite thorough clearing of areas of emotional and/or physical pain. I really loved this work.

This mental affinity with the dear Dimensional Beings during the healing, the sweetness of channelling the loving Rei-ki energy together was a joy. And kept me focussed.

Also, there was always something new, some subtlety to learn of and from a healing. Human Nature is fascinating. I'd add these in to my book, expanding on paragraphs here and there. There seemed to be always something new to learn from life's constantly unfolding experiences too.

I cheered myself when these 'extras' came up by hoping that *that* was why things seemed to be being delayed! Hadn't my Guides frequently reminded me that 'Timing was everything'?

But my book was however, written if not another word was added. I so wanted it published.

Then came several promptings and urgings, and dear Sheila naturally was the keenest, to write *another* book.

I took some convincing! I'd written my book on the body, hadn't I? There wasn't anything more I could write about, surely? And that one was still going nowhere!

But the thought intrigued as I really missed the challenge of writing. All this waiting had created a void again.

It took a while for the penny to drop. Ah! This could be on the rest of the body's systems. I already had all the necessary books at hand to delve into.

It would entail a whole lot more enjoyable study of course which promised to be quite a lengthy process. And there was a great deal to each system. Each one might be complete in itself but couldn't be studied in isolation - everything being connected!

There would then be all the associated and interpenetrative metaphysics to discover from the function and processes. There was a *lot* of work ahead. This could be the mental occupation I was needing to take my mind off the stasis of '*Essential Connections.*'

~.~

I was getting gradually into these studies however, and especially the writing up of notes, when I realised that a book on the systems, naturally in my chosen mode in order to have relevance, would be impossible.

It could not evolve as a separate book. There was too much cross-referencing needed because the energy system, described so completely in the first was irrevocably part of any and all other aspects of the body.

Not only that, separation defeated the whole essential concept of connectedness.

The other systems could not be separated from the core of the body or the chakra energy system through which they ran.

The best thing therefore was simply to create a whole new section for them to insert into the first book. This would make cross-checking easy. And I already had all the design, formatting and graphics to work with.

All these systems were quite complex of course. as each incorporated several organs and several chakras throughout the course of their functions. The interpretation, therefore was going to need a somewhat different presentation too. Naturally more illustrations would be needed as well.

In effect, this would create an 'advanced' version. Thus, one book of the Energy System itself, while the new version of the *whole* body would become my 'second book'; an extended book for more advanced healers, or even teachers.

Well, it would certainly give me something to get my teeth into meanwhile. I felt purposeful again.

Working out how it was to be inserted into my first book's pdf was for a much later date!

Of course, I was fitting all this into the various events and ramifications of everyday life, family and friends so the work in fact became rather piecemeal.

As always, thank goodness, I was well supported and encouraged by my lovely Guides and the dear ones of the network.

'Your heart vibration gave us joy dear dear one and will have its effect for the project.'

Khatumi was obviously keen on my efforts.

'....yes dear friend and helper of the network, it is Khatumi here. Remain focussed on the work you are doing dear friend. Believe in its purpose - the vibration is strong and gathering momentum.......your focus of positive belief and feelings of love for the purpose are great enablers – the network is always strengthened by such love and passionate commitment. This is always received with delight. The new work you are doing is giving us joy and our love is with you at all times.....yes Science plays its part too because it opens Men's minds to possibilities .....expansion of consciousness is essential dear friend and all things that enable that, are precious to Man's development.'

So, my 'extended' book, although in its infancy as yet, was under way and I had a lot of interesting work ahead of me whatever the outcome.

Chapter 28

Then in the July of 2008, another big change came into my life. No right-angled turn. This time it was a shock and an unhappy one.

I was, in fact, out one evening with a friend for a meal together at a restaurant. I was right in the middle of eating it, when suddenly I had a strange sensation on the top of my head. Much to my astonishment, I 'perceived' a broad beam of 'light' pouring into my crown chakra. This gradually became concentrated into a thin brighter 'light.' It took a few moments and was a very odd experience in the middle of a meal!

Luckily the friend I was with was also interested in the world of spiritual healing and actually knew more of esoterics than I did. Which was in fact, very apt at that moment.

Naturally she had seen me pause and my bemused expression. I was very puzzled as you can imagine so I was glad to be able to tell her what had just happened.

'Oh,' she said, quite prosaically, 'your Guides have just become ensouled.'

To say that I was utterly taken aback was an understatement. What on earth did she mean, I asked? I'd never heard of such a thing and I certainly didn't like the sound of it.

She told me that this had happened to that same lady who had recognised the Rei-ki energy in my hands. Her Guides had become ensouled also, hence my friend knew what had occurred. She explained that there is a point when their work is done and since they are a part of one's Soul template and have chosen this task of guidance, they then return to one's template to guide from within.

I was stunned! I didn't know how to take this.

On one level, it was extraordinary and quite outside of my understanding so far. On the other, to 'lose' my Guides....? I could scarcely believe it. She then told me how distressing it had been for her healer friend. I could well believe that. It was so odd that I was in fact, only half-believing the explanation, so continued with my meal and our evening out.

When I got home, the first thing I did was get out my notebook and 'listened.'

Nothing.

Perhaps I was tired or my brain shocked so the channel was unclear. Any explanation rather than nothing, no gentle voices! I went to bed, still in hopes that this had not happened, that I *would* hear them the next day.

The next day was full of silence.

I felt empty - bereft – as if I'd lost the dearest friends in all the world. They knew me, I didn't have to explain any part of myself to them. There was never a judgement or a criticism only a deep abiding unconditional love that I had tangible links to. What was I going to do without them to talk to?

I felt their absence acutely. Had I lost the gift of clairaudience too? Had I not been spiritually diligent enough? Had I been too involved in the ordinarinesses of life? Was I no longer worthy? There was a terrible void when I tried to listen. I was like a child in my agitation and sense of abandonment.

But they had been such a rich and constant part of my days. I 'spoke' with them and took down all they said on practically a daily basis for years.

But if they had really gone from my life at least I had some consolation; I still had all they had said to me, all their loving guidance, their sweet words of wisdom, reassurance and comfort. I could re-read their loving words. At least they would be with me that way. But what was I going to do now? I felt so sad.

But why just a void with no explanation? Then the realisation seeped into my dithering brain that it was my desolation, fear of and sense of failure that had created the void. I'd allowed *myself* to close me off by my mental gyrations! What a perfect exercise in futility.

It was the huge contrast as much as anything that had thrown me off my axis. I was deeply saddened, but I owed it to all their encouragement to disenable this negativity in order to pull myself together and face up to this. I *had* to face it. I had no idea what was going to happen now.

Having calmed myself a little, I had the bright, though somewhat belated idea, of asking my Guardian Angel.

So, I dowsed her with my crystal pendulum, and asked if I had indeed lost the gift of Clairaudience. The reply was an unequivocal 'No'. What a relief! I commented that I had been in rather an unnecessary panic. 'Yes!' came the reply with a very strong swing of the pendulum.

I also asked if my Guides had in fact become 'ensouled.' Again, the reply was 'Yes.' Now at least I knew for certain. I was full of questions but they required answers that were more than Yes and No so I had to be content for the moment. At least I had my Guardian Angel's presence and as always thanked her for her abiding presence, love and help.

In order to get rid of those blocks I had put up in my panic I knew I had to do some tie-cutting and quickly. So, I set about doing just that. I had to be prepared for what was coming next. 'Trust and believe' Samuel always used to say. So, trust and belief I had to have.

The following day I was out in my car on the way to a healing session. I was a little early and as I got there, I felt that 'nudge' I usually got when I knew my Guides had something they wished to talk with me about. Hardly daring to hope I pulled in a little way from the house and got out my book and pen.

Deep, deep joy! A voice came to me. It was Sophie, my lovely Parisienne friend. The relief was stunning! You can have no idea how happy it made me to hear her voice, indeed, to 'hear' again.

'Quelle problem my little chicken! It is Sophie here, all is good chere amie, - your Guides are now a part of your Soul and its consciousness - because you have developed your Soul-level ma chere – it is a *good* thing for you even though you are perplexed by all this – we know how you care Cherie – we can always speak with you if we are not busily engaged to tell you of what is happening – we have heard your perplexité and understand for you. The network are all filled with much happiness that you have made the transition so refrain from sad thoughts and know that if we need to speak with you we will do so with much pleasure. Yes Cherie because we are the Guides of others but when nessessaire we will always be able to speak with you. The connection to this plane will remain with you dear friend, nevair fear. It is good and sometimes we need a channel too. All is good eh? You are making *progress* ma Cherie. You have worked hard and are so willing. All is understood. Yes. I must go to my precious charge. We love you.'

As you can imagine my heart lifted several feet at dear Sophie's words. Ah! Their dear wisdom in coming to reassure me before I began my healing session! I was able to continue on in a much better state of mind. Focussing on the healing channel before commencing the session then came blessedly, very easily.

Of course, as soon as I got home, I sat down with notebook and pen and with a wonderful relief flooding over me, I heard Khatumi's dear voice.

'Yes dear Felicity, it is Khatumi here. We have been closely connected with you at all times – those of the network send love and blessings to you. Thank you for the joy you bring to our vibration – you have been most thorough in disabling any negative energy through your Soul-level and that of others. This is a great strengthener for us all – the celestial alignments are having strong effects on the planet to move it forward for the purpose – you play your part with your work and your healing and your insights – that is why I am here to bring comfort to you dear Felicity for it has been a perplexing time for you but be assured all is *good* and the path ahead will lead you to much light and love. The Masters and the network will give you help and love for all things and continue to guide you for the purpose you have been chosen for. We work at a different dimension for this because your beloved Guides have re-entered your Soul level to raise your vibration for the work ahead………you have a part to play for others who are ready to move on and also – yes – those whose Will holds them until a small shift is required by the Dimensions for them – you play this part as do many others who are the Lightworkers sent to help in the development of the planet's energy and vibration. Only experience of the Will by the personality in 'Will' situations can make good use of personality-level shifts – yes dear Felicity you are grasping what has been required – now the shift to this new level is a different phase which we will all guide you through. Make good use of your Guides' energy that has unified with your own Soul energy. We will talk of this deep subject when you are ready so think on these things and be comforted by us and our love - growing strong through love and the Divine Will is the task at hand. All is well and your love and joy will be passed on in the Singing Time. Rejoice in the Oneness with your Guides dear Felicity and strengthen the centre of your being with this knowing and the love of the Universe, the Masters and the blessed love of God. We will speak again soon dear Felicity– work well you are loved.'

You can imagine the relief and the feeling of joy I had at these words. Khatumi had come to comfort me; how beautiful. And I certainly was. The world was properly back on its axis again.

I was much taken with the fact of being sent help to comfort me. Something clicked in my mind. It went back to my very distant Latin lessons at school. Of course! Comfort – *con forté*. It meant '*with strength*'. How wonderfully appropriate. This was no 'there, there dear, everything's fine.' They were giving me strength to strengthen myself with. The word 'console' came to me too. That was obviously '*con *solé*', '*with light*', or enlightenment. I was immensely cheered at the essence of these words because they held real meaning for me. Perhaps this understanding was prompted from 'within'? Or dear Khatumi. It was so apt.

Here it is beautifully expressed as usual by these dear ones.

'…..we love to talk with you and warm your heart - it is a sweet exchange within the mind that we can share with you. This is good, for we have to work on the ether for the inner thinking of those we have under our care - so it is good that we can express love and happiness with you. Yes, the Oneness in the inner being and yes the mind also which is good for we are heard…….we all wish to encourage this to make life happier and strengthen the Love vibration we all live within on the network.'

I was so happy that I still had this wonderful inner connectedness with the wonderful Beings in the Dimensions. I was indeed comforted and consoled. I lost that abandoned feeling that made me feel so childish. But I missed them, my lovely dear Guides, my friends of the mind and Soul. It was going to take some getting used to a new reality, that they were a part of my inner voice now.

I had to give serious thought to the fact that my lovely Guides became ensouled at *this* point in my life. This indicated that their task was now completed. The only 'task' I had been involved in was discovering a new perspective on the body and writing a book on it. That the book was written, complete and ready for publication seemed to be that 'completed' task.

There might have been the odd typo to correct but it *was* written. All that was left was to get it into print.

There was no doubt at all that the book could *only* have been written, and in the way it was, *because* of the mental journey I took with my beloved Guides: it was the inner world of dimensional vibrational knowledge that connected and enlightened my studies. My changed perspective on the body with the whole world of our energy system came about only because they opened my mind to metaphysics.

Even all the metaphysics for the new book project was connected with all they had guided me to and taught me already. It even all fitted with the systems I was now covering. I was properly launched into this extended version now. That was in a way accomplished from their point of view. It would just follow a natural progression by its very subject and nature.

So, I presume that apart from what they could now impart to me through the inner, their presence on the mental plane was 'needed' for it no longer.

'Yes, Khatumi, - yes, the books are part of the purpose dear friend – your interest in writing, the skills you acquired through your University studies were all chosen as preparation – did you not find the writing easy? All threads were woven together for the purpose dear. Yes, - prompting you in the right direction, yes, then once on the path you carried all with you for the purpose of discovering and revealing the love within the body physical.'

It behoved me then to keep trying to get published. Try, try, try again. Having that task ahead of me helped, but I was still saddened and quite perplexed by their going.

Recalling this now, another realisation has come to me. I can now see the significance of the date, 2008: exactly the 'octave' from their coming into my consciousness. How apt! The octave is completion of course. Completion and a beginning of a new phase of what was required of me. I wish I had grasped that then, but I was deeply fortunate to gain strength and light from the beloved Dimensions to give me fresh heart.

The next time I felt that nudge to hear from the Dimensions another dear one came to help me. Her name was Martha and she was a blessed additional voice come to help me stay focussed and work properly on myself for what lay ahead.

'....for there is a great need that many have been called to answer. Your vibration must be kept high and bright so use all positivity and lovingness in every way to sustain it dear Felicity. We will help all that we can.......but know that your ensouled Guides and yourself are one and in serving yourself you serve them also and encompass that unity fully.......all strength is needed and helps all things – yes dear, the strength of lovingness...use it for yourself - imbue all that you do with it and it will be your strength and comforter for we are all within it – the Masters also who watch over all. yes dear it is an enabler for oneness of the Earthly Plane with our Dimensions which are to help Man to his development and evolution towards the Divine. Lightworkers who work with the loving lovingness create a network of love to encompass Man in his struggles with the Will and the dark side. All who play their part in that sustain it for all and strengthen it for all – it is this that moves Man and the planet on and this era is a new phase in that evolution.....so that ordinary people can move forward which is so necessary to the planet and the Dimensions as the vibration is raised.....Lightworkers are re-inforcing those who have chosen to look. Love is strength and God's loving arms enfold you and sustain you. All is *good* - love and blessings Felicity.'

I was, and felt, so blessed to be under the care of dear Khatumi and Martha. The whole 'network' was there too and frequently added their collective voice whenever I took up pen and notebook. They helped clarify, re-assure or advise me on whatever was needful and helpful about current things, 'keeping my vibration high and bright,' the progress achieved in healing sessions, use of seasonal energies and affirmation of insights.

'.....doubts do indeed create a barrier – fear has a strong vibration dear - it simply inhibits the light that *is*. Having the light in view is good for harmony and balance within – indeed. It is an illusion stimulated by the dark side into resembling reality. Knowing dispels fear, loving and trusting dispel fear. These are the tools. Only their negative energy shields them (**all men**) from the light and love that is there for them at all times.'

It was rather like talking things over with friends and at the same time being touched within by their lovingness, sweetness and total understanding. And of course, there was always some new viewpoint or some path to explore with them, especially with Khatumi.

'Indeed - thus Man learns of the Will which is his task as we have discussed dear Felicity. it is through this that the experiences created temper Man's spirit to discover the goodness within through courage, compassion, aspiration, acknowledging others, perception at a deep level of understanding. In this way he discovers his unity with Man and the Universe and God at Soul level and raises the Earthly Plane vibration in so doing. Good connection dear friend indeed – the level of survival as singular drive creates a strong vibration and continues at plant/animal level which joins with Man's instinctive survival vibration held by the Will/Ego. However due to Man's 'goodness' and compassion the vibration has been raised and because of the link to the animal level, that is raised also. Yes their (plants & animals) purpose is the physical survival of the planet and the raised vibration will and does to some degree create the vibration of interaction and unity so that there is no separation - indeed Man needs to develop past the 'them' and 'us' thinking into 'we' of the planet so that the vibration is one of love and honouring all that is good and true for the beingness of the planet.'

We spoke then of the connectedness, the connection with *all* creation. Naturally this got into deep waters.

'.....answers will come as needful - the infinity is beyond Man's thinking – yes glimpses because Man requires 'form' – the need to shape the thinking, yes dear! - your search for understanding is good for you seek the truth.'

Family, friends and healing commitments made time speed along with my clairaudience like a bright light enhancing my daily life. Then not long after the summer solstice I was having strange surges in my heart chakra. While I was wondering what if anything was wrong with me, The Master of the Third degree came to speak with me.

'Your vibration is being refined further dear Felicity. It is the quality that is changing slightly but the channel itself feels the change and your physical body hasn't adapted yet. The Angels of healing are making sure your system is fully able to receive the rise in the vibration in the heart chakra as that is the one being most stimulated by it. Yes it was responding in preparation for the change – it is because of the continual work you do to disenable negative energy – yes, expansion and stimulation was needed before their assimilation dear Felicity- their healing vibration was added to yours as they became one with your Soul vibration……..once it is ready we will come and talk with you further on this. Go with God's loving energy to strengthen and comfort you.'

It was a rather strange sensation but when I knew that it was as a result of my beautiful Guides becoming ensouled I felt quite reassured; my heart was in good order!

That aspect of them becoming part of my Soul-template had not crossed my mind. It was quite a humbling thought. It transpired that this meant I was connected to a very high healing dimension now. Zadriel was of course still bringing his gentle Angelic vibration to adapt it for human compatibility during healing sessions.

Over the next eighteen months, in between everything else, I was enjoying studying, collating and writing as I continued on my quest of the body's systems and especially the metaphysical interpretation for them. It did, however, fall by the wayside from time to time I have to admit. The non-event for *'Essential Connections'* rather slowed my momentum for this extended version. It sometimes felt pointless.

'…..losing intention becomes stored in the body and encourages that inertness that your mind wishes to overcome. It holds the Will in stasis so that it ceases to work for the 'doing' you are feeling the lack of - get into the stride of 'doing' dear and the vibration you are on will accelerate –

this will strengthen it and of good use to us who wish to help you. Yes dear, the law of reciprocity. God's strong loving arms keep you safe dear friend. We are happy that you ask for strength from us.'

It was mostly their wise and loving advice that put me back to work when I got a bit discouraged.

'…..all insecurities will create negative energy dear – all illusory because you are safe and protected and naturally supported by the network itself and God's loving arms. It is a natural psychological reaction dear friend so refrain from self-criticism and release the last vibrational link so that you can move into the momentum created by your 'project'.'

I was very lucky indeed to have such loving encouragement and support. I was also making my visits to the Temple now and then too, especially at the Equinox and Solstice as there were very potent times. I always had a task to perform on these visits.

Chapter 29

Then I had a bit of a delay to my daily life - with a fall that produced 2 little cracks in the neck of my right femur. For safety's sake it was pinned to prevent it breaking and I was off my leg for some time. I followed the surgeon's instructions very carefully! I was on one leg for six weeks for a start! Heigh-ho I thought. There's a surprise. So, all those years of seemingly fruitless endeavour and my precious book not 'going forward' was now strikingly manifested in my leg!

And the Right side, the masculine side of action and intention. My leg was definitely saying that I was cheesed off that nothing was happening.

I hardly needed reminding that, 'all things that need to enter the consciousness manifest in the physical.' So, I had some work to do looking for all those little attachments hidden in my psyche still! Hardly surprising given the number of years of failure to launch my book. As a friend once said, 'carry on clearing!'

Of course, once recovered from the effects of the anaesthetic, I was channelling Rei-ki into my incision and hip.

When I went to be assessed for the removal of the clips, it was remarked how beautifully and quickly it had healed! Ditto when they x-rayed me at intervals. I felt it best to keep my 'healing' to myself!

But I made good use of my enforced limited activity to proceed with my new 'book'. Imagine my amusement when I realised that I had actually reached the place in my work where the next chapter was to be on the Skeletal system! Don't you love metaphysics?

It proved to be engrossing. I discovered how little I actually knew about bones and was amazed at what I learned. The brain was fizzing again!

The metaphysical interpretation was fascinating too so it was all *very* satisfying. Just what I needed while I waited out the healing process. Synchronicity at its best!

Naturally my Dear Ones were happy that I was back to tackling my concepts on the systems with renewed enthusiasm. Then when I was writing on the interpretation for the joints, dear Jalal came to speak with me, interested as always in what the anatomy of the body told me.

'Yes dear friend, it is I Jalal come to speak with you I am interested in your work on the joints and the emotions that sit there. We don't carry fear as the Western people do – yes indeed it has been used as a spiritual weapon which is why it is deep in your psyche in the West. – we have a philosophy of the spirit as our guide to spiritual matters so we are much looser in the pelvis and limbs because of it.....experiences on the Earth Plane have many complexities because of the emotions we have with them. Yes indeed! Very interesting! Another connection you are making!'

Knowing of their interest, their enthusiasm and support was so cheering and made me feel that it really was a worthwhile endeavour.

I was still on crutches but able to walk on two feet when I was called in to the hospital to have the pins removed.

So, some more weeks of footery activity and those crutches. In all they kept me going for four months. But nothing is wasted. I had the best view of life for anyone on them; I was temporarily one of the 'disabled.' So, I found out personally what that was like.

I was surprised to find myself strangely invisible when out and about! It was a real eye-opener. But learning never seemed to cease. I even discovered how ingenious I could be around the flat. And a backpack carried my groceries very well indeed.

But I was happy to have got my enthusiasm back for my writing. I was really pleased at how much I had got done. There was still some rounding off to do but God wastes nothing, that's a certainty.

Although I still missed my dear Guides every now and then I had long accepted this change because it did mean that spiritually there was progress. Khatumi could always untangle my thoughts.

'.....we are with you in this valuable purpose. Our love for you is very strong and we are also filled with joy that your intent is now firm once again. Stay connected with us dear and we will help you – your Guides are part of your inner being - yes your Soul template dear and their voices are your inner voice now - Their wisdom is one with you and the Divine Essence.'

~.~

It so happened that in 2010 the news was occupied by those massive Icelandic volcanic eruptions that had affected so much air travel, (I was due to fly to Scotland).

This was very close to home and, coupled with other serious natural disasters of late, I wondered whether this was all of a piece with the prevalent upheavals of violence and disruption occurring globally between peoples. How could one not be concerned? How to fit this with the lovingness within? When I was connecting with the dear ones in the Dimensions, Khatumi came to the fore,

'We hear your questions and understand your perplexities. All is well. Man has many levels of development to go through to achieve the full connection to the Divine – that is with no Will or Ego connection with the Earth Plane and to dwell there in Divine Unity as he once did. Man is on the threshold of a new era towards the level of Universal consciousness which is also to comprehend the Divine of the Earth Plane and the earthly planet itself. There are those who have chosen to make this their life-path in order to aid Man towards realization and development within himself. The Earth is awakening to show itself to Man so that he begins to alter his thinking, needs, demands and expectations of the benefits he has become so attached to in this modern era. God and the Great Ones all have great patience for Man, knowing that it will be slow within the linear frame that governs the Earthly Plane..........there is much powerful work being done already dear Felicity which is enabling and strengthening the vibration that Man needs towards change.....there are many aeons of work and development for Man to achieve that part he plays in the Divine Plan.........Balance and harmony are the Laws of Nature and God has chosen Man to understand Will through Free Will therefore cataclysm would be a poor answer to Man's needs for God's Plan to come fully into being. It is for the 'unknowing' to become the 'knowing' ones. Then Man can dwell in love harmony and peace through knowledge of all things good. There is a long road ahead for Man towards the 'knowing' and dwelling in goodness. Man learns through adversity and there will be many Human Beings who will learn this way! They will all require circumstances for the experiences they need dear Felicity.'

'.....Each Soul makes its proper journey and any side roads, yes a good word – are used by God for part of the purpose also and always the Soul directs the Being back to the correct way forward. Thus Free Will plays its part for the 'knowing' dear/dear Felicity. It is this unpredictability that enriches the experiences toward the 'knowing' for the Dimensions as well as God who knows all but needs the 'knowing to be 'known.'

Oh! the wisdom of God.

Writing this out for you dear reader I hope reinforces the hope we all need in order to cope with the vicissitudes in our world.

~.~

There was much going on in my life and by this time I had discovered another symbol at the Soul point half way between my throat and heart chakras. I had become quite adept at activating all eight when I aligned them all to keep my own energy flowing as well as any healing that came my way.

Soon after finding the eighth, I 'knew' that I had to draw out and connect the energy from the energy field of each symbol to a certain point either side of me. They were now fully-fledged octahedrons as far as I could judge so I perceived them now as that shape. And of course, many lovely 'talks' with my dear Khatumi, Martha and the network were filling up my notebooks.

The endeavour to get my first book towards publishing was of course a background to it all. Life seemed to be cantering along nevertheless.

One day when we were talking about purpose, for I suspect I was rather doubting mine due to the non-event as I saw it for my book, Khatumi said,

'....each purpose fulfilled enables the next for Mankind and his evolvement towards the Divine. Each Plane has its purpose and place in the Divine Plan thus the Earth Plane is part of that evolvement – yes, the physical 'beingness' – only through the physical can the emotional be experienced because emotions are stimulated by the senses. That is why there is no emotion in the etheric planes and outer dimensions dear Felicity– what is used by the dark side is the negative response and manipulation of the negative in Man. There is no emotion involved. We experience the energy of love because it 'is' and that is naturally exchanged with the love within all beings. Ours is untouched by emotion and negativity which is why we function without emotional pain. It would not be possible otherwise. – we can 'see' all dark energy. We do not receive it. Our purpose is to help reduce dark energy so that the golden energy of Love is experienced by Man – indeed. When man contributes we are filled with joy which is an expansion of love – indeed. That expands our energy dear Felicity– this is what strengthens us. Yes. this is how we function and the vibration passes through the whole network to all. Let this be a conscious part of your function dear Felicity for it will sustain you in that we receive joy and it is sung of in the Singing Time.'

For a 'talking to', one cannot fault this for love and sweetness.

One evening some months later, preparing to visit the Temple, I was activating my symbols and found that now they were more complex. Within each plane of each symbol was now another triangle. This completely changed the shape in the process. I had not been 'building' them since the early work created the octahedron so I was surprised. Naturally I asked Khatumi about this.

'Yes, dear friend, eight were inserted into your chakras and yes, your development of them was essential to build them gradually so that your system could cope with their vibration, only as your system-clearing progressed were you able to carry all eight at their full development – yes we do dear friend, when you bring them into consciousness we recognise their heightened vibration and work through them for you. These were your healing symbols that were held for you until the correct time for your personality Felicity.

Thus, I had plenty to do working with them all and much to keep in conscious awareness for the network and the work I was doing.

But by 2011 I was *still* no nearer getting my book published. Somehow or another I had not hit the right note. It seemed to be a wide sea with no markers and I was just bobbing about treading water looking for one. After all this protracted effort to get a mainstream publisher interested in it, I was becoming quite despondent, despite my efforts to remain positive. It was hard not to feel it was never going to happen.

Meanwhile my lovely daughter came over on a visit with my grandson from Australia. She then told me that she had been attuned to Rei-ki and was in fact now a Rei-ki Master. She had wanted to keep it as a surprise until she had actually achieved Rei-ki Master level.

I was so pleased. It did indeed come as a surprise. I had no inkling that she had reached this point in her life. That she had, was beautiful.

While over here and getting in touch with other spiritual people and communities she was then attuned to a new energy healing vibration called Rahanni. This was attuned to the 5th dimension of healing and the Pink Ray. The way it is channelled and the method of Guidance is different, but it is naturally a beautiful healing energy.

My daughter really took to this and was keen that I be attuned too. I was I admit, reluctant. Rei-ki held my loyalty as it had chosen me so to speak. She was returning to Australia then so I was able to defer it. In any case she wanted to be the one to attune me herself.

As a result, my lovely daughter had much interesting work before her as she was very keen to teach this as well as use it in healing practice. I was very happy for her as she seemed to have come into her own in this new way of life that was opening up for her.

However, so many years having rolled past, getting my precious book out into the public domain was now getting to be an imperative: I had no wish to waste all my work and effort or my beloved Guides' work, by just giving up.

Moreover, despite the delays I still firmly believed that my book really mattered. Ja-San had once told me that ears had to be attuned in order to listen. Perhaps the waiting meant I was waiting for the eyes to be ready to read and the minds needing to accept what I had to say.

Someone had once suggested Self-publishing but up till then it was known, somewhat scathingly, as 'Vanity Press.'

For over a year I had dithered about with the idea unsure of the validity, the cost, the whole business in fact. Far nicer I thought to have a publishing house do all that and sort out the finer details with their expertise and back you with their reputation.

So, I dithered! But rising costs in the publishing world were now beginning to make it a viable option. It was not long before it had become increasingly the way forward for many writers.

Now that this method had lost most of its criticism, I made up my mind. Self-publish and be damned, I thought! Furthermore, I felt I didn't have any other choice now. That decided, unsurprisingly, it didn't take long to find a really good firm with very reasonable costs. At last, I was doing something!

It proved to be a very constructive move and went smoothly forward. There were a few workings out regard colour and correcting some errors and typos but it was soon all set., My clever friend Kim, had even designed a wonderful cover.

Wonder of wonders! In 2012 it was with the British Library in the five major UK cities and on the internet with several companies. It was out there at long, long last! Grin on face was huge!

Within weeks I arranged a little private book-signing/book launch party for my family and friends to celebrate this momentous happening. It was so good to see it actually in my hands, real and substantial and it looked just splendid. I was so proud and delighted and it was such fun signing all the books everyone brought. Without a doubt it was all being sung of in the Singing Time too.

Chapter 30

Woven through all these moves to launch my book were my lovely enlightening conversations with the beloved friends in the Dimensions. One autumn evening when I got out my current notebook Khatumi's dear voice came to me.

'Yes dear friend, I Khatumi am here and full of joy to be one with your thinking. This is a good concept. – yes dear friend it is to do with the structure of the network and the vibrations created by Man's thinking are of a different calibre to those of the actions of animals and Man – the living essence vibration from all that exchanges gases to exist is also of a different substance - all are visible to the Dimensions dear friend, yes. – thus we are able to ascertain the condition of the planet at all times. Many many Beings see these assessments and the Councils keep all informed of what is necessary for the well-being of God's Creation. Yes this is *good* thinking. Naturally the nature and quality of the vibrational network from Man's thinking will be in reciprocity with the vibrational influences of all celestial bodies. All changes, progress and development of Man will be interactive with these external vibrations so Man will be influenced accordingly. -The nature of Man's Will and Ego and the development and use of these will also play their part of course. – indeed. Whatever the collective thinking of Man's stages yes – 'Ages' (ie Piscean) is *good* – it will either respond or react accordingly – it was a *good* concept – this is exciting thinking for you! We are filled with joy when the light grows within you, (changes and fluctuations?) yes indeed.- ....'

'We impart as much as we can to the hearts and minds of Man who fulfils God's wishes *through* the Will and Ego. – yes indeed. Used well these elements move Man forward in experience which in turn gives 'knowing' to aid Man's Will and

Ego – yes it does swing dear friend in an eliptical way indeed! Yes, forward for progress and back against himself, - but this in turn dear friend – when enough pressure is exerted gives impetus for forward motion again – (energy force) yes indeed dear friend because the Earth Plane exists under gravity as all mass/celestial bodies do. Indeed - polarity also which you have explored in your mind.'

At all times they gave such enlightenment to the way for Man and the paths we tread or follow on this complex Earth Plane.

'…..the path for Man has many stones, rocks and obstacles so that he learns thoroughly all that is needed - these are not negative aspects dear one merely the way to learn all, yes, facets of each aspect of the Will and the Will of God-yes-yes—every hindrance is a positive because learning comes from everyone. …the learning has to be complete rather than skipped over-yes….will and ego need linear time to work out their purpose-yes-that is to learn all in order to reveal the beauty and truth of Love.'

We revelled in this kind of mutual mind exploring. Often the subject connected up with what was occurring as in a few days later after a particularly powerful meditation where I had to perform a task with collective consciousness on global energy.

'Yes Man will move forward. It is the Law of Nature that God in his wisdom and Love has set in motion for the Earthly Plane. – Indeed his Will and Ego is essential for good progress – yes it is his unconsciousness and negative Will/Ego that is the brake to all progress but the dear God has this all in his Love and compass for all things are for the purpose – yes it will always act as an impetus dear Felicity. The Law is forward motion and no brake will hold that back, merely create a build-up of energy to enable the next move to occur – excellent connection dear Felicity! yes indeed All is in microcosm of the macrocosm dear – yes just as your 'Blood' concept is also. All things are of God and his loving wishes, indeed the 'principle' is the reality as it is in all things.'

'…..fear inhibits Man if allowed to be nourished against the self – yes invisible barriers to the goodness and Love of the Universe. Each thought is a vibrational thread that entangles itself to form a strong bond that is holding all in place. This is the Ego used negatively dear friend – the dark ones waste nothing. Yes - They work hardest against those who work with us and for the purpose. Energy for forward development has been accelerating and has been full of disruptions due to the dissolution of those aspects for Humankind that are being prepared for change.'

It was always wonderfully reassuring to know that the dimensional networks and Beings were so closely involved and working for us with such diligence and loving commitment. Also, that everything was being made perfect use of for our time on this plane.

It is good to know that no matter how complicated we make things for ourselves all the little facets of these 'creations' are important to our progress as individuals as well as Mankind.

Knowing that mistakes, wrong turnings, follies and general all-round bad and appalling behaviour on Earth are all made use of for knowledge and understanding through all the planes including our own, does, to some degree, make bearable what we discover about ourselves and what we are capable of negatively.

'The purpose is to learn all in order to reveal the beauty and truth of love – yes, that which is within the Divine Love in the Soul for it shines there at every linear second of the time on the Earth plane no matter what negativity covers it or shadows it – only hidden dear – every tiny beam from every chink contributes to the Oneness, the unity of Love. Oh yes indeed – all help to dispel the energies and activities of the dark side are good for light shone upon an obstacle reveals it and gives pause for thought and in that thinking is progress rather than stumbling so believe dear Felicity that all that you do and have written plays its part in shedding this light, for the thinking on the Why of these obstacles is what we all wish to encourage.'

'…..thorough learning this way dear – yes mountains – yes Man feels the urge to climb which is prompted from the Soul to overcome and aspire, so you see dear all is positive – it is either slow or moving at a better pace, and all seeming 'stasis' is but a pause for finding the way no matter which that is for the path will always beckon. All those who shine even the smallest light are for the purpose and a new era increases the impetus which has been revealed by the work of the Lightworkers….there is much diligent effort from the Love Force from the Dimensions for the benefit of Man and the Earth plane peoples – all is in hand dear Felicity. Stay bright and be in loving Oneness with us for all comfort and consolation for the love is great and beautiful between us and this is good and a strengthener for all.'

Copying this out makes my heart sing again as it did when I first wrote those words.

~.~

Having launched my book into the world of the internet I was then caught up in life's usual fun and games. Then a remarkable chain of events occurred.

And this was thanks to my dear friend Sheila who had such faith in my book.

Sheila sent a copy of my book as a present to a friend of hers who had recently recovered from a serious cancer diagnosis and treatment.

This was Lorraine. She too was an ex-nurse – her field was Endocrinology no less - and only gave it up from being ill. She was slowly gaining strength and vitality in Slovenia where she and husband John had a holiday home. The fresh unpolluted air and the gorgeous countryside naturally drew her and played their part in her convalescence.

Lorraine had also been going to a beautiful healing energy resort nearby at Kamnik, Tunjiice and had become good friends with Katja who runs it with her father Drago and is a therapist there. She took the book to show Katja who asked to borrow it. She did. For three months.

Link four in the chain! Katja uses the diagnostic camera system of GDV (Gas Discharge Visualization) in her work. She also held workshops and conferences at her beautiful resort in her superb purpose-built healing 'clinic.'

She then contacted the man who did the training and the workshops and was the 'Main Man' for GDV in Europe, Lutz Rabe. He was instantly taken with my work and revelations of the chakra system and immediately contacted me to give a talk at the next conference workshop being held in Kamnik.

Hastily meanwhile, Sheila and I both looked up the GDV camera system on the internet as it was so new to us. It looked very interesting indeed.

When the official invitation came, I was overjoyed. So was Sheila. There seemed no question that we do this together! Lorraine and John offered to put us up in their lovely home 3,000 feet up into the Slovenian Alps. That was total joy in itself. Unbelievable scenery and wonderful companionship. What a start to a new door opening for me.

That was a wonderful experience for me and a great success. Sheila and I were both equally impressed not to say enthralled with the GDV camera system in action. I think it is a remarkable diagnostic tool.

It reads and prints out the condition of the energy of the whole physical body and, more importantly, a second 'reading' and printout of the condition and quality of the energy of the ANS (Autonomous Nervous System). Lutz was an exceptional teacher and able to interpret the readout most skilfully. It is so revealing of the condition of the whole body.

With the interpretative aspect of my book Lutz believed that much more could now be explained in the ANS readout. He felt that my work gave the missing dimension of knowledge and comprehension needed for the established GDV interpretative system. He called me 'the missing link'!

This was a tremendous boost to my belief in everything I had written about. The crowning part was that Lutz arranged for my book to be translated into German.

There followed several successful talks and workshops in Germany and Slovenia and a talk in Austria at the 3rd International Conference on Burnout.

Naturally Sheila shared them with me and we enjoyed every minute. These were amazing new experiences and I met and gave talks and workshops to very interesting people in the course of them: Engineers, Scientists, Therapists, University professors to name a few, from the UK, Europe and Russia.

These included Konstantin Korotkov himself who designed the GDV system. Sharing a conference with him was a real privilege. I felt as if the world couldn't get sunnier. Now I had the valuable experiences of being an International Speaker to noteworthy people on an important subject. This meant a great deal to me; it validated the work that I had put my heart into and all that precious comprehension from my Guides.

Lutz believed that there were so many possibilities and much progress to be made through the combination of the GDV system and my work. Both he and I had great hopes for these possibilities.

However, Konstantin went on to design a small personal GDV unit which used the internet and everything changed very rapidly. Cost was the nub of it but it meant just a print out through the internet not an in depth reading and assessment by a skilled practitioner.

Konstantin had recently recovered from a protracted fight with cancer and that probably played its part in that rapid change. It must have been a real disappointment not to say sorrow to Lutz after all his amazing work, training and the commitment given to the endeavour since its entry into the European field of healing. He was so knowledgeable and dedicated to the system and teaching its use and amazing benefits. Such a shame. A very real loss.

I loved every challenging minute and all the lovely people I met were a boon, especially dear Lutz and his lovely wife Tatjana who really believed in the combination of our work. I was really very sad that that phase came to an end. Every aspect had been marvellous.

I must confess that I felt very frustrated too and had to work quite hard on removing the disappointment and sense of loss. That the door so gloriously open and inviting had suddenly closed with such completeness was a real blow. I then had to accept that that was not the path for me. I found only recently that I still had links to it that needed removing.

During all this travel and excitement, the last leg of the new extended version on the rest of the body's systems had rather been assigned to the back burner. Now I decided to use this hiatus to renew my sense of purpose and get to it.

So, interspersed with all the illustrating and writing needed to complete it, I was in frequent contact with the Dimensions and my visits to the temple naturally continued.

The tasks required of me at the Soltices and Equinoxes were always extraordinary and quite outside any previous experience. Afterwards I always checked with Khatumi to make sure I hadn't imagined them. He always assured me that yes, I had played my part exactly as I'd perceived.

One of the reasons I omitted to make a note of these experiences was that it is very difficult to describe a perception. This gave impressions to the experience which were very subtle and I can only describe as 'felt' within my 'being'. They had a nebulous quality but very real at the same time. This made them both intimate and personal so it didn't seem something one could record as it were. Thus, it didn't occur to me to write down each event: the bare facts were simply inadequate. Anyway, I certainly had no idea I might ever need the details for a book.

I often 'visit' a beautiful little dell with a waterfall in a meditation to refresh my energy by releasing any negativity under the pure cascade of the waterfall. Invariably I encounter something profound.

On one occasion to my surprise, I was invited to take a horseback ride. What occurred was so vivid and moving that I can remember most of the detail even though it was about ten or more years ago. It was both extraordinary and the only one that involved emotion, hence writing of it here.

We trotted gently along a sunny country path, until, breasting a wide hill, found that there were massed trees on either side stretching back as far as I could perceive.

They were quite dim and deeply shadowed, but I was surprised to see that there were many, many horses between the trees. Suddenly a great wave of intense sadness poured out from the horses, flooding over me as they stood so still among those dark trees.

The horses seemed as hushed and shadowy as the forest as if it was one with them as they just stood, some with their heads hanging down. It was almost unbearable. I was quite at a loss, but then in my head I heard the horse answer my instant question; these were horses who had met only harsh and cruel treatment on the Earth Plane. Only when their fear subsided enough he said, would they emerge and allow healing to take place. - writing this tears at me anew – But that healing was waiting for them, as he would show me.

It was made clear that it was no part of mine to do other than know. We came down over the brow of the hill and vast undulating acres of the most beautiful paddocks with lush grass under warm sunshine lay before us. I remember being struck by the quality of the light.

There were many horses and foals grazing happily there and some of my sorrow lifted at the prospect for those dear wounded horses in the trees.

We continued down a smooth road to the bottom of the hill. There was a small and exquisite circular temple actually in the middle of the road which continued on beyond. I was told to alight and enter the temple which had a gentle iridescent glow within.

All I remember now is that the centrepiece was a large crystal bowl of white quartz on a pedestal and something suspended above holding a soft white flame. What occurred there I cannot precisely remember only that it was to do with the flame and the powerful vibrational field of the quartz and needed much intense focus. This was why I had been brought there for it was connected to the horses.

When I 'returned' I remember being quite disorientated and deeply moved which lasted for some little time. What I have retained is what I saw, rather than what I did that was asked of me. Since these tasks become part of the dimensional memory, I am somewhat consoled if the details slip from my own.

Of all the other visits and tasks preformed, that was the only one that involved sorrow or pain. But that was resolved in the task within the little temple.

Having passed through the crystal chamber at the Temple, sometimes I was taken to join others in the task appointed. I simply joined them in the endeavour as guided or requested to, which was always silent and needed an intense collective focus.

Sometimes the task was to do with my particular energy being put to a specific use. Keeping my inner focus and following the procedure took a lot of concentration so there was never time to speculate, merely do what was required. I was always aware of other-worldliness and cosmic energies. It was always something way beyond my imagining.

In all these experiences I perceived every figure, person or Being as having a bodily shape although this was a perception accompanied by a feeling of their presence. There were no discernible details or features as such. It is a very subtle reality. Everyone in the Dimensions is vibrating at a very high frequency so the form they provided for my comprehension was not fully substantial which is why I use the word perception. As Khatumi explained, 'the inner capacity of energy will generate a 'field' to encompass itself dear Felicity which gives us our semblance of 'form' for all is encompassed by love which since it is 'in being' has 'form' from the energy itself.'

Sometimes I was taken to the Council of Nine. They had great presence and I was very aware of their air of gentle authority when I entered their chamber and approached them. They were robed in vivid white with what looked to be smooth conical white 'head-dresses' that seemed one with their gentle serene faces.

One memorable time during a healing session with Lynn, we were sent for. We both had the Violet Flame placed in our heart chakra and instructed how to expand it and surround ourselves in its gentle power when needed. It was such a lovely experience and when we 'came to,' looked at each other in wonder! 'Well,' we said, 'that was a first!' An amazing experience for us both.

Sometimes I was sent for, sometimes I went for help or enlightenment. Because I took all this in my stride it didn't occur to me to keep a record of these visits either.

There was one place I was taken to for enlightenment that had the most enormous carved double doors. I knew I was to step forward from the Beings who had brought me and approach them alone. These swung open just as I did so. Before me was a vast hall with a very high arched ceiling. Both it and the walls were beautifully and intricately painted with what seemed to be birds and flowers in lovely colours. I couldn't see the details though because the place was so huge.

It was teaming with 'people' either milling about, some of whom looked at me with vague curiosity, or were talking intently together in groups. There was a long table at the far end behind which sat an imposing central figure with several others flanking him. They were all in white robes or gowns with white head-pieces but as always details were not clear. I was alone so making my way down through that milling throng was a little daunting as I remember being quite overawed by the place. The central Being had a serene sense of authority about him. Despite his 'presence' the Senior

Being was gently spoken and keen to help me. I don't recall what took me there however.

On the second occasion I was taken there because I was advised I could help previous members of my mother's family. It was an unusual experience so it is all still vivid to me.

I had asked my Guides to confirm that this was needed.

'We will all help you to clear the karmic links for your dear Mother's sake. – the knowing of the karma is unimportant dear friend – if you are willing to break these links to release them all then we can do this together. You will need to go to the temple and be guided from there - we will deal with the Akashic records dear friend. The task is to 'do' rather than 'know'. Cutting the connection dear, yes, the karma must not come to you. You will be protected by going to the Temple. Refrain from trying to 'see' all dear – the links are infinite – the only ones that are your concern are those for your Mother ...all else is the concern of other Beings. Indeed dear Felicity– release – that is what you are concerned with.'

So, I visited the Temple and was taken up to those imposing doors again which again opened at our approach.

As before I went in alone into that vast hall as full as before with busy figures. As I approached the table, I saw that the other members there were busy with other people but the central Being beckoned to me. He then placed on it a sort of structure that appeared to be a series of near-transparent 'shelves' which seemed to be suspended at intervals. I saw that there looked to be names floating on them. They were linked by many fine thread-like 'lines.' I was required to clear these 'links' of karma as instructed from these generational planes of the necessary part of my genealogical family tree.

He smiled and explained that it was my willingness that made this possible. I did all as directed, then again smiling gently, he thanked me.

Then I retreated and returned to the Temple. Once again far from my own imagining and unconnected to anything previously known to me during or after.

These were not the Lords of Karma. I had occasion to go to these Beings twice. I had been to them once on a memorable meditation with two healer ladies, who wished to take a petition to the Lords. I had never heard of them until then but I was happy to comply though I had no idea what to expect. This was entirely new to me.

We went up through many planes and came to some huge doors made of bronze. They opened part-way and revealed an intense golden 'power' in the form of light. That is the only way I can explain it! My companions were greatly in awe of the Lords themselves. Not having heard of them before I was just fascinated. We proffered our petition and left it outside then retreated. It was a very clear but unusual meditation.

The second time was not long after. Someone, as I discovered, was trying to attach their karma to me and it was very unpleasant. My Guides advised me to seek their help so I asked at the Temple if I could go to them.

I was taken aloft by an Angelic Being. On arrival, those huge bronze doors opened part-way again and within the light was a figure of normal dimensions whom I 'knew' to be an acolyte.

He was holding something, a scroll or book I thought. I had barely voiced my reason for coming, when a deep resonating voice sounded from well behind him.

'This karma is not to be put upon this Being. This will not, repeat, *not be permitted*!'

On the last ringing words, the acolyte retreated, disappearing into that intense light and the huge doors closed.

Although the 'presence' was really impressive, I was rather more taken with a feeling of relief and deep gratitude because of the *absolute* pronouncement that was given unhesitatingly for my benefit. It made me feel really safe. It is a very vivid memory.

As my Guides said regarding karma and the use of other's karma as a working surface for learning,
'.....allows for the loan of karma as we have described. This is for the learning to initiate knowledge therefore will remain that of those that help in this way – quite different dear pupil from the desire of the person to rid himself of its karmic burden and weigh your vibration down with it – but we know that this has been forbidden by the Karmic Lords – each must carry its own for the learning towards the 'knowing'.'

It is a strange experience entering Dimensions where one is known and nothing really needs to be explained by one. A great relief in fact. But one has been 'heard' and everything known in any given moment. Help is therefore always immediate.

Chapter 31

Whatever task I was given on my visits to the Temple was of course, self-explanatory in the given moment. This naturally made them unquestionable. Also, totally natural to the circumstances, extraordinary though they might be if one explained them to anyone.

It was always a case of 'do' rather than 'know' I found. Doing completed it I presume. Knowing leads to thinking and then 'connecting' thoughts; probably neither relevant nor needed. It has been 'done.'

No one in my immediate circle however has anything similar happening in their lives so I couldn't discuss these cosmic happenings with them. I could tell a very few if I wished but as I said, it is very difficult to describe a perception because one is 'experiencing' it on an interior level as well as doing what was required simultaneously.

One is aware in some way, of a different reality that is without the strict form we experience in life. Also, the mystery of these happenings could not I felt, be laid bare: that this would somehow reduce the experience, for it was very personal. Mere words would diminish the extraordinariness in some way.

The two layers, my physical, practical life and the metaphysical, flowed on as usual. The focus now was the completion of my writing and artwork for the new extended version. All the Dear Ones of the network were happy and interested in my progress. Their pleasure and enthusiasm, particularly as I completed the metaphysical sections, were a great boost to me.

And as always, they did much to encourage me to resist any negativity from everyday life. '...think on sweet things and nourish the heart chakra with the goodness that is all around. We are one with you dear precious charge so nourish yourself also with our love.'

I usually kept away from newspapers and the news as much as possible because it was invariably negative and speculative but I kept half an eye open so that I wasn't cut off from the most important bits.

One day Khatumi and I were talking about the point when the pressures exerted by these events put people's 'backs against the wall' as it were. A step too far.

'...it has become the pattern for Mankind in order that he rises and aspires. With only gentle harmonious energy Man readily succumbs to the comforts and inertia of the physical because its nature is dense vibration, ie. Matter – yes, the seed bursts from the pod, the chick breaks out of the egg, the infant through the effort at birth – all is against the physical constraints – yes dear, yes – aspiration as well as development and growth.'

And most of the time we need a really a hard rock in the way to get us to push at all!

Sometimes other 'friends' like Sophie and my own children's Guides visited to talk with me. It was lovely how they all worked together and for each other.

'.....yes, we can always call on extra help at any time. The network is 'one' and all who work in it are part of the whole and move for each other when something extra is called for – yes, this happens instantaneously because we work on vibrations but we do have discussions as you know to make sure our 'bases are all covered.' The unity we have here is a beautiful thing and is the manifestation of love and beingness – yes, we are individual but that adds to the beauty of the oneness for each part then is special not just anonymous. Like cells in an organ! For this we rejoice as each can share experiences in the Singing Time which is our nourishing time as you know. Love and blessings to you too dear. You are safe in God's loving arms.'

These encounters were always beautifully rewarding. We particularly loved 'making connections,' putting them 'into existence' which thus created a fresh vibration. Jalal loved this too and joined in,

'......this is why the work is important for all – yes us also – you are understanding it is eternal and greater than the mind can encompass dear friend, but very stimulating to think upon. We are filled with joy for this synchronous workings of our minds and the creation of good vibrations dear friend.'

It is always a very special experience doing healing with my dear friend Lynn. She is able to perceive and hear the Dimensions, although she does not take dictation as I do; it is in the given moment for her when needed.

When we were working through our healing sessions, we were frequently blessed with visits from someone special when we reached a certain point. Melchizedek has been overseeing her progress and came several times to share his joy in what we achieved for her.

We have had some amazing encounters with these lovely Beings who bless us with their help and encouragement.

As regards the work we do together, distance and opportunity are a very real impediment alas. However, this seems to be all a part of her inner work and the development along her life path. She has a very long past from aeons ago so naturally we do have some marvellous experiences in our healing sessions.

The healing work has made a great deal of difference to her life. We have journeyed thus-wise together over the years and it has been quite extraordinary so we have become close friends which has been an added delight. Not the least part of this is that she is the one person I can talk to (when we get the chance) for she understands it all. Rarely though at the time it occurs, so not quite as I'd like to.

That we can share these beautiful insights, perceptions and connections with these wonderful Dimensional Beings is joy to us both. The long periods between however, make the encounters we have together even more potent and profound.

When she does come to me for healing, we have a great deal to share in the short time we have together.

~ . ~

In my pragmatic life, the new, extended version of my book was becoming a reality. It was deeply satisfying seeing it all come together. All the necessary illustrations were finished as well.

I had put my heart and soul into every word, every shape, every image, every colour for people to truly re-evaluate the body and free that *lovingness within*. High hopes indeed!

Not to have written it as a complete work, finished it, and believed in it would be to have wantonly wasted the devotion from those dear beloved Guides who showed their love for me every day through their words, their wisdom, insights, guidance and patient teaching. And published it obviously needed to be.

By the end of 2014 it was as comprehensive as I could make it. The technicalities of fitting it into the original pdf however, needed an expert.

I found a very clever lady, Sue Portman, a professional designer and copywriter, who took this highly technical job beautifully in hand. The book could not have happened without it. I named it '*Body Mind Connections, the Essential How & Why Book*' and had a beautiful new cover designed especially for it by a clever young man.

Then at last by the spring of 2015 it was ready. It was published by the same company who were so good with my first. Once again having the book in its lovely shiny new cover in my hands was a great moment.

I realised then that it had, in effect become an *advanced* version. The first on the core of the body would suit those who were primarily concerned with the chakra energy system. The comprehensiveness of this one offered even more of the emotional impact on the whole body to those in wider fields of healing and hopefully teaching.

The year that followed was its usual mixture of life as I was living it. Then, as the year ended, things really began to change. The beginning of 2016 needed all my resources and the first few months were very difficult. As always though I was beautifully supported by Khatumi and the network.

Then, just as we were coming up to the Summer Solstice and when I least expected it, - naturally! - there was an extraordinary new development.

Lynn and her daughter took the long trip up to have some healing sessions with me. Both sessions were very profound and cleared what was ready to be released.

In the course of Lynn's session, we had a specific tricky problem to be rid of. Immediately I perceived the arrival of a Being who was tall, a dazzling white with a faintly perceptible form within.

I had never seen him before and I say, him, because although sweetly gentle as always, it felt like a masculine energy. And this was needed. We thanked him and he left in the subtle smiling way Beings do and I continued.

The same Being came to help during her daughter's healing the following day. Again, it had been a deep issue that we had arrived at when he came with his help. Both encounters were quite profound and quite new to me. I thought of him as a very high Celestial Being.

Since both Lynn and her daughter are spiritual and the esoteric is strong in their outlook and being, I wasn't surprised but very happy that someone special had come to help them through these significant releases.

As was usual at such times, at the Summer Solstice, I prepared myself for a meditation.

After activating all my symbols fully, I went to the Temple. The crystal chamber was Rose Quartz that evening, some pieces were really large and the energy was beautiful as it flowed round me.

When the chamber opened in front of me, I stepped out and found myself wearing a garment in a very elaborate cream material with embroidery all over it. I walked forward to find

Sandalphon and Uriel waiting for me and I believe that Metatron was there too.

Metatron led the way and the other dear Angels stayed either side of me. Then I saw a pyramid before me - it wasn't very big, perhaps 10-12 feet at the apex. It shone and gleamed and seemed to be made of the most delicate glass.

As I got nearer, I saw that it was surrounded by many like pyramids. It was all so beautiful and ethereal - they gleamed and shone, the light breaking into delicate prisms everywhere. I was taken forward into the first pyramid and immediately had the strangest sensation that the 'fabric' or substance of the pyramid and I were the same – a continuance of the vibrational essence I suppose. – that we were part of each other.

I could vaguely discern that the other pyramids outside formed a whole unit with the one I was within. Then a clear firm voice said. 'You will now be functioning from the purple diamond body.' Now I perceived that I was surrounded by what looked like one of my symbols but it was flashing and shimmering with a deep violet/purple light at all the points. Then it became smaller and smaller until it was in my body completely, edge to edge.

I was doing my best not to think but to remain focussed and still. Immediately I felt the most marked tingling on my crown chakra.

It spread outwards as if the chakra itself was expanding. Then the tingling sensation, which was still most marked, started to descend into my head yet some 'energy' poured like liquid crystal down over my face as well. It was incredibly tangible. The sensation of this trickling energy went right down through my core and down the front of my body. As it ceased, a voice said. 'You may return now.'

It took a lot of concentration to turn myself round to face the way I had come but I managed it. Then Uriel and Sandalphon returned me to the temple and I brought myself back to my surroundings.

From the moment when the voice told me about the purple diamond body that I was now functioning from, I experienced a very profound state of being and that was still with me as I opened my eyes and sat in some astonishment.

After a while, I found it all rather difficult to grasp so I immediately dowsed my Guardian Angel Michelle to ask if it had happened. 'yes' was the definite answer. I was still in a state of amazement, feeling humble and still trembling slightly. The whole experience was so profound.

The following day I decided to ask Khatumi to verify this to be absolutely sure! It was all true.

'Ah, dear Felicity- we are very happy to speak with you now – especially since your connections with the High Celestial Beings and the activation of the purple diamond body – this is an important transition for you dear friend – yes, much much joy from the network…..we ask that you dissolve all doubt, all barriers however frail for the way ahead is calling you forward. …………They come from beyond the Galactic Council and are Guardians of the knowledge beyond that which is comprehensible to most men and is given only through those who have been chosen to work with the highest Dimensions when we know them to be ready. (different collective 'voice') You are being prepared dear Soul for you have been chosen and we love you. Our voice is the one you heard in the pyramid and you are of the purple diamond vibrational body which we ask that you keep foremost in your consciousness for you are to accomplish things for us for the Divine purpose and Plan for the Earth. Our vibrational field is strong for we transmit through many Dimensions to reach those who have been chosen. Our vibration is in oneness with yours for the purpose you will fulfil. Yes, pure white. Yes we came to you for the release of these dear beings – you are one of us – be tranquil and believe for these are for your comprehension for the unfolding of your pathway. We will come to you when it is good we will come to you should you need us and we will know that need for our vibration is with you. Your diligence and obedience have made this perception possible for you to perceive us in 'form' so that we can reveal ourselves to you and hear our voice – we will speak with you further as the need arises dear Soul– this is sufficient for the moment. (the purple diamond body)….this is our gift to you and through which we can transmit all that is needful – you are chosen in this incarnation and have been sent for the purpose – trust and believe dear Soul for we are near and love you – be strong within – all are connections – all have the power of love and truth. We will speak again. Be at peace.'

That was when I realised that the beautiful 'white' Being who had come to help in Lynn and her daughter's healings had come to help *me* to help them. At the time, and for some reason, I had 'thought' of 'him' as The High Celestial Being. These beautiful Beings had now given me the purple diamond body to connect with me.

I was so astonished at this development that I skyped my daughter and told her briefly what had happened. '*Write it down Mum…as soon as possible! - every detail while it's fresh in your mind.*' That I did, which is why I have been able to relate it to you in detail. The feelings and intense perceptions I had though, are impossible to describe, so profound were they. Re-reading and writing it out astonishes me anew and my crown is tingling all the while too!

I found it amazing that I'd taken such a quantum leap after such a difficult start to that year. What I wondered would the second half bring?

Chapter 32

Needless to say, I was eager to be in communication with and take more 'dictation' from these dear Beings whom I now thought of as The High Celestial Beings. Also, ever-curious me was very keen to know all about them. They were quite new to my experience: their collective voice had a distinct timbre and a subtly different 'reality' when they speak to me alone. Now sometimes they blend with Khatumi and Martha depending on what is needful for me to 'hear'.

'We are where you belong dear Soul– we are all here and work for the Human Race and its destiny, its purpose, its development, so that the Human Intellect can work with true intelligence for this is a high vibration that we work with. Yes, not a coincidence a certainty for you to assimilate. Yes our intellect is from the collective energy of our being, unlike on the Earth plane where it is centred in the cerebrum – and indeed, awaits oneness with those 'cells' within the physical heart substance. Intelligence without love (yes – gently!) creates a vibration that is separate from the (energy) system – for the whole system should vibrate from Love. It is this separation that is our concern for the Human Race. Oneness is beginning to be understood but its true comprehension is needed. Your 'Chart for Development' interested us for we saw the beginnings of your true comprehension. We (collective Soul including Mind) show each step leading to the next – yes –...........thus we show those things to your consciousness through the analysis of your cerebral workings.........Yes, – the Human capacity for belief seems to require proof thus we offer the gradual building of the stages to comprehension for uniting these into one loving intelligence of the whole system so that it vibrates in its Oneness, so that it becomes part of the Earth Plane Matrix that you have already played your part in with your books - being the physical form of your concepts. ....yes – from the knowing within not the knowledge of the brain vibration. ....yes, this is a great deal to take in – just levels of consciousness which are parallels....be peaceful within and cherish your Being in all respects for thus you honour us and all who vibrate in the Dimensions for Man's enlightenment to development into Love and Truth. We love you, you are us. We will speak again when the need is there dear Soul.'

Can you imagine my reception of the revelation that I was originally from their Galaxy? I was both bemused and a trifle stunned. But oddly, I felt no denial, just astonishment.

The timbre of their dear voices and their 'presence' were unmistakably from somewhere different than I was used to. I had assumed therefore that they were from another plane of the Celestial Dimensions.

Right out of the blue, here were Beings from a far Galaxy speaking lovingly to me as one of them. They were undoubtedly vibrational and very advanced so this was obviously Soul-level regards myself, an ordinary mortal in all the complexities, contradictions and emotions of physical human experiences and earthly life.

This was a step further somehow than all the other marvels I had been experiencing.

These dear Beings were patently not from the Dimensions I had been aware of and the planes I'd learned of through my clairaudience. These were Galactic Beings, communicating to me through etheric realms and channels I had no knowledge of. Now I had discovered there were actually Galactic Dimensions. That curiously calm acceptance I had felt throughout these remarkable years was now really mixed up with several shades of amazement and '*can* this be true?' like bubbles in soda water. The dear Beings must have been amused at this.

I must admit this was taking a little getting used to. Here was a change I had no way of expecting. And brand new knowledge. All I could do was wait in patience for it to be revealed, to unravel, so that I could really take it in.

One thing struck me however. The Chart for Development they spoke of I had written way back in 2013 for my book *Body Mind Connections*. (on p381) I was delighted to hear that they had connected with this. And then to discover that this had a bearing on my purpose with these dear High Celestial Beings excited me too. It was rather reassuring in fact but there was certainly a lot to take in.

'…..yes dear Soul we are with you in Oneness and love….be at peace within for we are you and you are us and our love is great and boundless as your seas and skies and into the beyond of beyond – God hears all and all is Love. Continue with your activation, it will strengthen you. - Keep your heart open to all dear Soul. The love intelligence is your beingness in us. Yes, feel our love – it will heal the sad places for you are precious to us and the work you do with us…..we will speak to you again about the work ahead for now your mind has earthly concerns…heed our words and be in peace dear loved Soul.'

'….your name is 'our' name dear Soul and as such unpronounceable in your language as is our 'home'. We use a Portal for we come from beyond, yes, the upper plane of the ninth dimension is where we enter through the Portal. Yes, that which the human brain can comprehend. Yes, we have parts of Being which gives us our individuality as you conceive. Yes, planes of connectivity for the purpose for all is One – yes infinite – yes where energy has become matter (planets) for 'form' carries vibration added to it for the purpose. Yes, indeed dear Soul, hence the influence on the Planet Earth and the Human Beings there. yes, for pattern without vibration is just that, thus patterns have a frequency creating a determined vibration for the purpose. Thus 'matter' plays its part also. Yes dear Soul. Yes, variety for there are infinite strands to knowledge and wisdom. Yes dear Soul. Our 'form' is created from the oneness of the white light field of our Love

Intelligence. This therefore has its vibration and frequencies are created from that part of the field that is in use for the purpose. Yes, pulses, - that is a good concept to understanding dear Soul. This has been a *good* conversation dear Soul........we love 'us' and our Beingness is in perfect Oneness dear Soul. Be peaceful within dear Human Being, for that is which carries our dear Soul.'

Once again this is a joining of thoughts and learning at lightning speed so that both seem simultaneous, while I perceive the images their words conjure up. Now as soon as I heard them, I felt totally connected to them.

I had called them High Celestial Beings, but these Dear Ones were a different reality. Well, here was a definite and extraordinary enlightenment. How marvellous. These were from a very distant Galaxy, vibrational yes but inhabiting another part of the Universe.

I'd heard of the Hathors, Beings from Venus who love and wish to help us, through my friend Sheila but I hadn't given much thought to them and automatically associated them with the celestial realms. There is a difference in hearing about something and actually experiencing a new reality oneself because all my experiences so far were with Celestial Beings. Now here were Galactic Beings in my conscious experience. This flung back the horizons even further although I knew for a fact that the Celestial Dimensions were deep into an infinity I could not comprehend let alone conjure up.

But we have photographs of space and galaxies to grasp a little the infinity of the Universe. This is easier for the mind to comprehend, a physical reality of things unseen. We know it for vast beyond comprehension but those images give one a picture so to speak because we rotate physically in it. Hence horizons. But it is still, 'out there,' distant, removed from Earth. Now it wasn't any more.

Having settled now into that calm acceptance, this new connection seemed naturally consistent with all the revelations that had been coming my way. Everything segued together. Now and then, I did still marvel at it all though.

However, having named these wonderful Beings, that was how I thought of them and it seemed to have been accepted, just as my names for my Guides had.

Now here was a fresh conscious awareness, that of activating the purple diamond body and my symbols plus creating a mental 'pathway' from the cerebrum to the neural tissue in the heart. This I needed to do frequently, regardless of a healing situation. It took a lot of concentration and I worked on it quite diligently in light of my wonderful new connection with these loving High Celestial Beings.

However, I did have considerable distractions as the events of the early part of the year made a few waves. As a result, my health over the year did hit a bit of a low and there were complicated and rather trying periods to contend with.

As a consequence, I was not as diligent as I should have been with my activations as the year ran on. There were times when I felt as if I was not really progressing.

Nevertheless, I continued with as much spiritual work as I could, healing, writing, talking with my dear Guides and carrying on in much the same mode as always. Never critical, they just kept lovingly advising me to strengthen myself within with my activations so I did re-energise the Amethystine energy from time to time. The many calls upon my time and attention as well as things in general however, were not conducive to going quite deeply within.

It was not long after this that I made an amazing discovery through my daughter.

Since her return to Australia, she had been developing into an incredible healer at a level that I was unaware could be reached. That is her story however.

It was late in the summer of 2016 when we were skypeing each other. As if I could no longer be surprised at anything, she said, *'Mum, I can speak Light Language,'* in a pleased voice.

I have to confess that this didn't really register with me. Partly because I had never heard of such a language and I was more caught up with the clairaudience and channelling that she had been gifted with and partly with the amazing stuff she was doing in her healing. To me it seemed all of a piece with how she had developed as a healer.

I asked her about it a few days later when we skyped however. It seems she had been able to do this for 3 years at least. At first, she just thought she was muttering away to herself. Suffice it to say, she soon came to the realisation that this was a language and it was being channelled through her. For myself, since so many amazing things were happening for her, I accepted this and asked her to speak it for me.

Well. Although quite unintelligible, I felt no trace of resistance in my mind. Instead, a profound feeling of rightness and beauty, and the wish to just go on listening to it filled me. She said that a beautiful feeling of love flowed through her as she spoke it so she loved speaking it. I was blown away by this. I saw that her hands moved too.

It is Soul language and therefore an inner response was utterly natural she said: purely a language of sounds and symbols. It is quite beautiful. It is the original 'language' of all communication. All our Earthly languages developed from it: one can even hear traces of Native American, Polynesian, Russian, French, Japanese, Arabic in among the 'sounds.'

She explained that it comes through her from the Galactic peoples who have a care for us and our planet's destiny and development. It has subtle differences for all occasions. Each time, the language that comes through is singular to the purpose. My daughter uses it in her wonderful healings; it heals on a very profound level.

What surprised me after this was my acceptance of a vocal connection with 'Galactic peoples.' I had only recently discovered there were Galactic Beings but I believed her unreservedly. I was thoroughly fascinated and wanted to know more.

I thought I'd try the internet. To my astonishment I discovered on YouTube *so* many people able to speak it! Also, who freely gave transmissions from *their* Channelling.

I was amazed to discover that these come from Sirius, Arcturus, Lyra and the Pleiades among others. Not only that but some had been channelling Light Languages for 20, 40 years or more. And here was I, only just heard of it.

I was utterly riveted by all this. That there were people, including my own daughter, bringing the actual voices of Galactic Beings through to us on Earth was phenomenal. I had no idea spiritual connections had been moving by leaps and bounds to such a degree.

This was such a different perspective within my awareness. Now suddenly many presences from whole star systems out there are in our compass. A yet further expansion of my awareness of the scope of the Dimensions connected with our planet. And now lately, into my comprehension, the Universe itself.

Having been contacted through clairaudience by Celestial Beings made this a lot easier to assimilate. Though it did astonish me nevertheless. Horizons were diminishing to the point of non-existence! Which really seems an actuality. Simply knowing there was a vast universe full of stars planets and Galaxies out there beyond the night sky hadn't impinged on me, being bounded by the realities of our life here on the Earth. Now my own reality was unbounded by the astonishing knowledge it was peopled by vibrational Beings.

I had a real longing to be able to channel this wonderful language from those Beings who were so eager and happy to communicate with us and send healing to us here in the Earth Plane. I was clairaudient yes, but I had no real expectation of becoming a channel myself.

I couldn't wait to skype my daughter again. I so wanted to hear her speaking Light Language again. I then asked her to ask them to speak it to me. Came an outpouring of fascinating language. She said she hadn't spoken that language before. We were both delighted by this. Glad that they were willing to talk *to* me and being rather concerned about the many distractions that were intruding into my life, I asked her to ask them if I was still on the right path. A short, very fast burst of

Light Language was the response. *'You could say that was a 'Yes'*, she said! That made us both laugh.

She was amazingly fluent! So, whenever we skyped, I asked her to channel it for me. It was so beautiful to listen to. Very often the voice was really excited and very fast. This amused us both as we and the 'speaker' all seemed to be enjoying it!

Caroline knew I longed to be able to speak it myself. She said there was no reason for it not to be activated in me. Accordingly, she placed some symbols in my upraised palms over the ether as we spoke.

I had no idea if this would activate it but Caroline was sure it would come through when I was ready.

Buzzing with this new discovery, I naturally asked my friend Lynn if she had heard of it. Like me, she had never heard of it. I suggested she too have a look on YouTube. She became as fascinated as me.

Because the High Celestial Beings spoke to me in my own language, I asked them about 'Light Language'.

'...We too speak in this language you call light for this is how we speak to one another across the galaxies and sing of our joy of all things good together. (commenting on them speaking in 'English' to me) Yes for we need to impart exact information to you and this is easy for us for you are us also – we have been speaking in our language to your Soul all your existence on the Earth Plane – yes you recognised that but realise also that you are us so this came from 'us'. We are the Love Intelligence and that is our task for the Earth Plane at this time. Yes, we are of the highest plane of the 9th Dimension and work on different and subtle levels of vibrational energy. – yes, white energy. - We come from a galaxy far beyond those dear Soul– we will find a way of translating it for you – it is yet to be identified by your astrological astronomers thus the name has no word in your language – yes you can speak it but it remains unawakened as yet. Yes, on a subtle level rather than as a mouthpiece channel – all things are to the purpose for the purpose. If this is necessary to the purpose you will be enabled dear Soul– yes in patience! We are star people and our home is bright with the love vibration and the wisdom we carry and work with – yes we have children who work with human children – our vibrational bodies have great longevity and our children have much time for there is much wisdom to learn before they become fully adult in your sense. Then they continue in us so that all our vibrational energy is renewed. Thus we are 'we' – yes and the wisdom held and carried by using a strong vibration……..thus we are prompted to awaken Man and open his ears to hear of our love and receive some of our wisdom or re-connect with that which is held for them – yes, it is very strong – yes it is needed in the density of the Earth Plane vibration both to deal with it and rise above it….Man must see all even in this darkness (of negative energy) for he will know the truth for his Soul is pure and is speaking our language with us through all the Dimensions so truth is always known. Thus Souls are not alone or struggling in isolation for this is the language of God the creator and 'known' in the darkest of dark places – *all* is One, dear beloved Soul - all work where needed for the Earth is a special Planet and physical Man has developed great skills in all manner of fields from a low vibrational body through the nervous system and the body corporate – yes great beauty and loving creativity – yes through the Ego impulse and the Will energy applied to aspire, achieve and pass on those things of the beauty within – in this transition from one aeon to another confusion is experienced as 'form' is changing into a new beingness for Man to make better use of himself and his planet home. All is in the Creator's hands dear Soul and Man is guided by we of the Dimensions. These are for God dear Soul– yours is for the purpose you have been chosen for which we will aid and guide you at all times. Be nourished by our love and the food you give yourself dear Soul. Be good to the vessel you have been blessed with. Go gently and be at peace dear beloved Soul. We will speak of much again.'

Such conversations from these beloved Beings were always deeply interesting as well as beautiful and nourishing and I was continuing to learn from them. Their explanations were always so clear, 'moving the thinking into comprehension.....' which is so stimulating.

It was in the same month that I found a ninth symbol had appeared in my energy system. This time in the hara.

'Yes dear friend, it is I Khatumi. You wish for confirmation dear — yes, the ninth symbol has been placed within your system — this has raised your healing vibration to the 9th dimension where it has been held for you by The Great Ones. We are happy to see you making use of your symbols for these are the connections dear and the chakra you vibrate from gives us the intention for the healing needed. We are one dear so all is known, all is understood. We ask that you use daily contemplation to align the chakras for the Solstice turning of the year. Zadriel is still your potent Healing Angel to enable acceptance into their physical body and energy systems for those you help. Yes, he will always be with you. There is much joy here for you and us all....then a different voice came from deeper in the Dimensions....*for the soil is fertile and the cosmos carries a deep vibration for the Earth. You are within this vibration dear as are all those whose conscious awareness is increasing at this time of the beginning — release all negativity dear for God has all in His hands and his knowledge is infinite for He determined the Purpose out of Love and Love is within the Earth and all who dwell on her for the Purpose is Love and Truth and the ascendency of Man through knowing the Will and knowing Love — for Love with the Will aspires to great things which is God's Will for the purpose of Man, the Earth and the Divine Plan that He 'is'. These are great things beloved One and we wish you to hold them in your heart for Love must reside there with truth and Goodness — all are*

Divine and for God's purpose. Rest and leave all to God. May sweetness be with you beloved, sweetness and grace of being for these are who you are and we are one and beloved of God. Be strong within and call on us beloved one precious to us – there is work ahead for the purpose. We know this is your wish from the heart. Visit us through the Temple when you need of us, Melchizedek bids you adieu for Khatumi is here again….we are with you and God's loving arms are keeping you safe.'

Words cannot describe the intense sweetness and beauty of this encounter. I felt very privileged that Melchizedek had come through to speak to me. His 'presence' was an added deeper dimension. My heart chakra could not have got wider. Even as I re-read this and write it out for you it fills my heart anew.

Also, I'm getting used to the tingling activity in my crown chakra whenever I add a quotation from my collection for this book.

So, more focus and work to be done with my symbols and chakra alignment especially with the Winter Solstice approaching. Since these are Portals for knowledge each one is important. It was only a week or so after this that when I started to activate them I 'saw' that the symbols were even more complex. They had such tiny facets added that I couldn't really grasp their actual shape.

*'…..the stages were required for your comprehension and bringing them into your consciousness gradually for you to encompass – yes very complex – yes that which is easy for both cerebrum and mind to realise (**bring into reality**) They have been revealed dear Soul/dear Felicity. Their existence was always there….'*

It seems that they were part of my Soul template and were brought up and placed into my physical chakra system for me to use and were revealed in slow stages for me to work with. I imagine it was the only way that my brain could take their perception.

Everything has been on a 'need to know' basis. Keep it simple was obviously easier! It was certainly easy to accept the little-by-little method. That they comprised the octave had seemed appropriate. Now a ninth was added to the hara raising the vibration for healing was, I assumed, due to all the work I'd done on activating the full octave. There was always something new to take in.

All the time I was activating each stage as was revealed it seems I had been actually activating each symbol in its entirety. I'd obviously needed this gradual exposure so that I could achieve this properly myself. As always, one was required to work and play one's part.

It had really made me focus and concentrate. Now I was seeing all that was perceivable and this was obviously sufficient. That it had also honed my focus and concentration for any tasks or visitations I was called to was also apparent. Everything for its purpose indeed.

As I worked with what I could perceive yet another aspect was revealed that I had to work with and then another. Now I saw that they were part of quite a complex system in itself now.

Once again, a lot of concentration was needed for all that was required to fully activate all nine and encompass the system itself before a healing or any visits to the Temple. This I felt was a necessary part I needed to play. One needs to make a contribution with willingness and diligence for the Dimensions give so much. It is also part of the Oneness with the Dimensions and one's inner being for that was where the work lay.

At the Winter solstice I did my usual meditation. No sooner had I activated the purple diamond body and the Violet Flame than I was taken up and entered the translucent pyramid again. I stepped through it and I was part of an amethyst vibrational field. I was directed to hold my arms out beside me and the field assumed a huge crystalline-type cube reaching forward from my fingertips.

I was instructed to bring my hands forward palms towards one another. As I did so the 'energy' grew stronger until, as my palms almost touched, a great beam of amethyst crystal energy shot forward from my fingertips. I was told to focus and hold it as this was activating the energy and enabling the intensity to stay in 'form' until it could continue generating without me.

A little while later it assumed a peak and separated from my fingertips. Once separated it stayed in place. I had no idea or what was occurring only that it was a part of who I was.

I was told that this was Amethystine crystal healing energy. I began to put certain pieces together. I remembered Anthony and Tibetan Grandmother helping me to develop my brow chakra, the amethyst-edged gossamer gown, the amethyst cube I'd had to help rotate. With the Violet Flame in the heart chakra and the purple diamond body as well it was apparent that the quality of this particular energy was significant to me somehow.

Now there was this extraordinary potent experience where Amethystine energy was part of me and had created some important vibrational force.

Then I was requested to re-charge this at intervals. This I did and each time I could sense that it had pulsed forward to another point. It took a lot of focus but in the stillness required it was a beautiful experience. To enable this intense healing vibration was both humbling and wondrous.

Chapter 33

As the year turned into the next, I found I was quite washed out from the practical and earthly demands and vicissitudes of the previous year. Therefore, when out of the blue, and thanks to my lovely son and his wife, an extraordinary chance came for me to move house, I took it. I really was seriously in need of a change; a change of scene, energy, even lifestyle. It happened very swiftly and the Universe found me exactly what I needed. I was moved out and in in one month!

My beloved friends, Khatumi and the network were unsurprisingly very happy that a change of energy was imminent even though I viewed all the necessary packing and clearing with some dismay.

'Refrain from being daunted by this dear/dear friend – all will run smoothly determined by the correctness and the intention so keep that clear in your energy to enable all dear friend...then to my delight, dear Sophie joined in – reste tranquille little chicken – yes Sophie here, we are all connected still and full of great love for you, so life is good with us, no? We are all one, we are Love and Truth together – yes, expand the heart dear with our love and guidance, for in oneness there is no aloneness for you. Help will be given. All will be well and it will be *good*!'

Always a comfort and their joyousness during my move was a great boost as I surveyed the increasing number of boxes and organised chaos of the home I was having to take apart!

In the midst of this upheaval was the Spring equinox. I did not want to miss this so I prepared myself for my Meditation.

Just as I'd activated the purple diamond body and the Violet flame, instead of holding my hands forward, I felt them again going out-stretched to the side, level with my shoulders. The Amethystine energy was flooding out of my whole body and arms in a great wave of violet energy centred from my heart chakra. I could feel the weight there. Once again, I had to bring my arms together and focus it once more into a tight beam and wait until it detached. It took much concentration.

I worked like this for several more sessions. They always felt profound. Nevertheless, I always checked that these tasks had occurred and as always was reassured.

~.~

By the April, I found myself in my new home here; another fresh about-face. This rallied my spirits. It had all been so swift and smooth. I felt really happy to be living in this new neat house.

Now I have been here 18 months and much has happened. Between the many events, comings and goings, I have been writing as diligently as possible.

For the first few months I was very busy with settling in, the new joys of gardening again, having family and friends round and enjoying my new environment. This was as well as all the other things that occupied my time and needed my attention.

The months were flying by. I was being a bit indulgent and basking in the changes the move was making. Nevertheless, I was told that my moving house to this fresh energy was all part of preparation as development for my work ahead. However, what with one thing and another I was not being very consistent with my activations, but I was also writing my book, talking with my loving Beings and meditating at certain times so these kept me in conscious awareness of my spiritual work.

As July arrived, that night when I picked up my notepad and pen, much to my surprise I had another visitor.

'Running Brave is here. I came to sing you the Calling Song, the drumbeat, with the pulse of the heart of the Earth. You need to come. The people need to hear you, feel your energy, be with you in numbers, yes, I am Navajo, but I am just one of our nation it does not matter which tribe or people I am just of the true nation who wanted to sing you into the Earth's heart. Your words, your vision of what you call negative energy that lies like a pall on my people – on all peoples – wherever it is understood, wherever it is lifted will play its part in the negativity of my nation. The disconnection through the chase for and demand for money, power and possessions is very potent in our country. It is the cultural blanket thrown over the land and stifling the heartbeat of the Earth and stopping her breath. The understanding in basic and simple terms is needed. – yes, all that is above the word not what is beneath it and which powers it. We peoples did not experience this so it has been doubly heavy for us and held us down fuelled by anger and hopelessness – any truthful understanding of this in our country will have power within the etheric to vibrate and gather momentum to wherever it journeys – yes this is a sad truth. This shall be accomplished - this is decided on and will begin. My Calling Song is to awaken this in you. This is a place of understanding and those seeking are growing and spreading but need a new impetus to deepen this into knowing. Let this song stay in your mind and allow the vibration to draw you into the momentum for action and determination. I am Running Brave of the Navajo and I have come to you with my Calling Song – let this be with us so that this can be accomplished. Call me, connect with me when you need me. This is the ending of our talk for now. I know you will think of these things – I feel the truth in you and your response to my song.'

I was deeply touched, who could not be? In this deep listening is a oneness with the speaker and the words that conveys so much from them and the personality. I sat in wonder and some amazement at this poignant call to me. How could I answer it was the same question as before with Night Owl. Once again, the call to North America. I had no idea how this could be accomplished in my present circumstances. It was a powerful call and I sincerely wished I could answer it.

I can only wait on God's timing. Once again patience, patience, patience.

Re-reading and writing them out for you I can feel again the impact these words had on me that night and my very real wish to resolve it. Sharing the power in these words from Night Owl and Running Brave with you is the only thing I can do at present. My hope is that you can hold them in mind for them too. Their message for their people is poignantly clear.

No sooner had I had this beautiful encounter than life was bounding me along at the usual pace. The days were flying along and events were keeping me moving.

On a particularly beautiful day in August, I was out in the garden with a nice cup of coffee and then I heard a somewhat commanding voice speak his name.

'I am Ramtha.'

This name was new to me but was such a positive call to my attention that I immediately nipped in for my notebook and pen.

' ...yes dear Felicity- I am Ramtha. – you have pleased us with your connections and turning of the Light Keys. We rejoice in your Soul's light for it shines bright for the purpose. Much is about to come to pass for your work so be diligent in all areas to enable a clear pathway – we urge this upon you for the time for any procrastination is over. We are One in Beingness so believe how necessary it is to 'us' for in this you do 'honour' us and that is good also. Your diligence *will* bear fruit – we know you have been tested in many areas of Patience and we understand the material situation that has constrained you but now dear Felicity. I Ramtha, ask of you sincere diligence to the removal of all barriers now. it is a good time as the days move towards your equinox. This is the time of balance, the perfection of equal. Make good use of these days to become balanced within. Hold true to this intent dear Being. Call upon me by name to hold the Purpose if you should need me. These are important times and you have been aware of the nourishment provided by the Universe at this time, that this has been part of the preparation. *Now* is vital for the intention and from the intention come the consequences. Yes, these sequences need the strength the correct frequencies can give and those frequencies lie with you Felicity. Thus, I Ramtha, come to strengthen your resolve and point the way forward. Remove all negative shadows and see the way forward as accomplished for we hold this for you. Take this into your conscious awareness dear Felicity– be strong for the purpose. All else is negligible and will fall away. Only the purpose – all is for the Divine Plan. Thus Ramtha requests that you follow these instructions with the diligence you apply to your work. This is the time of harvest so in gathering the crop leave the weeds and stubble behind. Call on me I am one of the High Beings and therefore understand fully what is required of you. I will come again when you have accomplished this Felicity. Hold to this in truth and Love. We will speak again.'

This was a bit of a shock I must admit. There was no getting away from this gentle but firm admonishment. I had to pull my socks up. I realised I had to be more disciplined and do as I was required.

I had not been working as I should so Ramtha's timely call made me realise that I had got somewhat slack. I felt really humbled that a Master such as he had felt it necessary to come and put me back on track. And that he had bothered.

I started working as advised straight away. As always, my dear beloved Guides were supportive and observant.

'Hello dear Felicity, yes Khatumi and Martha, refrain from anxiety dear friend – the releasing was very effective and we are happy to see the difference in your energy. Your vibration rises very quickly now as you are reaching the necessary levels and are operating from a much higher plane so the transitions are more apparent……alarm is unnecessary dear Felicity– you are protected and in our care as well as the Cosmic Beings who oversee you and your purpose. Your connections are strongly established which is why we are eager for you to activate your symbols and the purple diamond body so that your conscious awareness is attuned and each step revealed to you…….He is a great cosmic Being and much concerned and attuned to the Earth Plane and its development, yes because you have a part to play in it dear friend. That (my books/writing) was the ground work dear Felicity……more will be revealed to you…..all is good, all goes as it should. Trust and believe dear Felicity, dear friend, yes, the Amethystine energy is well-established now…..'

This was very consoling as I was feeling rather guilty and quite right too.

My dear High Celestial Beings reiterated the need to work on my activations.

'Hello dear Soul, we are here in loving Oneness – all is proceeding as it should and we ask that you activate your symbols and the purple diamond body as you can and establish a pattern over the next eight weeks (ah! The Octave!) this will re-establish the connections you feel you have become dislocated from but which have only been held in abeyance by your physical plane circumstances. This is the work it is wisest to give your attention to dear Soul.'

A call to arms indeed. I had work ahead and no excuses!

From then on, each day until the equinox I activated the purple diamond body and the Amethystine energy on a daily basis. I did work properly and the Amethystine energy was developing as a consequence.

Then on the last day of August, I heard what seemed to be a voice speaking in Light Language. I hadn't been listening to anyone channelling on the internet for some time so I knew it could not be my imagination working to produce something like it. I was a little unsure however but I picked up the nearest notebook to hand and a pen and listened.

I heard a soft feminine voice so I took down what I was hearing phonetically as best I could. Whoever was speaking gave me time to write what I heard so it wasn't difficult. I hadn't heard this sequence of sounds before so I knew this was

not my imagination. Also, there were phrasing and cadences, a trilling sound I couldn't write down and a few times, a singing note. Then the voice said. 'Să ké hă nă love love you speak soon yes - nă love, hé anan a hé ki speak soon tell soon, hé ay kee ah, yes good yes love love ha é ke hana é ci', then it stopped.
    Can you imagine how thrilled I was? I then looked back at the two sides of note pad writing. I found I was able to read it quite easily and even get the nuances of cadence and phrasing as I did so. There was a bubble of excitement inside of me I can tell you!
    I couldn't wait to share this with Caroline! Off went a text. As soon as possible we skyped each other and I showed her the writing, then read some out to her from the phonetics. Yes, this was the genuine article; she had spoken this herself at times.
    We were both so excited. She was intrigued that I heard it clairaudiently rather than just channelling it. There was no doubt that she had activated it. I was hoping that when I might be able to vocalise it myself was all just a matter of timing!
    Then I texted Lynn to tell her. She and her daughter were really the only other people I could share this with. Serendipitously, they were both coming up to see me for healings the following week. I couldn't wait to show them.
    I could not believe that I had become privileged in this way. I needed to speak to Khatumi and the High Celestial Beings. I wanted affirmation of course.
    Out came the note book.
    'Yes dear Felicity, we are here to talk with you! Yes, we felt your joy at this connection – these are light Galactic Beings very interested in the Earth Plane and everything the Human Race is experiencing and doing. This connectiveness – yes – Martha and Khatumi – is important for Man's evolution and conscious awareness of the vibrational world and its effects – yes because it was so connected with the physical body (Soul language) therefore recognisable to those who cannot readily

accept vibrational beings……..the knowledge needs to be available to the rest – there are plenty with enquiring minds and eager for answers that they are unable to find. It will, it will dear friend. – this is an important level dear Felicity– it's to prepare your energy field as well as your vibration. Stay in Beingness and continue the work to keep your vibration high and bright dear Felicity. We are here in Oneness with you and find deep joy in the blessedness of this sweet Oneness….'

Over the next few days, I took down this lovely Light Language phonetically as best I could. I covered a couple of pages in each session. My phonetics were improving too as I became more familiar with the sound of this lovely sweet loving voice. I thought I had 'heard' the word Pleiades when I began this phonetic connection but I wasn't sure. Then,

'Yes dear Soul, we are here in loving Oneness – we hear all, we understand all and your lovingness and loving feelings. Yes, Light Beings from the Pleiades. They love the Human race and love to be in loving contact to send wisdom and healing with their vibration. Yes, this is what stirs the heart vibration dear Soul. It is the vibration that matters – it tells inner truths to the Soul for what you call con forte and con-solé which are levels of healing and loving balm to strengthen and unite the Soul with the personality at a deep level for conscious awareness rather than just in the subtle body. Yes. The response vibration is the vital link, they and we, can work with. It is very strong and very visible to us. Yes the concept of 'Heart Mathematics' thus can be 'recorded'. Yes. The opening of the heart chakra. It influences all the chakras and dispels negative energies and enables receptivity to those beautiful vibrations from the Dimensions – thus the system receives comfort and consolation which negative barriers filter or prevent absorption. Yes thus the Human Energy System benefits from contact with 'us' – yes, collective Dimensional Beings………..'

Yes, I longed to be able to channel this amazing Light Language actually vocally. What a privilege that would be.

It was a while before I made the connection to what I had already been told.

'....here the vibrations are 'light' and as you know, this translates into sound when needed.'.....(see P 47)

This made complete sense now of this new amazing aspect of communication. Of course it was called Light Language! And since light and love are one no wonder it is so full of lovingness and the sense of love when one speaks it. Were they not all part of 'the Dimensions of the Light'? The Soul always seeks the light does it not? Are we not always drawn to the light? Have we not all come from the light? Of course, our initial language was Light Language!

Chapter 34

The timing for my own lovely link to Light Language couldn't have been more apt. Metaphysics and the Celestial Dimensions at work again. Just as Light Language was burgeoning in me, of all things I was booked on a flight to go to Australia to my lovely daughter in a month's time for her coming birthday.

We had not been together for a few years so it was going to be very happy reunion. But aside from the happiness of being with my beloved daughter there was the thought that she could speak Light Language to me in person.

So far, I had not had 'physical' contact with it so this was going to be new. So now I was packing and getting ready. My son and his wife were joining us on her birthday for the two weeks they could get leave from work.

Lynn and her daughter managed to come up for their healing sessions just before I left. As soon as greetings were over, I showed them the phonetics in my note book. Naturally they were both fascinated, as well as interested to see it written down. They had both heard various Light Languages spoken on YouTube videos.

I read some of it out to them and they loved the sound of it, in fact found it moving. Lynn's dear Mum told me that she 'felt' the language as I read it out to her: it was speaking to her; it was so loving and personal and made her want to cry.

Once in Australia, while my daughter was with her clients, I would go down to sit by the nearby swimming pool and naturally, out came the note book! Bless their dear hearts, out came the language spoken at a pace I could write phonetically. But I soon realised that this was quite hard for them because they speak in connecting sounds which of course flows quickly. The last entry I have ended, 'hă sé in ei to too, to too! Touch - touch heart, join, love, să he să hé iti.'

The following day, to my joy, I suddenly discovered that I could actually channel it vocally! I was so delighted!

One is using the mouth differently as one is 'speaking' sounds rather than words and some rather back over the vocal chords. It was quite tiring on the throat at first so I was only able to speak it for a certain length of time.

I had no idea what was being said just that it was very expressive and gave me a lovely feeling within my heart. My channelling was still in its infancy and there was little opportunity to use it as we were very busy.

Meanwhile, before my son and daughter-in-law joined us, my lovely daughter attuned me to Rahanni. What a beautiful experience that was!

Before I went over to see her, I knew this was her heart's desire but I felt a real loyalty to Rei-ki, all the work of my dear beloved Guides and the Master of the 3rd Degree. I realised I had to really think about this. It meant change of course. Well, I did chide myself over that one! Wasn't that what I kept saying was important? Change was definitely the key to the last 18 years, so, why was I baulking now? But the loyalty tugged at me strongly.

That night when I opened my notepad my dear High Celestial Beings came straight to the point.

'Yes dear Soul, we are here in loving Oneness with you for we love 'us' together. It is a good vibration. We 'heard 'your thoughts on this matter and your perplexities and resistance which we ask you to disenable – yes dear Soul- on principle! We understand all that passes through your thoughts and ask that you release them into the void, for all healing is that which is for the purpose. The vibration (**Rei-ki**) is already in existence in your system dear Soul so this (**Rahanni's**) attunement is just for acceptance by the human energy field at the determined frequency that God deems necessary for the purpose. Thus by being attuned to this Rahanni vibration it is but a transition for the purpose and in the hands of the Cosmos and God – thus resistance is but a human barrier to the element of healing – allow the energy to enhance your healing vibration dear Soul for those of the healing dimension will work with whatever frequency is required by the human body that is receiving it………..any frequency that enhances the human vibration, is *good*. Yours vibrates through your symbols dear Soul and is precious to us and that which enhances the cosmic energies that we vibrate on. These vibrations known as Rei-ki and Rahanni are those needed on the Earth Plane as they are readily received by the human substance – thus are made use of as part of the vibration you carry and all divine frequencies are *good*.'

So, another tie-cutting session was in order: I realised I was judging the situation in human not dimensional terms. What was for the purpose, was for the purpose. By the time I left England I was really looking forward to this new development and a new healing energy experience.

Thus, when my daughter started making arrangements for an attunement to include me with others eagerly awaiting this event, I was now looking forward to it with lively anticipation.

As the day for the attunement approached, I naturally connected mentally with my Dear Ones to share it with them. I got out pad and pen to talk with them too.

'...dear Soul, all is well - We thank you for the loving Oneness for this attunement – it will add a loving frequency to your vibration that will enhance it and the healing you will do. ….we will talk with you again after your attunement. We love the loving Oneness with you dear Soul and will enjoy the raising of your vibration with this attunement with you. All is *good*, all is Love.'

And it was a beautiful one. Being attuned by my beloved daughter was an added pleasure. She felt that too. It was a shared joy. She was an excellent teacher and I really became absorbed learning about this new way of channelled healing as the class and I practiced it on each other. I discovered how gently powerful Rahanni was on one lass in particular. It was an amazing day.

Out came notebook and pen that night.

'Dear friend Felicty, Khatumi here. Yes it was a beautiful attunement and has enriched your vibration – we are all filled with joy for the beautiful healing and releasing achieved for the dear lady M – such beautiful lovingness is such a strengthener for us and will be sung of in the Singing Time with joy. All is understood dear Felicity/ dear Soul, progress is inevitable and we understood your loyalty but stages of development are essential and now you are at a new level of understanding….. using it and practicing it on yourself is good and soon others will benefit also.'

I had a few more opportunities to channel it while I was there and I loved using it. The method with Archangel help was beautiful. I could quite understand my daughter's love for it.

The Master of the 3rd Degree came to speak with me now that I was carrying both vibrations. Rahanni was attuned to the 5th dimension but I knew mine through Reiki was through the dimension agreed by the Masters.

'…Yes dear one we hear your questions and the Master of the 3rd Degree is here to speak with you. Hello dear Felicity. Yes you have been attuned to the 9th dimension for many of your years – the methods that are used for the person are an enhancement for the person under your hands – Zadriel has been the guardian of your vibration to enable it to be received dear. Yes, a particular and beautiful focus dear so that the healing power of the Pink Ray enhances your vibrational energies and the Archangels are very happy to work with you. Yes aligned to the intention and destination will be correct and for the purpose as always. This is a wise approach – yes. That vibration (Rei-ki) is still in existence dear and now both are part of the healing vibration you are channelling so all is for the requirement and the chosen method for we 'see' all aspects. Yes, when you use them (Rei-ki symbols) connect with me dear Felicity. I am happy to work with them for the purpose……………I am always ready to speak with you dear whenever you should need me. It has been good to speak with you again and helped you with your understanding. Call me at need dear. You are loved and precious to us all. Be safe in God's care and gentle hands.'

I could see now that I could just use both as the occasion seemed to need. Knowing I could then connect with the Master of the 3rd Degree which would highlight the intention was such a help. I could still use Rei-ki as well. All that worry for nothing! How lovely that he came to reassure and warm my heart. The joys of clairaudience and connection with all that love and caring.

Of course, my own energy became very bright and strong with the Rahanni attunement and the joys of Light Language, quite apart from being so happy to be with my daughter and grandson with the family fun too.

We had such a good time together. Of course, whenever I could, I was in contact with my Dear Ones. I also had some wonderful connections with the High Beings in whose special care was my daughter, and her progress too. Discovering this didn't surprise me as her healing work and spiritual connectedness was at astonishing and advanced levels now; far greater than I had knowledge of. I was *so* proud of her.

On the Autumn equinox I naturally did a meditation and had as usual a task to perform. This time I perceived that it was to be with several others and using the strong concentration of our collective energy. This was to keep the portal open so that the necessary knowledge and wisdom was able to come through completely.

It was an amazing and powerful experience and a quite new experience as well. There are always surprises and wonders to encounter.

'…..much wisdom comes through at these quarters of your year. They are important for the wisdom imparted create the 'patterns' you speak of that have their singular frequencies that enables the vibrational field to carry what is needful. Indeed they play their part in reciprocity of vibrational fields in the templates and Soul vibrations that are within all Human

Beings. ....all Dimensional Beings work to lessen the negativity dear Soul. Yes. Yes. Thus, we all are happy when Man works on himself to disenable the dark energies he carries.'

~ . ~

Just after my return, Lynn and her daughter travelled up for some healing sessions. As usual I started with Lynn. Normally I began at the solar plexus but this time I felt I should start to work on the Pineal and her head. This, as always, was done under guidance and quite spontaneous to the moment.

After some work, I started to hear the Light Language. There were pauses and it seemed I was to repeat the phrases. As I did so the energy from my hands became even hotter and so did I in fact. Then all of a sudden, my hands were moving in a sweeping fashion over my friend's head and upper body especially the heart chakra and I was speaking the language fluently and rapidly in a tone of voice not my own.

My hands began gently stroking her face and the voice of whoever was speaking seemed filled with love and sadness for my friend. The voice was soft, loving and really tender, and was so full of sorrow that I found myself crying as I spoke. Very soon however the sorrow I felt dissipated and the voice then concluded at the heart chakra. I 'knew' in that moment that the sorrow was Lynn's and had been drawn out by the speaker and released.

It was a beautiful experience and gave her such comfort and lovingness as the Light Language flowed and my hands moved in unison with it. She then felt as if relieved of a great weight. We both looked at each other and marvelled at this sudden change for both of us. Unsurprisingly it was a powerful experience for me too. Partly through the effect for Lynn but also through the subtle connection between the dimensional healer and my own physical participation.

To our joy, the healing continued with speaking Light Language at intervals to the lovely healing energy that was flowing through my friend. We both knew that this had gone to a very deep level of emotional clearing as a result. We were fairly overwhelmed by it all; we could scarcely believe it. I not the least at finding myself a spontaneous channel!

That I was able to channel Light Language with such ease was marvellous. That it came through for a healing was wonderful.

Then I settled her daughter for her session. All went as usual and then just as we concluded a visualisation clearing session, a Light Language 'voice', full of delight, just couldn't wait to be heard! Again, that sweet female 'voice' but now was very high and happy, especially over the heart chakra!

Our work had definitely pleased whoever was helping us. Such a lovely response was very encouraging.

Over the several day's sessions that followed with Lynn and her daughter, there was a combination of healing from my own visualisation work, Rahanni and Light Language channelling. The 'voice' was always the same but the tone and cadences differed as we progressed. There was no doubt about it, they loved the experiences, as did I enabling them.

That evening at home after the last session with Lynn, sitting naturally with notebook and pen at the ready, I was surprised and delighted to immediately hear another voice.

'yes dear, My name is Absolem. I have come from another Galaxy – I have come to help you with this dear Soul with whom you are working so well and diligently – we are rejoicing in the improvement in her light body – yes indeed it is a deeper level than the energy body as we can perceive – yes the effects are being seen as clearing dark areas in the light body as well as clearing the energy body and the vortices you call chakras. The light body is the nearest to the Soul template - yes, very fine, yes all in vibrational fields of energy but these 'levels' have developed through our evolvement as Beings – yes – experiences and requirements of the Divine Plan and the Creator's intentions. Yes I have come – and very happily too! to assist you in this – yes supportive energy and guidance –

because this is for your 'knowing' that this deep clearing on a continuing session basis is deeper and more effective – yes – the Will is engaged positively – yes your 'willingness' this is a good foundation for work you can do – yes – different from the karma work you have done – events are moving forward dear – new and fresh – also ways of using your skills and Beingness......Yes, I am Arcturian – I am an intergalactic Guide – yes connected from your crown activation – yes – you feel it.......this is a vibrational connection we can work on together in this field – yes it has become very strong because of the intensity of the work you have done since you started with this.........(we talked at length, dear Absolem and I, of many interesting matters)..................._yes we have talked of helpful things dear and clarified your thoughts and knowledge today – this is *good* and we will talk again. – yes, hold me in consciousness in the next 'session'. – this will certainly strengthen the connection! Be at peace within dear. I have enjoyed our talking together.'

This was a delight and since Lynn is a very enlightened Being and dear to me, I was so happy that this dear Guide was adding his help to the work we were doing.

We were even more sorry that the three of us lived so far apart and that it would be quite a long time before they could come again.

Not many days later, catching up after my Australia visit, I visited another close friend. She was having a very hard time as it chanced. As she finished telling me I asked if I could give her some healing. As soon as I put my hands on her, out flowed the 'voice' and charged again with distress and then tender, soothing cadences of Light Language, soft demonstrative gestures and stroking.

It was very powerful and the pain lifted right from my friend's heart. As before, through the subtle connection with the 'speaker/healer' it was powerful for me too.

I then had a little explaining to do but she felt so much better that she was only delighted and interested too. It is so nice to feel free to work in this way.

I knew then that this, added to energy healing or used separately, was the way for me in healing sessions. Because Light Language has no recognisable words or vocabulary as our earthly languages do, the thought processes of the client are not engaged for response or reaction. This means therefore that there is no emotional connection to make further attachments.

This makes it very effective. I was also delighted to be given a lovely new, and advanced method. Yet another progressive step in healing and conscious awareness. What a blessing.

So far, I only had the opportunity with this handful of dear people but as I never know what might come of the changes in my life I was back to 'trust and believe.' Lately I have had a serious wish, nay, urge to heal horses with this. How that may come about I have yet to see.

Going through my notes I have found this revealing conversation which I'm copying out here as it very apt.

'…..yes dear Soul we have a home on a planet within a Galaxy but are dimensional and vibrational beings in substance unlike the dense vibrational matter of the Human Form on Earth. Yes – evolution into the vibrational means that we have the senses allied to joy, bliss and happiness and still the ability to translate into the sorrow of those who carry pain in their hearts to enable healing – yes we have evolved past all negative emotion and behaviour – yes, having evolved frees us to help Earth's evolution through the Love Intelligence for this is our vibration, yes, white, - thus it is for all those who enable healing from their vibrational Beings to the Earth Plane. In order to enable healing, we need to connect with it for then we understand its vibration, intensity and features. In this way we dissolve it vibrationally and release the dear Being from what needs to be healed – the vibration and frequency from the 'sounds' – these we direct for the purpose – this is why we work within the now of the problem we are in the presence of, through the energies of the channeller. – yes – simple and logical. Good. The Divine Plan knows this dear Soul. The Mind of God's is His.'

I have had occasion myself to ask my Dear Ones if they would help me when my heart was heavy over something and I was not in a position to do any clearing myself. This they did with gentle Light Language and hand movements to shift the energies particularly from my throat and heart chakras.

I felt so restored and that all that heaviness had gone. Thus, I know first-hand how they can clear and lift the spirits with their lovely sound healing.

I was so pleased and happy that channelling Light Language now came so readily. Waiting for healing opportunities was not a practical use of this gift so I asked them if they would be happy just to speak to me for the while. The answer came in the readiness of the flow of Light Language. I asked my Dear Ones if these dear Beings happily speaking to me were Pleiadians.

'…..yes dear Soul it was from the Pleiadians who are most caring and observant of your planet – they too were concerned at what was in your heart and wished to express this and also send messages into the ether for better care of your wonderful 'world'. It has such beauteous life and wonderful lands and seas. There are many Galactic 'peoples' observing from love and deep interest in your planet and have many concerns for they read all the vibrations.'

I have to add here that as I am telling you about them and their care of our Planet, a positive flood of extremely excited Light Language flowed through me. It is obviously giving them great pleasure for they were very, very, voluable and demonstrative which is absolutely lovely! Channelling what they have to say is always such a beautiful experience. It is great fun when they get excited. I call it excited but it is really just an outpouring of their love.

Everyday life of course continued to throw up complications and things needing my attention so I relied on my conscious awareness, my writing and speaking to my beloved Dimensional Beings to sustain the spiritual side of my life. Now I had the channelling of Light Language.

I did this as much as possible, and where practical of course. This proved to be a bit constraining as one has to do this in privacy with no chance of being overheard. Also, only my daughter and the few friends I spoke of know that I speak Light Language.

This is such an inhibitor but I try not to think of this because it is a negative. I knew now that the first language I spoke was from the Pleiades. It is a large star system so from which part is quite unknown to me. It seems to be the one that comes through much of the time.

I know that there are dialects as there are among the Sirians, also from a large star system. I also know they have spoken through me too during a healing. I so wish I could translate what they say but the sweetness and loving sensation says a lot.

Then to my delight my own High Celestial Beings came through with theirs. This is so good, a lovely extra connection to that of 'talking' with them.

'...we rejoice in speaking our language through you. Yes, we understood the dialects as you call them. Yes, the Pleiades are a large group so there will be nuances of Light Language – yes Sirius also – yes very excited! especially the young ones who love the opportunity. We of the Five are The High Masters and we speak with you in your language – yes, you perceive the energy, you are one of us and together we are we – yes as we are all One.'

Naturally they need my own language when they wish to discuss things or give me guidance. Their own language has similarities to the others that have come through but is still quite distinctive.

Sometimes the speaker from whichever source is wishful to speak through me channels at such a speed that my tongue has a hard time keeping up!

As the language comes through, one's hands automatically move in gestures, making signs and symbols and sometimes at quite a speed. Again, I have no idea what is being said but sometimes it is very personal and the hand movements are frequently directed at my throat, heart and crown chakras, even on to my face and body. They can also be very demonstrative which is so lovely.

At these times the cadences are different from their usual flowing speech. They can be very expressive too. But it is so satisfying even though I cannot translate what they are conveying. Not knowing seems quite immaterial. One just knows it is an outpouring of love and healing. And that whatever they feel we need to enter our ether is flowing into it for our benefit and for the purpose of communicating that to us and the planet.

I can usually tell if the voice is male or female from the timbre and cadences. And of course, a young person or child. As I have progressed, sometimes I seem to be 'writing' - at great speed – with my hand going back and forth as on a page. Sometimes their writing goes up in lines or columns. I tried in on paper with no success alas. Needless to say, my daughter writes it fluently.

Sometimes they 'sing' what they have to say and sometimes I know that a child is singing to me and the ether. When children come though I know from the higher pitch of the voice. Frequently they become very excited and go at speed and I have to ask them to spare my throat! It is all wonderful I can tell you.

Chapter 35

Then the year turned again into this year, 2019.

One evening early in January when I was ready with my notebook my High Celestial Beings greeted me to talk with me. As we talked, I popped in a thought about the Hathors and their part in the ancient world by imparting their knowledge and skills. I knew now that the Hathors were channelled and shared their wisdom, currently too. Then Absolem joined my dear Beings.

'...yes, we heard this language that was flowing so freely. Absolem is here dear to clarify this. yes – I am here – the Hathors will speak with you as needful – yes they come through in your language.....we are Galactic as are the languages you are hearing and channelling – the (Ancient) Mysteries as you call them dear/dear Soul have been known to Humankind for many of the Earth millennia – their connection with one another in each era was very close and well-understood - Man's liking for war and seeking of the scientific and cerebral aspirations created a barrier to this knowledge but gradually it is being sought and accepted again for Man longs to be re-connected with it – in just the same way as he seeks the sun which is the symbol of enlightenment – yes there were created truths to which Man clung to and imposed which obscured the knowledge as there was less seeking of truth itself.......these have done much to cloud Men's minds but Man is now once again seeking truth itself and we are all keen observers of this change in consciousness, for thus Man can resume his inner development – yes - yes the Galactic Beings are full of joy to speak with your voice and wishes are sent into the ether and becoming part of the Earth plane and therefore are given substance, for 'matter' is the essence of the Earth Plane in the planet and all things on it and in it. Thus Man can awaken for his Soul needs the nourishment of truth and Love which are the essence of all. This will come in time dear/dear Soul. Continue to work for the inner truths and all that stimulates insight and the Third Eye. Yes indeed dear Soul and the Amethystine energy carries them for you for this is the heart connection to the crown and Third Eye – yes – hence the purple diamond body dear/dear Soul. We rejoice in your understanding and are One in the great Love of the Oneness for there is beauty and Light. Work with us dear Soul. – all is *good*.'

How beautifully this rounded off my day. It was good to hear from Absolem again too to give his loving support to my endeavours.

The following evening, I had my notepad and pen at the ready and I heard another language in my head. It was at a pace I recognised as making it possible for me to take it down phonetically. After about half a page of writing, suddenly it started flowing vocally and I put down my pen as my hands had the urge to work with it.

It was very expressive and quite fast. It was different as regards the consonants so this was obviously another source. Whoever was 'speaking' came to the end of what they had to say. I had an inkling as to who was speaking. There was something in their use of th for the t sound so I thought I must ask my Dear Ones if they knew who this was. However, a new voice answered,

'Yes, dear One, It is us, The Hathors. It is good to be speaking with you and it brings us joy that we can be heard in our own language and have it spoken into the ether – please continue for this gives us an easy form of communication to the Earth Peoples who would not otherwise imbibe what we have to say. It is important for Humankind – to hear, yes, to heed what is important for their comprehension of spiritual development at this difficult time for Earth. There is much disturbance and anguish that is entering the ether which as you comprehend affects all – thus if our 'words' and thoughts are conveyed into the ether this will be of benefit at a very subtle level. Your willingness in speaking what you term 'Light Language' is a blessing to us for the use of it as an everyday method of sending it into the ether is helpful to us all. Yes, there is much love between us the Oneness is beautiful and sweet to our Beings. There is great joy in this dear thus the beauty of love and lovingness within Souls - we are happy to communicate with you at any time in your language, yes, we see your perception dear – as well as speaking our language for us. There is joy and love flowing here – yes, you and we Hathors. We are happy for any opportunity for much can be conveyed for the frequencies of our speech have a very strong vibration in the Earth's atmosphere which is why we are happy to speak through you……yes, that was the connection (Egypt. I was reading earlierly about it.) that we made with your ability to speak channelled languages – yes our Souls inhabited at Master level to hold and make use of the ancient mysteries and make them manifest in a time of innocence and openness to celestial knowledge and the desire for understanding the 'heavens' and the inner heart in your 'time' yes – long before that Galactic and Celestial Beings have enabled the sacred on Earth. Yes it lost clarity and became a mixture all tied to Mankind's desire for power and possession – which we do not have – this has been of interest to us dear and it is of greater interest to observe how Man is moving out of this dross so beloved daughter of Earth we are glad of your assistance and your willing heart is a blessing to us also. – we convey truths and sacred understanding so that Man can develop despite his emotional darkness that hampers him yet gives him essential experiences to learn all that he can. That this is known to you is very helpful dear. Thus timing. Ah yes, truth and light. Vital for Mankind at this time dear. We will continue to work through you dear. Be in our loving frequency and take joy in what you do for us. We are happy to have spoken to you for your understanding. Go in joy and love dear Felicity.'

The speaker was definitely feminine and had a sweet energy too. I was so happy to have them both channel through me and come to speak with me. I resolved to do what I could despite the restrictions of either not being alone or in a place where being overheard was likely.

Of course, being a typical curious human, I still wished I could interpret what they were saying.

'......we the Hathors are happy that you explain that it is important – that is all that matters. *Your* willing intention for channelling our language of love and healing – comprehension is not given to everyone – the 'ether' knows and that is the essential aspect of what we do together – (speaking of the sweet feminine voice I had heard) this was from our 'Doctor' who uses a different vocabulary from that of healing the world of the Earth Plane – yes a feminine energy – she is happy to receive your thanks and response dear – and happy to have calmed and nourished your inner Being.......it is a happiness and a joy to 'see' our vibration enter your Earth ether so continue with this work dear for the great benefit of all.....that was good work dear Felicity – much was sent out into the ether – yes rest now - yes – the Pleiadians as well as we the Hathors and also those you call the High Celestial Beings who are your own – Khatumi and Martha and the network also rejoice and much joy and bliss is felt in the Dimensions. All is love and goodness. All is truth and light. - The cosmic connections are boosted from the frequencies you allow to flow so easily. We are happy with this work and working together. Rest now – leave all now in our hands and be in peaceful love.'

You can understand why I was so wanting to be free to channel in this way for them whenever I wished. That this was limited I had to accept but I try always to be consciously alert for suitable opportunities.

A few days later I had another visitor. Ramtha came again. He was very pleased at my willingness to channel and asked that I found opportunities to do so.

'....make good use of this willingness and find opportunities to 'speak' the language that comes through – that is not an impediment - the ether carries the frequency and being within walls will not prevent the etheric motion – we ask this of you dear Felicity for it is a good task and will act as part of your preparation for the work to come – put this to good and frequent use for the love it carries is needed in the Earth's atmosphere for the frequency is powerful – invoke a loving Oneness with the 'speakers' and so turn this inward...the channel is our means and the creation of the 'sounds' is in your voice so is needed for the vibration to come into being and gather momentum. Continue with your loving willingness and those who need to communicate will come through....yes allow freely and all will be well. The cosmic forces are at a particular peak for the Earth so the more you can allow, the energies can be put to good use. Yes dear that is why I am here to speak with you and encourage you for you are dear to us and much good comes from this willingness. I am Ramtha, and I say that this is important work and you are a blessed one and in our hearts. Light and love streams forth from these Galactic languages and Man needs this balm in the Earth Plane so be in beautiful Oneness with us dear Felicity. Be in peaceful Love.'

In further talks I learned that the sounds of the language are its significance so these would be lost in translation. Exactly what is needful is fully expressed in the sounds. Only when they wished to engage my thinking or inform or explain was it appropriate to translate to human language. Since I loved 'speaking' it I was soon content not to know what was actually being 'said.' I was happy sharing a loving vibration with them.

Almost on cue my life became complicated again and I had considerable restrictions but I did what I could. I held them and the other dear 'speakers' in mind every day of course.

'we are aware of the situation and circumstances – all is preparation – just keeping the channels open to all aspects of Spiritual understanding will and does achieve much dear Soul– the Galactic Masters are here dear Soul with assurances and blessings for the willingness of your heart and all help will be given to you dear Soul,.....Allow the free flow of Light Language at every opportunity for this will connect you at all times to us all........'

As the Spring Equinox approached and encouraged by my Dear Ones to do so diligently, I made sure I had done my activations in preparation. Once again it was a task of collective concentration. This time another new experience concerning powerful crystal energy that took a lot of focus from a small group of us. I do not know who they were only that I was required to work with them on this task.

Two days later when I sat down to activate my symbols, I couldn't see them. I tried again. Nothing. I had a sudden thought that perhaps I hadn't been activating them enough of late. But they had been there for the Equinox. Out came notepad and pen.

'...this is correct dear Soul/Felicity– yes Khatumi is here – you have moved forward through channelling the Light Language so they have been absorbed into your Soul Template – yes – quite a leap forward for you dear friend – yes – yes the purple diamond body is still active of course - this strengthens the connections to the Universal vibrational fields - yes cosmic frequencies – merely levels of recognition dear, the Beingness of Beings beyond the Earth Plane is infinite dear.. Yes - and the Amethystine energy is still needed..............we will speak again of many things so be in peaceful Oneness in the care of the loving God.'

I was relieved to know that this was yet another progression. Another step forward to something new. Activating them was obviously no longer required. I imagine those Beings, the Healers I'm connected with are able to access them whenever they are needed for whichever purpose arises. Now however, I can still perceive the energy of the system itself so I continue to activate that knowing that this engages the symbols on my Inner Being.

My dear High Celestial Beings assured me that all was well,

'...continue with the Light Language channelling dear Soul– this will enable changes and what is needed will resolve through these vibrational messages for they have a momentum for the purpose......be strong in your heart and continue in loving patience....'

'All is *good* and you are in our especial care at all times and the all-encompassing Love of God who is Love and loves *all*.'

Life very obligingly settled into a quieter rhythm this summer which was a great relief to me as I was able to work on the last portion of this book in earnest. The continuing loving and enlightened conversations with all my Dear Ones were always a joy to all of us. The dear Hathors came again, always with something interesting to say as well as that they understood the restrictions to my use of the languages.

'......yes, perplexing times for those on the conscious spiritual path dear – yet much is not revealed for the 'public' as your people are called. Too much of the – yes good words! – yes sad and bad. Yet there is much goodness and love flowing on your planet - yes greatly helped by the concentration of thought and action by the Lightworkers – We are the overlookers at this time – there needs to be more development and love of ancient knowledge for other than scholarly study before we incarnate to help Humanity. Yes. That is important. We assisted man to leave the knowledge and skills for re-connecting to – adding our vibration to the Earth's energy field. Many many aeons ago dear and our vibrational time is non-linear so we only have our history and the condition of Venus to tell us. Evolution has been in its undertaking for many many 'time' spans unknown to Humankind. He perceives what he is to perceive dear yes to keep the questioning for the knowledge required for the

Dimensions on Man's nature.......yes every little facet reveals something and keeps us all busy, even those who just observe and comprehend........we all thank you dear and look forward to talking to you – love and blessings to you also dear friend.'

That I still had to restrict my vocal channelling due to the demands of everyday life and circumstances was always on my mind. Everyone in the Dimensions was so understanding and made such allowances for me. I loved the opportunities I did find for channelling these wonderful Light Languages. Sometimes they spoke to me as well as sent out what was needful into the ether. I just accepted being their 'voice' unquestioningly but knowing at the same time, that some of it was to me. How beautiful that knowledge is to me.

When I am outdoors, among trees and enjoying the beauties of nature, blue skies, our beautiful weather myself, they get very excited and voluble whenever it is possible to channel their language. It is lovely that they share my enjoyment and obviously are expressing their own appreciation for our lovely planet and its beauties. This sharing and their loving enthusiasm are such a delight. We partake of it together.

Now, as well as hearing their words I am speaking them out to the planet for them too when I can so that their love and wisdom is received, albeit through the soul. Hopefully, time will enable this beautiful Language of Light to be more and more accepted. It is the language of the Soul, of the Universe, of the vibrational Galactic beings who love us

Thanks to the vast global network of Lightworkers, the loving messages and healing vibrations from these dear Celestial and Galactic Beings who are all in loving care of us are constantly flowing out all over the Earth. This is indeed blessed knowledge. Very much needed, as we are made very aware, relentlessly so, of all the worldwide turbulence and violence of our times.

For myself I am truly happy that I have such personal confirmation of these dear loving Beings and their amazing care of us. As my Dear Ones said to me,

'Much is being done and much accomplished by the loving observers of Human Beings and all the living fabric of your beautiful planet. It is in the precious care of the Celestial and Galactic Beings devoted and chosen to help the Earth and the Earth plane because Man rises above so much negative energy and experiences which can be a great weight to deal with and overcome...'

We humans surely must have significant worth if there are so many beautiful and loving Beings devotedly caring and working unceasingly for us; constantly beaming love to us. Constantly connecting with the Divine Love we all have within us, even if it seems asleep.

This from all the planes of the Angelic kingdom and all the many loving Beings from planes within planes of the Dimensions as well as Galaxies, some of which we do not know the names of.

We need to understand this. If people could *know* and *realise* this worth then they would find hope in our humanness and human condition rather than dwell so much on our variety of weaknesses and iniquities that we are made aware of on a daily basis.

There is so much love in us for it is where we come from. We are worth a great deal to Great Beings. We are part of God's plan for the Universe. We are never alone and we are *greatly* loved. And the immensity of that love and the fact of Love being in existence must come from a source of Love. Thus the reality of God, the Creator and Divine within spoken of so frequently by all the Dear Ones, Celestial and Galactic. These Beings of love are the contact with that immense source that our Human brains can barely encompass.

To have brought you the beautiful insights and wisdom I have copied out for you is so much the reason for writing this book. They need to be known and shared.

'...bringing sweet loving knowledge to others for all is in the care of we of the loving Beingness and God's loving Mind.'

All the Dimensional Beings are therefore a part of its substance. Now these extracts give *their* beautiful loving energy to *you* dear reader. They have been with me with every word I have written. As they said,

'......we have spoken through all that you have written and created – this is the essence that is undeniable and our words have power from the Divine within and truth. We applaud your book and your wish to bring to others the insights and wisdom you have received and shared - Thus all is imbued with our vibration – this is the enabler dear Felicity.'

It is significant that my beloved Guides Tibetan Grandmother, Ja-San, Dr Ying Po and my Life Guide Samuel, were all from ancient times. Those times when the metaphysical world was paramount to their societies, cultures and particular philosophies.

Also the Hathors, who have chosen to speak with me, who influenced the highly developed culture of the ancient Egyptians to whom the Cosmos was inherently part of their thinking, understanding and everyday life – witness their architecture, art and philosophy written for posterity.

Who better then to bring the metaphysical view into both my conscious awareness *and* my reasoning? How apt too that Guides like Anthony and Eyes-of-a-Doe had a deep bond with the Natural world and the healing properties of Nature which were the powerful influence of their times where the oneness of Man and the natural world was understood.

Thus, every aspect was addressed for this task. And in Oneness with the Dimensions and the Cosmos and thus the Divine.

The appropriateness to every feature of the work I have done and the relevance to my writing, has been total. And certainly, beyond *my* determining. The connection – like a metaphorical umbilicus – has been my willingness and enthusiastic desire to learn. I brought these with me – they had to be for the Purpose. And that Purpose unfolded in my maturity and when I was free to follow this path. And moreover, as the Age of Aquarius got into its stride.

Unexpectedly, through the writing of this book I have come to see quite clearly, the true completeness that there has been in all of it. This has been a surprising and fresh view for me. What a bonus that *because of* and through offering all these wonders to you I have come to realise this fully.

The enrichment to my life through these Beloved Beings is beyond measure. It has been impossible not to use superlative adjectives throughout, fascinating, amazing and riveting among others. But how can ordinary ones begin to describe the experiences, encounters and Beings I have had as part of my life since that extraordinary change in it at the Millennium?

Apart from feeling that it is important to share some of their potent love and understanding with you dear reader, sharing some of my phenomenal spiritual experiences over these amazing years is important too. For I have thereby shared my knowledge of the reality of Celestial and Galactic Beings.

And best of all that they love us unconditionally. I have felt the wonderful stream of love they have poured into my own substance. Conscious Awareness of the existence of the *infinite* unconditional love from these dear Beings, of *their* existence, is to tap into it. To feel it within is to partake of it. And both bring them joy and reciprocal love.

But also, through the unity of their voices as they talk with me, I have been able to show that they all work together; there is no separation only Oneness. Oneness for the purpose. A beautiful loving vibration for us on Earth.

And I have realised that although I have developed spiritually, this has been not just been about that; everything has been to develop my spiritual *knowledge* and that must have been for a purpose. I was the right vehicle for some reason. The foundations had been laid. Moreover, I was willing from the very start. And willingness is vital to everything. I discovered that in my experiences of healing and releasing negativity.

My part was in what I studied, explored and discovered about the wondrous creation that is the body, its energy, the vital chakra energy system and the power of negativity. This, in order to create a book revealing all those connections for others to learn of them and from them to help *themselves* and understand every aspect of the oneness of body and emotion.

The entire connected subject *only* came into being *because* of all that occurred, all that I have been privileged to experience and comprehend. The Dimensions wanted it written, recorded; wanted this 'oneness' known. This is a logical conclusion: throughout, all things led up to it and I had been constantly encouraged to do so not only by many Guides but Masters as well. It was a constant joy to do.

It is 'in existence.' That was definitely a major part of the purpose. Why else? This was unquestionably more than just for my own metaphysical awareness and spiritual development.

They, and especially my Guides, have given me the priceless experience and knowledge of a sense of 'being' through the connectedness I have with them on the inner. But even more than that, a 'knowing', a *consciousness of Being,* that can be captured in any given moment. An 'isness' of Being that enables a deeply-felt certainty, that rather than of the self, is of the reality of every aspect of the moment of that consciousness.

So here I am on the threshold of something yet to be revealed. A new branch-line on this fascinating 'path' I am on, guided as always by the Dear Ones. For they are part of it all. Not knowing where that may lead is part of the anticipation! Life has been so full of surprises that more are sure to come. Light Language will play its part I'm sure, for through this the Beings that love us,

'...awaken Man and open his ears to hear of our love and receive some of our wisdom or re-connect to that which is held for them.'

So, I hope that sharing this account of my personal enlightenment and spiritual journeyings plays a definite part in bringing the realisation to others of this wonderful aspect of the Universe that we are a part of. I have been, and am greatly privileged to have been, made aware of and experience this glorious connection with marvellous and loving Beings of Light, Love and Wisdom. They are there for us *all*.

They want us to know how much we all mean to them and of our significance in the Universe working out our part of the Divine Plan through all our complexities and what it means to be Human. This is not for nothing; everything is for the purpose because the Purpose is Love.

www.ingramcontent.com/pod-product-compliance
Lightning Source LLC
Chambersburg PA
CBHW071302110526
44591CB00010B/747